THE
HUMANITIES
HANDBOOK
PART I

THE
HUMANITIES
HANDBOOK
PART I

JOSEPH SATIN

Midwestern University

HOLT, RINEHART and WINSTON, INC.
*New York   Chicago   San Francisco   Atlanta   Dallas
Montreal   Toronto*

34253

FOR MY WIFE
through whom random events acquire purpose and meaning

TO THE STUDENT

The study of humanities that you are now beginning may well be one of the great courses of your college career. This handbook is intended to facilitate your study, and a few early words on its purpose will help clarify some practical points. The handbook sets up patterns of relationship from ancient Greece to the present among philosophy, literature, architecture, sculpture, painting, and music—all against a backdrop of historical events. Its scope is probably larger than that of the course you are taking. Its presentation will certainly be less detailed because this handbook makes no attempt to parallel your professor's lectures; rather, it focuses upon the core business of humanities—the interrelationships among arts and ideas—and it provides a framework in which you can understand arts and ideas within their proper historical and cultural settings. Your classroom lectures will embellish that framework with esthetic, biographical, historical, and critical insights, thereby complicating it and thus making it believable.

The humanities course can properly include anything and everything, from cave drawings to a Scarlatti sonata to a miniskirt—which is its special value and, for teachers, its special problem. There are no requisite materials that must be used and no central way to set up a humanities course. Your particular course, however, will probably cover some periods of Western civilization and be some variant on one of two approaches. The first approach relies upon a team of professors, each a specialist in one area—art, music, and literature professors form the nucleus of most teams. Each specialist presents his subject chronologically within a given period. In studying Greece, for instance, the professor of art will offer a survey of Greek art; and professors of music and literature will contribute similar surveys. Often, though not always, weekly discussion periods will attempt to tie together the presentations of the various lecturers. The second approach relies upon the services of only one professor, who must juggle the many areas of the course as best he can and who must in most cases lean heavily upon his own area of specialization.

Each approach offers certain advantages. Team teaching can provide a fuller and more comprehensive presentation of materials; solo teaching can concentrate more upon links between ideas and subject matter. Both, however, by their very nature must leave the student with unanswered questions. Team teaching in hour-long lectures does not allow for time to set up a section of framework to include, say, the motivations shared in common by

Edmund Burke, Goethe, Rousseau, Géricault, Beethoven, Schopenhauer, and architects of Neo-Gothic buildings. Solo teaching is also bound by limitations— of the clock and of the scope of the particular course.

Hence this handbook by providing a wide range of humanities inter-relationships sets up a framework to stand alongside either type of humanities course. You, the student, may use this framework in several ways:

1. You may measure a particular work against the framework to assess the manner in which that work reflects the temper, mind, and stance of its own age.

2. You may use the framework to compare the effect of traits, ideas, and forms of one branch of art on other arts in the same period.

3. You may use the framework to examine the manner in which the total complex of traits, ideas, and forms shape and color a variety of works produced by that age.

In sum, by using the categorized traits, ideas, and forms in this book together with the detailed classroom lectures and examples provided by your own course, you may confirm and perceive a range of syntheses that is the special gift of the study of humanities.

Wichita Falls, Texas
October 1968

J. S.

ACKNOWLEDGMENTS

I owe thanks to many people for help in the writing of this book: to my colleagues in humanities courses, Stephen F. Crocker and Frank Manning of West Virginia University, the late Edward Emley of Eastern Michigan University, and Delsie Holmquist and Gerald Ippolito of Moorhead State College; to Professors Ivy Boland and John Carson of Midwestern University, whose advice as specialists filled in several gaps; to Midwestern librarians Calvin Boyer and Louise Gregg, whose cooperation was unstinting; to the Piper Foundation of San Antonio, Texas, whose Piper Professorship award made possible a research trip to Europe; to Dean N. W. Quick of Midwestern, for his awareness and concern; and as climax, not resolution, my warmest gratitude to the editorial staff of Holt, Rinehart and Winston, Inc., most notably to Kenney Withers for his vision and to Jane Ross for her monumental tact and understanding.

J. S.

CONTENTS

LIST OF ILLUSTRATIONS

PART I

CHAPTER 1
THE HUMANITIES
APPROACH

One of the classics of Confucian philosophy is *I Ching*, the *Book of Changes*. It holds that all seemingly chance events in any moment of time are not random but part of a pattern. For *I Ching* today's campus beards and protests, electronic music, roar-shock novels, and commitments to existentialism mean something *together*. For *I Ching* elements like those, contemporary with one another, are like a bundle of sticks thrown into the air. When they fall to the ground they seem to the literal observer to be just a chance scattering of sticks; to the more imaginative observer they will suggest a recognizable shape or perhaps an emotion; to the one who understands they become a related part of the profound and total pattern of their own moment of time, the pattern of interrelationships which are the primary concern of the humanities course.

Humanities as a course came into being because of the urgent need for something that offers maximum breadth and fluidity to offset the ever-increasing emphasis on specialization in today's colleges. It marks a vital and high-level innovation, which is not surprising in view of some of its impressive forebears. As early as the sixth century B.C. Pythagoras explored interrelationships among mathematics, astronomy, philosophy, music, and religion for the Greek world; the *De ente et uno* of fifteenth-century Pico della Mirandola proposed to encompass Greek, Hebrew, and Christian culture within one comprehensive pattern; the seventeenth-century philosopher-scientist René Descartes thus explains his method of interpreting the emerging modern world: "Perceiving those long chains of reasoning which geometers use to accomplish their most difficult proofs led me to think that everything which might fall under the cognizance of the human mind to be connected together in the same manner." Humanities stems directly from syntheses like these, but is aimed at a far larger and more diverse audience.

To accommodate that audience humanities has foregone the traditional type of course in favor of a method, which we may call the humanities approach. For the purpose of analysis we may subdivide the humanities approach into the following steps which together blueprint the structure of humanities courses and of this book. These steps are theoretical and presumably no course will follow them literally any more than one would consult a blueprint inch by inch; but the steps, like a blueprint, can provide ready reference whenever needed.

1. As a first step the humanities approach places contemporaneous examples of works from different areas side by side to find their common elements. For instance, during the Age of Reason (approximately 1600 to 1775) *The Spirit of the Laws* of Montesquieu proposed a three-part system of government structured upon a symmetrical balance of power; the Classical symphony form which crystallized during this same period relies upon similar

symmetry and balance, so that political theory and music of the Age of Reason contain structural qualities in common.

2. As a further step, this common element may then be traced across all areas of culture during a given period. In the poetry of the Age of Reason, the heroic couplet reflects the same reliance as do political theory and music upon symmetry and balance. In painting, the rules laid down by Charles Le Brun for the Royal Academy of Painting and Sculpture in Paris likewise stress symmetry and balance. The universe of Isaac Newton rests upon a symmetrical and balanced interaction among forces. Even the planning of gardens during the Age of Reason required precisely symmetrical designs, thereby mirroring the same balance of forces as in *The Spirit of the Laws*, the Classical symphony, the heroic couplet, the rules of Le Brun, and the universe of Newton.

3. Every period has a number of characteristic elements which affect all areas of its culture, and the next step in the humanities approach is to identify those elements and to examine the recurrence of each in area after area. For example, a rationalistic element pervades the culture of the Age of Reason, and this together with symmetry and balance further enriches our knowledge of its arts and essence. And as other elements such as scientism, Deism, social contract, and a new attitude toward physical nature are discerned and traced one by one across areas of knowledge we come to understand the total pattern of the Age of Reason and to experience its full savor.

4. Slightly outside the scope of the humanities approach is the final step: assembling the patterns of all periods to form a total structure. Tentative attempts in that direction are made in Part II.

Humanities materials are well nigh limitless, but the humanities approach in every case narrows down the use made of them to one result: a moment of illumination. The Pythagorean number theory that eight symbolizes perfect harmony viewed alongside the Pythagorean development of the eight-tone scale spells discovery; so too does the disappearance of receding planes in seventeenth-century Baroque painting—in the Renaissance depth was marked off in discrete layers—viewed alongside the contemporary theories of democracy of John Locke; and so too the perception that the objective correlative of T. S. Eliot reflects the same depersonalized form as Constructivism in sculpture, the International style in architecture, Cubism in painting, the tone-row in music, technocracy, and the sociological bombshells in Spengler's *Decline of the West*.

Humanities has no monopoly on these moments of illumination. Specialist courses are aware of them too. Where humanities differs is in the way it examines parallel perceptions, not from a central concern with music or architecture or literature or painting but by setting all areas alongside one another in peer relationship. Where specialist studies stress the vertical line of chronology or the pinpoint of depth, humanities is uniquely horizontal.

It sweeps across broad areas and harvests the common elements among them, and by matching up those elements side by side achieves discovery through a widening of vision.

Each of the nine chapters that follows[1] deals with one of the distinctive cultural blocks that builds from Greece up to the present time so that the full range of Western civilization—the usual outside limits of any humanities course—is covered. Each consists of a historical overview and a horizontal scrutiny of the given period. The "Events" sections provide the background needed to set the culture of a period in proper perspective: the thirteenth-century B.C. Greek sea raids, for example, explain the setting of Homer's *Iliad* and *Odyssey*, and nineteenth-century imperialism points to the exoticism of the North African paintings of Eugène Delacroix. Historical interpretation is kept at a minimum and relationships between history and culture pointed out wherever feasible, so that the historical summaries feed directly into the central concern of this book, the humanities approach.

History is a study of what goes into the make-up of an age; humanities is a study of what comes out of it. What does come out is at least as rich and various as history and as difficult to reduce to simple formula. Nevertheless this handbook does turn to formula, in order to provide a useful framework— the swarming, endless elements of humanities demand some kind of compartments into which they can at least be sorted. Therefore the humanities materials of every age are here divided into three categories: traits; ideas; forms and techniques. Traits include all of those elements of a period that shape and reveal its way of life, its temper: balance and symmetry, for example, are elements of the temper of the Age of Reason. Ideas mirror the view of life of a period: for example, the Greek idea that a man's will is limitless and free. The forms and techniques characteristic of a period reveal its physical attitude to life: an example would be the technique of liturgical symbolism that permeated every work of art in the Middle Ages. The humanities approaches that follow will survey the traits, ideas, and forms and techniques of each period from the horizontal viewpoint of interrelationships among philosophy, literature, architecture, sculpture, painting, and music. To provide the fullest possible experience of a period each humanities approach makes its survey a piece at a time. It approaches temper trait by trait; it deals with ideas one by one; it does the same for forms and techniques.

TRAITS

The first full scale humanities approach in this book is applied to the Greek Golden Age and typifies the method used throughout the text. The

[1] Chapters 1–5 make up Part I and Chapters 6–10 make up Part II of *The Humanities Handbook*.

approach begins with a consideration of Golden Age traits, and its handling of the first trait, of passion-and-control as a unit force, is typical. Table 1 outlines this handling:

TABLE 1

Trait	Introduction	Philosophy	Literature	Architecture	Sculpture	Painting	Music
Passion-and-control	Nietzsche and the Orphic myth of Dionysus Zagreus	Heraclitus and tension of oppo-sites. Plato, *Phaedrus* myth and Demiurge	Homer: war and peace; character conflicts. Aeschylus: Furies and Apollo. Sophocles: character of Oedipus	Symmetry and subtle imbalances (the Parthe-non)	Serene faces and off-bal-ance bodies (Praxite-les, Skopas Parthenon frieze)	Proces-sionals counter-balanced by strug-gles (vase painting: the Three Maidens painter)	Soothing lyre and exciting aulos; Doric and Phrygian scales counter-balanced

The trait is discussed, shown to be reflected in contemporary thought, and then traced across its appearance in all of the salient art forms. This same procedure is used for each Golden Age trait to show how it affects—*similarly* affects—the various arts.

Traits tend to repeat themselves, although with variations, from one period to another: there is Greek reason and seventeenth-century reason; Greek coldness verging on cruelty and Medieval brutality. Such repetition reminds us that much in man remains unchanged and cautions that while a humanities approach to a single trait can be intriguing by itself, it is only through a cumulated cluster of traits that any given period takes shape. That cluster, however, can reveal the temper of an age remarkably well. Against its backdrop every key work of art becomes a prismatic glass. For example, Dante's *Divine Comedy* mirrors the hierarchical order, formalism, dualism, faith, and brutality of Medieval temper; so does the Gothic Cathedral of Our Lady at Amiens, so that the Italian epic and the French edifice reveal a profound and special kinship when viewed from the vantage point of the humanities approach.

IDEAS

In each humanities approach in the text the survey of traits is followed by a survey of ideas. The boundary between traits and ideas, however, can seem sharper than it really is. Traits frequently slope over into ideas, and the formulated judgments characteristic of an age usually reflect its temper. Why, for example, should we label faith a Medieval trait but call love as ritual a Medieval idea? To answer broadly, divisions between traits and ideas are arbitrary and the reader may redesign them as he chooses. In defense of the present alignment, traits being buried deep in the psyche of an age would permeate all of its areas of art and learning; ideas, which are more cerebral, probably would not, so that in cases where the line between traits and ideas is blurred their humanities applications determine where they are assigned. For example, the trait of faith colors every Medieval art form; the idea of love as ritual has a marked impact on Medieval literature, sculpture, and painting, but it has little or no impact on architecture and music.

Though less pervasive, ideas also appear in parallel patterns in the art forms of any given period and hence are presented in much the same way as traits. Table 2, for example, outlines the treatment of the first idea presented in the humanities approach to the Greek Golden Age.

TABLE 2

Idea	Introduction	Philosophy	Literature	Architecture	Sculpture	Painting	Music
Free will	Not in orient; originated with Greeks	Heraclitus: man's will as his destiny. Plato applies Heraclitus to meta-physics	Homer: Zeus' speech in *Odyssey*. Sophocles: Oedipus as free to choose		Indepen-dence in attitudes: Polyclitus: *Spearbearer*		

The idea of free will appears so sketchily, if at all, in Greek architecture, painting, and music that the text does not discuss it in those areas.

FORMS AND TECHNIQUES

Besides its native temper and ideas, each period has forms and techniques characteristic to it: no modern painter, for instance, would content himself with literal representation or with portraits of the Madonna and Child repeated with variations which make them symbolize a full range of topics and concepts. Although more easily distinguished than traits and ideas, forms and techniques nevertheless sometimes shade into the other categories. Hellenistic satire, for example, which partakes of temper and idea, is placed in the text under technique since the Hellenistic Greeks themselves considered it as such. Since forms and techniques can be nearly endless, only a reasonable amount of showcase ones are presented in this handbook. Included, however, are enough examples to make it clear that form and technique are vital to the humanities approach.

Chapters 2 to 5 (and 6 to 10 in Part II) propose, then, to suggest how the temper, mind, and stance of each period reveal themselves throughout all aspects of total culture. Against so vast a claim the size of this book suggests limitations. Only the more salient traits, ideas, and forms of each period are presented. Some, which are subtler and perhaps too private, have been omitted; others have undoubtedly been overlooked. The reader may well turn up a number of searching traits and ideas not covered here. Another limitation is the choice of examples. These could include any and every work of art, literature, and music ever created, but they have been deliberately restricted in most cases to the standard ones in survey books in order to match as closely as possible the materials the usual course will cover. However, additional materials covered in your course as well as any further examples you choose to examine on your own can all be fitted into the humanities structure presented here. A further limitation derives from the nature of the arts themselves. Sculpture is not painting, and literature, architecture, and music are even less alike. That is, the arts do not lend themselves to precise analogies, and none will be attempted here. But all of the arts do reflect the characteristic traits, ideas, and forms of a period—some reflect almost all, others only a few—and these reflections will be explored in detail, often provocatively.

A final limitation might seem to be the arbitrary order of areas presented in the text: that is, unvaryingly philosophy, literature, architecture, sculpture, painting, music. One can justify putting philosophy first, since its function is to articulate the newest directions in our thinking. The remaining order might just as well have been shuffled or reversed. A music historian might, for example, construct a full portrait of Medieval temper out of the motet and then go on to show how all of the other arts in the Middle Ages echo the same traits found in the motet. An art historian might do the same with the Cathedral of Chartres. Humanities can be taught, then, from any starting point. What is more, there is really no such thing as a humanities professor, only a humanities person, a genus rather than a species. He is special not through specialization but through his ability to perceive and to profit from the horizontal view. One major American historian manages to build up a rounded picture of American civilization out of fluctuations in the price of wheat.

In the course of your studies you will probably meet professors of art, music, literature, history, or even "unlikely" subjects like science who teach humanities (the universal field theory of Albert Einstein is an archetypal humanities approach). The humanities course has no monopoly on the horizontal view or on the illumination that comes from the parallel patterns turned up by that view. It is special only in that *it concentrates upon the horizontal method* and thus does more than any other course to insure the breadth and illumination nurtured by that method. As a result it is sometimes the target, and victim, of exaggerated claims. It should be noted at the outset therefore that humanities does not teach you everything. It merely makes it possible for you to understand everything you learn.

SELECTED BIBLIOGRAPHY

The selected bibliography below consists mainly of books whose scope and contributions are broad.

GENERAL

History

Brinton, Crane, John B. Christopher, and Robert Lee Wolff. *Civilization in the West.* Englewood Cliffs, N.J.: Prentice-Hall, 1964.

Burns, Edward McNall. *Western Civilizations.* New York: Norton, 1963.

Easton, Stewart C. *The Western Heritage.* New York: Holt, Rinehart and Winston, 1966.

Fisher, H. A. L. *A History of Europe.* 3 vols. Boston: Houghton Mifflin, 1935–1936.

Johnson, Edgar N. *An Introduction to the History of the Western Tradition.* 2 vols. Boston: Ginn, 1959.

Knoles, George H., and Rixford K. Snyder. (Eds.) *Readings in Western Civilization.* Philadelphia: Lippincott, 1960.

McNeill, William H. *The Rise of the West.* New York: Mentor, 1963.

Toynbee, Arnold. *A Study of History.* 12 vols. New York: Oxford University Press, 1934–1961. (See also the one volume redaction by D. C. Somervell, Oxford, 1947.)

Social and Intellectual Background

Barnes, Harry Elmer. *An Intellectual and Cultural History of the Western World.* New York: Reynal, 1941.

Brinton, Crane. *Ideas and Men: the Story of Western Thought.* Englewood Cliffs, N.J.: Prentice-Hall, 1950.

Collingwood, Robin G. *The Idea of History.* Oxford: Clarendon, 1949.

Commins, Saxe, and Robert Linscott. (Eds.) *The World's Great Thinkers.* 4 vols. New York: Random House, 1947.

Copleston, Frederick. *A History of Philosophy.* 2 vols. London: Newman, 1946–1950.

Durant, Will. *The Story of Philosophy.* New York: Simon and Schuster, 1933.

Edman, Irwin, and Herbert W. Schneider. (Eds.) *Landmarks for Beginners in Philosophy.* New York: Holt, Rinehart and Winston, 1941.

Fleming, William. *Arts and Ideas.* New York: Holt, Rinehart and Winston, 1968.

Fuller, Benjamin A. *History of Philosophy.* New York: Holt, Rinehart and Winston, 1945.

Hayes, Carlton J. *A Political and Cultural History of Modern Europe.* 2 vols. New York: Macmillan, 1933.

Jones, W. T. *A History of Western Philosophy.* New York: Harcourt, 1952.

Lamprecht, Sterling P. *Our Philosophical Traditions.* New York: Appleton, 1955.

Randall, John H. *The Making of the Modern Mind.* Boston: Houghton Mifflin, 1940.

Robinson, James Harvey. *Mind in the Making.* New York: Harper & Row, 1921.

Runes, Dagobert. *Dictionary of Philosophy.* New York: Philosophical Library, 1942.

Russell, Bertrand. *A History of Western Philosophy.* New York: Simon and Schuster, 1945.

Smith, Preserved. *A History of Modern Culture.* 2 vols. New York: Holt, Rinehart and Winston, 1930–1934.

Smith, Thomas V. (Ed.) *Philosophers Speak for Themselves.* Chicago: University of Chicago Press, 1934.

Wallis, Wilson D. *Culture and Progress.* New York: McGraw-Hill, 1930.

Windelband, Wilhelm. *A History of Philosophy.* 2 vols. New York: Harper Torchbooks, 1958.

Wissler, Clark. *Man and Culture.* New York: Crowell, 1923.

Literature

Buck, Philo M. *An Anthology of World Literature.* New York: Macmillan, 1951.
_____ . *The Golden Thread.* New York: Macmillan, 1931.

Chadwick, Hector M., and N. K. Chadwick. *The Growth of Literature.* 2 vols. Cambridge: Cambridge University Press, 1932–1936.

Everett, Edwin M., Calvin S. Brown, and John D. Wade. (Eds.) *Masterworks of World Literature.* 2 vols. New York: Holt, Rinehart and Winston, 1955.

Guerard, Albert. *Preface to World Literature.* New York: Holt, Rinehart and Winston, 1945.

Hibbard, Addison, and Horst Frenz. *Writers of the Western World.* Boston: Houghton Mifflin, 1954.

Highet, Gilbert. *The Classical Tradition: Greek and Roman Influences on Western Literature.* New York: Oxford, 1950.

Hornstein, Lillian H., *et al. The Reader's Companion to World Literature.* New York: Holt, Rinehart and Winston, 1956.

Horton, R. W., and V. Hopper. *Backgrounds of European Literature.* New York: Appleton, 1954.

Locke, Louis G., John P. Kirby, and M. E. Porter. (Eds.) *Literature of Western Civilization.* 2 vols. New York: Ronald, 1952.

Mack, Maynard, *et al.* (Eds.) *World Masterpieces.* 2 vols. New York: Norton, 1965.

Moulton, Richard G. *World Literature, and Its Place in General Culture.* New York: Macmillan, 1911.

Trawick, Buckner B. *World Literature.* 2 vols. New York: Barnes & Noble, 1958.

Warnock, Robert, and George K. Anderson. (Eds.) *The World in Literature.* 4 vols. Chicago: Scott, Foresman, 1967.

Architecture, Sculpture, Painting

Bazin, Germain. *A History of Art from Prehistoric Times to the Present.* Boston: Houghton Mifflin, 1959.

Chase, G. H., and C. R. Post. *A History of Sculpture.* New York: Harper & Row, 1925.

Cheney, Sheldon. *A New World History of Art.* New York: Holt, Rinehart and Winston, 1956.

Fletcher, Banister. *A History of Architecture on the Comparative Method*. London: Batsford, 1956.

Gardner, Helen. *Art Through the Ages*. New York: Harcourt, 1959.

Giedion, Siegfried. *Space, Time and Architecture*. Cambridge, Mass.: Harvard University Press, 1954.

Gilbert, Katherine E., and Helmut Kuhn. *A History of Esthetics*. Bloomington: Indiana University Press, 1953.

Gloag, John. *Guide to Western Architecture*. New York: Macmillan, 1959.

Gombrich, Ernst H. *Art and Illusion*. New York: Pantheon, 1960.

———. *The Story of Art*. New York: Phaidon, 1957.

Hamlin, Talbot. *Architecture Through the Ages*. New York: Putnam, 1953.

Hauser, Arnold. *The Social History of Art*. 4 vols. New York: Vintage, 1951.

Janson, H. W. *History of Art*. New York: Prentice-Hall and Abrams, 1962.

Malraux, André. *The Voices of Silence*. New York: Doubleday, 1953.

Newton, Eric. *European Painting and Sculpture*. Baltimore: Penguin, 1949.

———. *Masterpieces of European Sculpture*. New York: Abrams, 1959.

Pevsner, Nikolaus. *An Outline of European Architecture*. Baltimore: Penguin, 1960.

Read, Herbert. *The Art of Sculpture*. New York: Pantheon, 1956.

———. *Art and Society*. London: Faber and Faber, 1945.

Robb, David M. *Harper History of Painting*. New York: Harper & Row, 1951.

——— and J. J. Garrison. *Art in the Western World*. New York: Harper & Row, 1963.

Roos, Frank J., Jr. (Ed.) *An Illustrated Handbook of Art History*. New York: Macmillan, 1954.

Taylor, Francis Henry. *Fifty Centuries of Art*. New York: Harper & Row, 1960.

Upjohn, Everard M., Paul S. Wingert, and Jane Gaston Mahler. *History of World Art*. New York: Oxford, 1958.

Music

Bacharach, A. L. (Ed.) *The Music Masters*. 4 vols. Baltimore: Penguin, 1957.

Bauer, Marion, and Ethel Peyser. *Music Through the Ages*. New York: Putnam, 1951.

Boyden, David D. *An Introduction to Music*. New York: Knopf, 1956.

Cannon, Beekman, Alvin Johnson, and William Waite. *The Art of Music*. New York: Crowell, 1960.

Davison, Archibald T., and Willi Apel. *Historical Anthology of Music*. 2 vols. Cambridge, Mass.: Harvard University Press, 1947–1950.

Einstein, Alfred. *A Short History of Music*. New York: Vintage, 1954.

Ferguson, Donald N. *A History of Musical Thought*. New York: Appleton, 1948.

Finney, Theodore. *A History of Music*. New York: Harcourt, 1947.

Grout, Donald Jay. *A History of Western Music*. New York: Norton, 1960.

———. *A Short History of Opera*. 2 vols. New York: Columbia University Press, 1947.

Harman, Alec, Anthony Milner, and Wilfred Mellers. *Man and His Music*. New York: Oxford University Press, 1962.

Harman, Carter. *A Popular History of Music*. New York: Dell, 1956.

Lang, Paul Henry. *Music in Western Civilization*. New York: Norton, 1941.

Leichentritt, Hugo. *Music, History, and Ideas*. Cambridge, Mass.: Harvard University Press, 1938.

McKinney, Howard D., and W. R. Anderson. *Music in History.* New York: American Book, 1940.

Sachs, Curt. *Our Musical Heritage.* Englewood Cliffs, N.J.: Prentice-Hall, 1948.

Strunk, Oliver. (Ed.) *Source Readings in Music History, from Classical Antiquity Through the Romantic Era.* New York: Norton, 1950.

Zuckerkandl, Victor. *Sound and Symbol.* New York: Pantheon, 1956.

CHAPTER 2
GREECE

EVENTS

Pioneer farmers settled the peninsula that would be known as Greece as early as 6500 B.C., and about 5000 B.C. a race of short, dark-haired neolithic settlers moved into Crete from the Levant. By 3000 B.C. the fusion of these groups produced what is called Early Helladic culture. By 2600 B.C. brown-haired invaders armed with bronze weapons swept westward into Crete and then north across the Aegean to found the city of Mycenae in the southeastern corner of the Greek peninsula. The fusion of these invaders with the Early Helladics generated an ornate and sophisticated Bronze Age culture in Crete and Mycenae which by 1900 B.C. was urban, literate, and unfortified.

About 1950 B.C. the first Greek-speaking people invaded the peninsula. They came from the northern plains, probably Macedonia, and were primitive in comparison to the earlier inhabitants, having achieved little more than the domestication of horses. But by 1550 B.C. they dominated all of Greece and established Mycenae and nearby Tiryns as major capitals. This period is termed Middle Helladic and is marked by the rule of petty kings (Homer's Menelaus and Agamemnon were just such Middle Helladic rulers), by the emergence of a thunder-wielding Zeus as head of a family of gods, and by free expansion into the western wastelands. However, the Middle Helladics were blocked off from the rich trade with the East. Crete monopolized this trade, and although Mycenae and Tiryns developed rapidly as cities, they could not compete with Amnisos, the chief port of Crete, which lay across the Aegean. By 1400 B.C. invaders from the east overran Crete and destroyed its culture, probably after a devastating earthquake. Even the palace of Knossos with its lush decorations and legendary labyrinthine structure was burned and razed.

Mycenae now entered into trade with the Levant and soon became the chief western city, inheriting the burdens as well as the blessings of wealth and fame. From 1300 B.C. on she was peppered by sea raids, mainly from the Philistines, then Egyptian subjects. She retaliated in kind, against the Philistines (who may have given Palestine its Greek name) and against other harassers like Troy (Hissarlik), which lay across the Aegean to the northeast. These sea raids provided the subject matter of Homer's *Iliad* and *Odyssey*.

THE DARK AND MIDDLE AGES

In the end it was not eastern sea raids but a northern land invasion that overcame Mycenae and Tiryns. About 1100 B.C. Greek-speaking Dorians conquered the entire southern peninsula and made Sparta their central base

16

and new home. Like the northern invaders of 1950 B.C., the Dorians were primitive and brutal. The culture of Mycenae came to an end, writing disappeared, and plagues overran cities such as Thebes (the Oedipus myth derived from this time).

Over the next 200 years the Dorians spread southward and took over the islands of Melos, Rhodes, Thera, Crete, and Kos, while emigrants from central Greece sailed eastward across the Aegean Sea and settled the region of Ionia on the west coast of Asia Minor. These settlements established the structure and geography of classical Greece.

By the eighth century B.C. the Greek communities thus formed in the central and southern peninsula and in Ionia clustered into city-states, separate and complete societies each independent of and hostile to the others. They did so both for surface and searching reasons: the Greek terrain consists of mainly fertile plains cut off from one another by mountains; and the Greek polis (city-state) became not merely an economic group but a vital self-contained organism whose public affairs became the personal concern of all of its members.

By the eighth century B.C. literacy had returned to Greece and spread rapidly throughout the city-states. The Olympic games were established in 776 B.C. Greek colonists expanded westward into Sicily and founded Syracuse, then northeast and founded Byzantium. These colonies provided new markets for trade and hence a rise in living standards. In this century and the next most of the city-states were controlled by "tyrants," mainly enlightened rulers whose active interest in all aspects of the city-state reflected that of the average citizen. Outstanding among the tyrants was Periander of Corinth whose reign was succeeded, typically, by a wealthy middle-class government.

The only major cities which did not follow this pattern of tyrant-to-oligarchy were Sparta and Athens. Sparta, the core Dorian settlement, adhered to the laws of a shadowy figure named Lycurgus, who may never have existed. These laws called for Sparta to remain a military aristocracy, nominally under two kings whose limited powers were further curtailed by a council of five supervisors. The backbone of Spartan government was a council of twenty-eight elders, all over sixty years of age, chosen from the noble families and elected for life. The Spartan Assembly, consisting only of males over thirty belonging to the few thousand Spartist or full citizen families, passed on all key decisions. No other Spartans had a voice in their destinies. Spartan life reflected this hard, exclusive type of government. Infant boys who seemed weaklings were left outdoors to die; the remainder were taken from their mothers at the age of seven and brought up in camps. At twenty they were elected into army platoons of fifteen members with whom they spent the essential part of their lives. Required to marry at thirty, they continued to sleep in the platoon barracks. Discipline and stability formed the code of their lives, and that of Sparta.

Until almost the sixth century B.C., Athens remained comparatively dormant. Untouched by the Dorian invasion she developed no colonies and produced no tyrant. She lived under the Code of Draco, a collection of laws that favored the rich and decreed death as the penalty for every misdemeanor. At this time Ionia led Athens and all other Greek city-states in cultural matters. It had already produced Homer. At the turn of the seventh century it became the birthplace of Western philosophy. Even Hesiod, the only significant name in ancient Greek literature besides Homer, wrote in Ionian dialect, although he was from the region of Boeotia.

Then, in 594 B.C. in Athens, Solon, a nobleman of modest means, was given near dictatorial powers and a mandate from the people to effect reforms. He abolished enslavement for debt, forbade the export of grain during famine, gave status to the Citizens' Assembly, and established a People's Council of 400 citizens so chosen as to include all classes. His reforms were backed up by the sword of Peisistratus, who ruled as tyrant from 546 to 528 B.C. Reform in Athens led in turn to great cultural advances in the areas of sculpture, vase painting, and drama, which began about this time.

THE WARS WITH PERSIA

In 546 B.C. the Greeks had their first clash with a massive, centralized empire when Cyrus, king of Persia, made the long march westward and subdued Ionia. Cyrus placed all Ionian cities under Greek governors loyal to him and collected yearly tribute. He then turned his attention eastward and conquered Babylon. Cyrus was killed in 529 B.C. and in 499 B.C. Ionia revolted against the Persian tyranny. Darius, a despotic nephew of Cyrus and a brilliant organizer, was king of Persia at the time of the revolt. His armies marched upon Ionia and began to destroy it systematically while Athens debated fiercely whether or not to help her neighbor across the sea.

In the generation between the death of Cyrus and the Ionian revolt Athens had made giant strides in the direction of democracy. Under a new and liberal tyrant, Cleisthenes, all free men who were permanent residents of Athens were declared citizens, the People's Council grew in number from 400 to 500, and the city-state was subdivided into thirty wards, each containing a cross section of the population. The chief remaining vestige of aristocracy was the Council of Archons (best men), whose members were still elected from the patrician class and who, at the close of their year of service, were appointed for life to the Areopagite Council (a kind of supreme court). Themistocles, an intense liberal and one of the great political manipulators in Athenian history, was elected Archon in 499 B.C. He argued for aid to Ionia, and at the very moment that he was swinging the assembly over to his side a Persian army crossed the Aegean and took up a position at the north end of the plain of Marathon, a coastal city northeast of Athens. An Athenian army, led by Themistocles' choice, a refugee Ionian general named Miltiades, marched to meet them. Miltiades formed his troops in a line thin at the center and massed at the flanks, and when at the first onslaught the Persians burst through the center of the line the Greek flanks cut them off from behind and slaughtered about 6400 of them. The survivors fled in their ships and Athens emerged from the Battle of Marathon the chief city-state of Greece, a distinction she would retain throughout the entire century.

In a final effort to regain power the Athenian aristocrats tried time and again without success to get Themistocles exiled. But they did manage to bring charges and levy a huge fine against his friend Miltiades for "deceiving the people"—that is, for failing to overtake the fleeing Persians. At that time, however, a wound he had gotten in the Persian pursuit gangrened and he died. In 487 B.C. Themistocles arranged that henceforth Archons would be chosen by lottery—the coup de grace for the patricians. Then in 485 B.C. he persuaded the state to assign revenues from a new-found silver mine to the building of mammoth triple-decked warships in preparation for the next Persian invasion, which he termed inevitable. It came in 480 B.C.

The new Persian king was Xerxes, who succeeded his father Darius in 486 B.C. A stern, decisive ruler, Xerxes prepared a full-scale invasion aimed at the total destruction of Greece. Athens, a few nearby islands, Sparta, and her Peloponnesian allies banded together under the leadership of Sparta—a bitter pill which Themistocles persuaded the Athenians to swallow. The first encounter came at Macedonia where a Persian army routed an Athenian-Spartan one. To allow time for a sea raid on Xerxes' navy at Artemision, on the east coast of central Greece, an army composed mainly of Spartans under the Spartan general Leonides delayed the Persian army at a high rocky pass at Thermopylae, in central Greece almost due west of Artemision. The overwhelmingly larger Persian army was held at the pass by Spartans fighting in relays, and although every Greek soldier perished there the sea raid at Artemision was successful. At this juncture Themistocles persuaded Athens to move all warships to Salamis, an island a short distance west of the mainland and separated from it by a narrow strait. Meanwhile Xerxes' army marched unimpeded through Greece putting all cities to fire and sword. Athens was leveled and the Acropolis burned. Xerxes, in a hurry because of the approaching winter, grew careless in his haste and followed the Greeks into the shallow waters around Salamis. While he watched from a throne set up on a mainland hill, the heavier Greek ships grounded and destroyed his navy. Two hundred Persian ships were sunk and Persian corpses blackened the beaches. Athens lost only forty ships. The following summer a combined Greek force wiped out all that was left of the Persian army within its borders. This occurred in 478 B.C. and launched Greece upon its Golden Age, which would last for only fifty years.

THE GOLDEN AGE

After the Persian War Ionia petitioned Athens for protection, and city-states in other regions followed suit. The Delian League was thus formed under the protectorship of Athens but with its treasury at Delos, an island city off the east coast of the Greek mainland. Kimon, whose father had been Miltiades, was appointed general of the league. Athens went to war against Corinth, defeated it, and demanded a protectorate over the whole Greek mainland up to Thermopylae. In 455 B.C. the Athenian navy confined Sparta to the southernmost section of the Peloponnese.

Paradoxically, as Athenian imperial power increased so did its zest for democracy. The Assembly deprived the Areopagite Council of most of its powers and turned over decisions on constitutionality to the people. Moreover Athenian art now reached a high point with the poetry of Pindar, the bronze sculpture of Myron, the fixing of the Greek temple form, and the development of tragedy by Aeschylus.

In small ways, however, Athenian zeal began to slope over into excess, and the causes of Athens' downfall can be traced back to the very start of its Golden Age. In 471 B.C. Themistocles was exiled on charges of accepting bribes during the war against Xerxes. Ten years later Kimon, married to an Athenian aristocrat, was exiled in an outburst of democratic passion, and at the same time Athens broke off its alliance with Sparta. In 454 B.C. Athens transferred the treasury of the Delian League to its own city. In 451 B.C. it decreed that no one could be a citizen whose parents were not Athenian born. These strictures led to rebellion in Boeotia in 447 B.C., and Athens lost its hold on central Greece in a matter of days. Meanwhile Sparta made warlike gestures, but Athens wisely appeased her and in 445 B.C. obtained her promise of a thirty years' peace.

Over the next fourteen years Athens built the Parthenon and adorned it with sculptures directed by Pheidias; Sophocles and Aeschylus vied with one another in the writing of tragedy; Herodotus emerged as the father of history; and Anaxagoras, Protagoras, and Socrates gave fresh impetus to science and philosophy. In politics Pericles gained and held the trust of the people as no one else would do in the history of Greece. An aristocrat with democratic convictions, Pericles was never a top political leader—though he was elected general almost every year—but his was the voice that the assembly listened to more than any other. To the great good fortune of democratic Athens, Pericles placed her interests above all else and did for her the best that any individual can do for a state: he abetted her glory; but he could not prevent her decline.

In 431 B.C. the "thirty years' peace" between Sparta and Athens ended after only fourteen years, and these two leading city-states embarked upon their most decisive war. Known as the Peloponnesian War, it lasted until 404 B.C. It was probably started by Pericles who believed that such a war was inevitable and that, from Athens' point of view, now was the best time for it. From the start the war went badly for Athens. A plague brought in from Egypt struck the city in 430 B.C. and killed one fourth of its population, including Pericles, during the next three years. After this the fortunes and in a sense even the character of Athens declined. The following two events exemplify that decline: in 428 B.C. Mytelene, a city on the eastern Aegean island of Lesbos, revolted unsuccessfully against Athens and was crushed. Cleon, Pericles' successor, persuaded the assembly to condemn the entire male population of Mytelene to death. The assembly agreed, but the next day it relented and sent word to spare the Mytelenes. But when the northern city of Skione revolted unsuccessfully in 442 B.C., the assembly ordered all males killed and the women and children sold as slaves. This time no humanitarian second thoughts intervened.

In 421 B.C. Athens and Sparta agreed to a fifty years' peace which was broken in 416 B.C. when Athens sent a large army to western Sicily to help non-Greek Segesta against Dorian Selinous. Athens in 419 B.C. had found a new hero to replace Pericles. He was Alcibiades, a demagogue whose chief concern was himself and whose chief asset was his winning personality. He and a merchant named Nikias led the army that invaded Sicily, until Alcibiades fled to Sparta after Athens recalled him to face charges of heresy. In Sicily Nikias, left in sole charge, besieged rich and powerful Syracuse while Alcibiades persuaded Sparta to come to the aid of Syracuse against his erstwhile homeland. In 414 B.C. a combined Syracusan-Spartan army crushed Nikias' troops and drove them into the sea. Those Athenians not killed were put to work in the quarries of Syracuse where most of them soon died.

Athens went on with the Peloponnesian War for nine years longer. Alcibiades, in trouble in Sparta, returned to help lead the Athenian fleet in its final series of major sea battles. He lost at Samos and fled to the palace he owned at Gallipoli. In 404 B.C. the bulk of the Athenian fleet, incompetently led, was crushed by Sparta at Argospotamai; 170 ships were captured and 4000 Athenians were executed on the spot. That same year the city of Athens surrendered under siege to Sparta. The Peloponnesian War was over. So was the Golden Age of Greece.

THE HELLENISTIC PERIOD

During the war Greek culture had teetered between the last phases of Golden Age classicism and the opening phases of Hellenistic humanism. The Propylaea and the Temple of Nike on the Acropolis were constructed.

Sophocles wrote his last plays while Euripides and Aristophanes wrote protest plays; Democritus formulated atomic theories, while Hippocrates put new emphasis on scientific observation.

Sparta set up a protectorate in Athens that was run by thirty Athenian oligarchs. The oligarchs, who were led by the Sophist Critias, purged all extremist democratic elements and then turned upon the moderates. The moderates then revolted and killed Critias, whereupon Sparta restored at least an appearance of democratic government to Athens. However, the trial and execution of Socrates in 399 B.C. shows how timidly puritanical Athenian democracy had become. Athens subsisted thus in the shadow of Sparta until 379 B.C., when Thebes under its brilliant general Epaminondas challenged Spartan control of central Greece. Many mainland cities joined with Thebes, but Athens, jealous of Thebes, allied herself with Sparta. In 362 B.C. a massive Theban army faced one of equal size composed of Spartans and Athenians. Early in the battle Epaminondas was killed and the fighting stopped. Instead of a decisive victory by one dominant city-state the deadlock that had held Greece at a standstill continued, but events were building in the north that would change all that.

Macedonia, at the northern crest of the mainland, lay open and exposed to the regions of Thrace and Thessaly on either side of it. Despite political changes in the rest of Greece Macedonia had remained a monarchy all these years, largely for the purpose of defense against its neighbors. In 349 B.C. Philip, the present king, felt strong enough to shift from defense to attack. He marched upon Athens which for one final time produced a hero worthy to oppose a great invader: Demosthenes, the finest of all Greek orators, who thundered warnings against Philip and urged a general mobilization. Philip marched southward conquering as he went, and when at last in 338 B.C. he faced a massed Greek army at Chaironeia, on the western border of Boeotia, his victory was so decisive that the opposing army turned and ran away.

All of the major Greek cities except Sparta declared allegiance to Philip; then, as he was preparing to invade Asia, he was stabbed while marching in a victory celebration. His son Alexander succeeded him in 337 B.C. Though he was young he swiftly established himself as an icy military genius by crushing a Theban revolt in 335 B.C. and by razing the city, leaving only the temples and the estate of Pindar standing. He then sold the entire population into slavery. He moved eastward and conquered Darius, king of Persia, and then embarked on a march of conquest all the way to India, establishing cities named Alexandria at a dozen different places. He returned home to marry a daughter of Darius, symbolic of the marriage of East and West. While in Babylon preparing a vast sea campaign in 323 B.C. Alexander, now famed as Alexander the Great, caught a fever and suddenly died at the age of thirty-three.

All of the principal Greek city-states (except Sparta, which had remained uncommitted) united in a league against Macedonia, but even under a succession of shaky rulers Macedonia managed to stay in control. In a major sea battle soon after the death of Alexander a superior Macedonian fleet annihilated the Athenian navy off the Dardenelles, ending Athenian sea power forever.

Athenian democracy was abolished in favor of a military protectorate and its common ranks of citizens were all disenfranchised. Demosthenes, hunted down by Macedonia, took poison. Athens languished under Macedonian rule until 266 B.C., when it revolted. The revolt was led by Chremonides and became known as Chremonides' War. Athenian military power was ended when the city-state was besieged and starved into submission by the Macedonians. In 229 B.C. Athens raised enough money to bribe her military governor into leaving and then proclaimed her friendly neutrality toward everyone.

Sparta, reacting to its decline in fortunes by punishing itself, became a tight, legalistic oligarchy with an impassable gulf between rich and poor. In 222 B.C. she finally stirred herself to revolt against Macedonia, but was crushed as totally as Athens had been.

Eliminated as a power, Greece still flourished as a torchbearer of civilization. Hellenic culture had given way to Hellenistic—from *hellenismos*, meaning *imitation* of the Greeks—and had become the property of the world. More individualistic and materialistic than Golden Age culture, it flourished brilliantly in Athens and in such other centers as Alexandria and Priene. Hellenistic philosophy produced the Cynics, the Stoics, and the Epicurians; Hellenistic literature produced Theocritus, Aristophanes, and Menander; Hellenistic science produced Euclid and Archimedes. Greek professional people became valuable properties, and from the third century B.C. on, conquering nations despoiled the city-states of their most vital citizens as well as their art works.

In 217 B.C. while the titanic conflict between Rome and Carthage was shaping up delegates from all of the Greek city-states met at Naupactus, a town on the Gulf of Corinth. There they pledged amity among themselves, neutrality toward both countries, and encouraged one another to avoid this holocaust as much as possible. Typically, within a few years half of the city-states had pledged themselves to Rome, the other half to Carthage. In 212 B.C. Syracuse, siding with Carthage, was overrun by Rome and wiped out. In 86 B.C. Rome besieged and brutalized Athens and made the Greek mainland a battleground for three of its civil wars. In 31 B.C. a shortage of mules during the war between Marcus Antonius and Octavius Caesar caused Antonius' generals to hitch Greek citizens to sacks of their own grain and drive them over 100 miles of mountain paths so that their betters might be fed.

THE HUMANITIES APPROACH

THE HEROIC AGE

General Characteristics

Classical Greece was divided into two sharply defined ages which were preceded by an earlier, less definitive era known as the Heroic Age. Although Greek civilization owes few essentials to earlier cultures, the Heroic Age (1400–1100 B.C.) does reach outward to include the rise of Cretan civilization, the fall of Troy, and backward to still fresh memories of its Eastern origins.

Many of our insights into these origins and into the Heroic Age rely upon the inspired guesswork of Homer and Hesiod. But the view reflected in their writings lacks the full focus that only a wealth of detail can supply, and accordingly the humanities approach to the Heroic Age will be at most a preliminary sketch— impressions and snatches of evidence suggesting general characteristics.

To make the sketch still vaguer the Dorian invasion of 1100 B.C. destroyed Mycenae and ushered in a period of migrations, plagues, and suppressed culture which historians call the Greek Middle Ages (1100–700 B.C.). Since Homer and Hesiod both lived in the Greek Middle Ages, their recollections of the Heroic Age are understandably filtered through the darker lens of their own time. Nevertheless the characteristics to which they attest, laid out in horizontal humanities approach, can serve to broaden not only our understanding of Homer and Hesiod but also of Heroic Age architecture, archaic sculpture, early Greek vase painting, and the origins of Greek music.

Eastern migrations, trade with the East, and the eastern sea raids of the twelfth century B.C. brought Greece into contact with Eastern culture (especially Egyptian), the most advanced culture of that time. As a result of this influence the Heroic Age is in part characterized by a FORMAL, MASSIVE, STYLIZED way of life and art, and a SUPERSTITIOUS AWE OF ANIMALS (many of them monsters) AND WATER since the Nile was literally the Egyptian source of life. The formal, stylized epic speeches of Homer, the Trojan horse of the *Iliad*, the monstrous Scylla of the *Odyssey*, and the central role in that epic of Poseidon, the ocean god, all bear the mark of Eastern influence.

Figure 2.1   Reconstruction of the Megaron at Tiryns. (Original structure 1400–1000 B.C.). [New York Public Library].

In architecture the Tholos (treasury) of Atreus at Mycenae with its stylized horizontal beehive tombs below the earth, closely imitates Egyptian tomb decorations; and the Megaron (palace fortress) at Tiryns (Figure 2.1) with its heavy overhanging roof, its thick supporting walls, and its flat enclosed façade conveys the same oppressive massiveness as the Temple of the Sphinx at Ghizeh or the Temple of Amen Ra. Further, the Megaron is only interesting frontally, connoting the elaborate Eastern ceremony of a formal introduction.

Archaic sculpture got under way later than its sister arts, and its beginnings too were shaped by Eastern influences. The stiff frontality of seventh-century B.C. figures like the *Auxerre Goddess* (Figure 2.2) and the *Youth from Sunium* (Figure 2.3) is Eastern. The *Auxerre Goddess* stands flat and heavy, her weight resting equally on both feet, suggesting Eastern massiveness. She is highly stylized; her hair is a double row of temple columns plaited into a square design; her robe is an elaboration of this design. Her right wrist and hand forego anatomical accuracy, duplicating the shape of her waist and upper torso. The ears, lower torso, and kneecaps of the *Youth from Sunium* are patterned designs that make no attempt at all at realism (the ears in fact are Ionian volutes).

Figure 2.2   *Auxerre Goddess.*   (c. 630 B.C.).   Louvre,
Paris.   [Hirmer Fotoarchiv Munchen].

    The prevalence of sculpted animals also indicates Eastern influence. The
famous lions on the castle gate at Mycenae, whose massiveness is emphasized
by the heavy rocks they seem to brace, were copied in miniature and used
on the pediment of the Megaron. Also common in the eighth and seventh
centuries B.C. were hammered bronze figurines of lions, deer, and centaurs.

The stylized designs and figures on geometric vases resemble the frieze and design work on the portico wall of the Megaron. Many eighth century B.C. vases make considerable use of animals, including horses, dogs, goats, deer, griffins, centaurs, and the monstrous chimaera with its goat's head, lion's body, and serpent's tail. The amphora shown in Figure 2.4 combines formal design, animals, and stylized human figures. The torsos and arms of the charioteers form geometric designs; so do the legs of the horses pulling the chariots. The upper front of the horses is an inverted version of the lower half of the charioteers, thus interlinking horse and rider on the basis of formal design. The grazing horses above the chariots are formal geometric exercises; above them, the massive lion crushing the doe is at once an exercise in triangles and an echo of Eastern superstition. The decorative, geometric bands are also stylized and formal.

With no record of the nature of music in the Heroic Age, our knowledge rests mainly upon conjecture. Most music historians believe that the cult music of Egypt passed into Heroic Greece and that the hymns to Isis and Serapis were in widespread use there. These latter seem to have been solemn, formal chants and dances accompanied by *sistra* (raucous clappers) and giant tambourines.

In the Heroic Age mankind saw itself as the product of DETERMINISM, will-less, the course of its life being determined by all-powerful, whimsical gods. While Zeus early in the *Odyssey* claims that man's will is free (p. 48) and Odysseus shows a certain resourcefulness in escaping from the Cyclops, his fate is largely determined throughout the epic by opposing gods. Homer had the genius to glimpse the way of the future, but his heroes in the main were ruled by *moira*, destiny. In the *Iliad* the entire Trojan nation is made the predestined victim of spiteful gods, and Zeus speaks of man as follows: "Lo, he thinks that he shall never suffer evil in time to come, while the gods give him happiness and his limbs move lightly. But when, again, the blessed gods have wrought for him sorrow, even so he bears it, as he must, with a steadfast heart, for the spirit of men upon the earth is even as their day that comes upon them from the father of gods and men." Homer's contemporary, Hesiod, implied this same fatal inevitability in his cycle of the Ages of Man: Gold, Silver, Bronze, Heroic, Iron.

Archaic sculpture, stylized as it is beyond all possibility of human empathy, reflects this same sense of determinism. If the *Auxerre Goddess* conveyed the idea of God, then it was a God unapproachable by man.

Still another characteristic of a civilization determined by whimsical gods was the SHARP DIVISION BETWEEN RELIGION AND MORALITY. Since early worship involved no moral sanctions, Homer's gods could quite properly cheat and trick both sides during the Trojan War. Funeral services like those for Patroclus in the *Iliad* unabashedly included human sacrifices; the souls of the dead whom Odysseus visits had dwindled to pale shadows none more favored than the rest. Without moral standards to follow, life no matter how pious was stripped of purpose and ultimate reward.

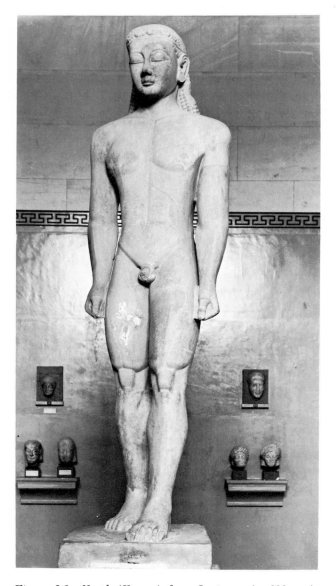

Figure 2.3 *Youth (Kouros) from Sunium.* (c. 600 B.C.). National Museum, Athens. [Marburg: Art Reference Bureau].

Lack of ultimate purpose and the hard life of the Greek Middle Ages is described in Hesiod's *Works and Days* and serves to explain another characteristic of this period. The Greeks turned toward THE PAST AS A MEANS OF ESCAPE into a more spacious and exciting world. Homer's world of heroes with their freedom from mundane responsibility represents just such an escape. In the fifth century B.C. Pindar, who was a conservative, reflected this same characteristic in his odes. *Works and Days* too harks back to an Edenlike Golden Age as the time of man's greatest glory and then traces his decline through ages of Silver and Bronze, a temporary surge in an Age of Heroes, presumably a tribute to the *Iliad* and the *Odyssey*, and a present fall into an Age of Iron.

Eighth-century vase paintings on craters (mixing bowls) and on funeral vases frequently recalled heroic events like the procession of charioteers depicted in Figure 2.4 and funeral games like those of the *Iliad*. (A seventh century B.C. relief vase in the Mykonos Museum depicts the Trojan horse filled with soldiers.) Cavalry too abounded in seventh-century B.C. vase paintings, although by that time cavalry had become outmoded and had given way to hoplites, heavily armed infantrymen.

One final characteristic less easy to analyze than to perceive by intuition: the Heroic Age seemed always in a STATE OF BECOMING. Where the Golden Age will suggest a state of being, through its balance between ideal form and realism, the Heroic Age seems always on the move, or about to move, in the direction of near realism. Homer's heroes waver between outsized cartoons and human beings, like figures in and out of focus. Achilles, often so alien in his petulance, becomes suddenly close and alive when he elects to battle Hector despite Thetis' warning that he is fated to die shortly after Hector. Odysseus in a later epic is more consistently approachable, so that Homer's own development reflects this sense of becoming, this trend toward realism.[1] Homer's genius, as we will see, also carries him forward into the state of being of the Golden Age.

In architecture the semifunctional façade of the Megaron suggests the purely functional buildings that were to evolve in the Golden Age. The façade wavers between open display and closed fortification (the real purpose of this building). The guardian lions further suggest fortification as the purpose despite their being a part of the irrelevant central ornament. In sculpture even the works of the archaic period border closely enough on the human to propel sculpture toward a greater realism. The face and the upper body of the *Auxerre Goddess* appear to be human, and the *Youth from Sunium*, with his spread stance in contrast to the joined feet of the *Auxerre Goddess*, points toward the more dynamic realism that was to appear in Golden Age sculpture. In vase painting the development beyond geometric figures is

---

[1] Whether or not Homer wrote the *Odyssey* after the *Iliad* is in this case immaterial, since the subject matter of the *Odyssey* postdates that of the *Iliad*.

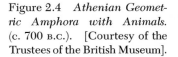

Figure 2.4 *Athenian Geometric Amphora with Animals.* (c. 700 B.C.). [Courtesy of the Trustees of the British Museum].

summarized in the Athenian Amphora which contrasts the pure formality of protogeometric design with the activating realism of the lion and the semi-representational charioteers. Along with the development of realism in the eighth century B.C. came a significant impetus toward movement in Corinth, where vase painters made the hitherto formal silhouette figures more plastic by incising details like facial features or hair. In music the ninth (or perhaps the tenth) century B.C. nomes of Olympos moved music away from ritual and toward a real identity of its own. The pastoral music of the Middle Ages played by shepherds on the syrinx probably filled out that identity with realistic emotion. With that conjecture we have gone about as far as possible with a humanities approach to the Heroic Age. With the Heroic Age a process of becoming, we may now turn to its fulfillment, the Greek Golden Age, which runs approximately from the time of Solon to the death of Alexander the Great.

THE GOLDEN AGE: TRAITS AND IDEAS

Perhaps the most intriguing facet of Golden Age temper was the trait unveiled by the nineteenth-century German philosopher Friedrich Nietzsche in his book *The Birth of Tragedy.* In it Nietzsche holds that the Greek temper is at once Dionysian (after Dionysus, god of fertility and wine) and Apollonian (after Apollo, god of contemplation and moderation).[2] Nietzsche defines Dionysian temper as emotional, active, and communal; Apollonian temper as placid, contemplative, and individual. While Nietzsche favors the Dionysian, he admits that both traits are poured into the single vial of Greek temper. Ever since Nietzsche's interpretation was presented, classical scholars have been quick to perceive PASSION-AND-CONTROL as a unit force in the arts and society of the Golden Age. Actually, two millenia before Nietzsche the Greeks themselves had discovered this aspect of their temper and articulated it as the Orphic myth of Dionysus Zagreus. Core of the Orphic religious creed, this myth tells how the child Dionysus, son of Zeus and Persephone, was torn to pieces by the Titans. His heart was afterward consumed by his father, who also reduced the Titans to ashes with his thunderbolt. Then Zeus created mankind out of the ashes of the daemonic, communal Titans and the blood and heart of his gentle, unique son, that is, out of Nietzsche's Dionysian and Apollonian forces.

Hellenic philosophy reflects this fusion of passion-and-control early in the writings of Heraclitus, who held that all of man's deepest beliefs involved a tension of opposites. He wrote, "The dissonant is in harmony with itself," and "Men do not realize how what is at variance agrees with itself." Plato in the *Phaedrus* describes the soul as a combination of a white horse of "modesty and temperance" and a "plunging" black horse, the two *together* in the grip of a charioteer, thus expressing the essential importance of passion-and-control in the Greek temper. In the *Timaeus* Plato describes how all matter in space was in a state of chaos until the Demiurge imprinted it with controlled shapes: for Plato all of the shapes that form gives to matter re-enact the fusion of passion-and-control.

LITERATURE.   Homer shows us in the *Iliad* a world at war, yet only seventeen of the twenty-four books involve actual fighting; the remainder concern themselves with councils, religious rituals, and domestic scenes. The setting of this epic, though on the surface purely one of violent passion, is in essence a blend of passion-and-control. Homer's *Odyssey* is essentially a story of homecoming, a celebration of the peaceful (controlled) aspects of life. Yet at least seven of its twenty-four books center around battle scenes, so that the unified blend of passion-and-control penetrates this epic too, although viewed this time from the opposite end of the telescope.

In the *Iliad* the passion of Achilles is offset by the calm of Nestor, and all developments in the *Odyssey* depend upon the intervention of two gods equally vital to the epic as a whole: Poseidon, passionate with rage, and serene Pallas Athena. The shield of Achilles in Book XVIII of the *Iliad* depicts two cities, one at war, the other witnessing a bridal procession; it depicts two fields, one a dancing place (for Nietzsche, the Dionysian impulse was best expressed through dance), the other a place for the reaping and binding of grain.

[2] As per the famous admonition "Nothing in excess" in his Temple at Delphi.

Aeschylus, who calls his own work "slices from Homer's banquet," closes his greatest dramatic trilogy, the *Oresteia,* with a conflict between the frenzied demands of the Furies and their calm rebuttal by Apollo. The resolution of the trilogy, a truce which permits both parties to coexist, is in perfect keeping with the trait of passion-and-control. Aeschylus' successor, Sophocles, also reflects this trait in the character of many of his heroes, most notably in that of Oedipus who combines a passion, almost a frenzy, for truth with a calm and monumental nobility.

ARCHITECTURE.   Golden Age architecture tended to blend the Doric style, whose simplicity suggests formula and control, with the Ionic style, whose flair suggests dynamism and energy. The Parthenon (Figure 2.5) uses both Doric and Ionic columns. The use of symmetry for the exterior offers at first glance an appearance of placid serenity. The outer columns on each side are even-numbered; the apex of the frontal triangle neatly bisects the building; the outer and inner columns form matching rows. Yet careful scrutiny reveals that this seeming symmetrical control is offset by a kind of restlessness. A number of factors tend to tilt the building subtly off balance: the columns are not straight up and down but swell slightly toward the bottom; nor are they set perfectly perpendicular but lean slightly inward so that the spaces between them seem perpendicular but are subtly, disturbingly slanted. The bases on which the columns rest are not precise horizontal planes but rather curve upward a couple of inches or so in the center and at the ends, giving the building a thrusting vitality beneath its surface appearance of serene repose. (Some of this imbalance *might* be explained by the slope of the Acropolis on which the Parthenon rests, but not the swelling columns nor the thrusting stylobate below them.) Similar harmony of balance-imbalance may be seen in all of the buildings of the Acropolis: the Propylaea, the Erechtheum, and the Temple of Athena Nike (Figure 2.6) whose miniature delicacy might seem at first glance to offer contrast to the restless principle of the Parthenon.

SCULPTURE.   Golden Age sculpture offers the same surface appearance of majestic repose as does the Parthenon, but careful scrutiny reveals the characteristic blending of passion-and-control. The apparent poise of the sculpted bodies clashes subtly with the tension evoked by shifting the weight of the body onto one foot. This effect of tension-in-repose gains in power with the famous "S" curve of Praxiteles. In his *Hermes Holding the Infant Dionysus* (Figure 2.7) Hermes' hip is outthrust in a way that clashes contrastingly with the serene straightness of the head. The infant's clutching fingers provide similar contrast alongside the god's calm, almost dreamy facial expression. The near legendary work of Praxiteles' successor, Skopas, brings the trait of passion-and-control into dramatic prominence. The *Raving Maenad* (Figure 2.8) probably based on an original by Skopas, is almost dominated by passionate gyration except for the drapery in front which hangs serenely like a thing apart. Also dispelling the first-glance impression of majestic repose is the way a sculptor like Praxiteles concentrates on figures in the round instead of in relief, using twists of the body to lure the viewer to move around it, thus blending the viewer's own feeling of restlessness with the sculptor's surface illusion of calm.

PAINTING.   Our knowledge of Golden Age mural painting is too sketchy to do more than conjecture about how it might have reflected the control-and-passion of Greek temper. Nothing survives of the great wall paintings of that time, our most notable losses being the work of Polygnotus in Athens and of Mikon in Delphi. We may with some validity, however, assume that contemporary vase painting is in general a miniature version of the work of the mural masters. Vases such as the red-figure amphora (two-handled vase) (Figure 2.9) by Oltos and the Corinthian crater (mixing bowl) by the Three Maidens Painter combine the effect of passion-and-control. The upper band of the former depicts a girl tying on her sandals, and the lower band depicts a nymph struggling with a satyr. The upper band of the Corinthian crater portrays a procession moving in stately calm while on the lower band animals move restlessly about. Note too on the vase by Oltos how the horizontal design in the band below the sandals is counterbalanced by the vertical design of the lower band. A similar two-tiered synthesis may be found in the sculpture on the walls of the Parthenon. The metopes above the outer columns depict a savage struggle between centaurs and lapiths (the victorious lapiths symbolize the victory of the civilized over the beastly nature of man); and the frieze above the inner columns depicts a solemn procession in honor of Athena. This majestic combining of passion-and-control may well parallel the themes of the lost mural paintings.

MUSIC.   Although fewer than twenty fragments of Greek music survive (none of them earlier than the second century B.C.) we can nevertheless find evidences of passion-and-control in music of the Golden Age. The two instruments used almost exclusively were the lyre from Ionia, and the aulos from the East. The four-stringed lyre, associated with contemplative Apollo, induced a mood of calmness and restraint; the aulos, with its exciting reed-pipe sound, belonged to Dionysus. The aulos was the only instrument accompanying the dramas presented at the festival of Dionysus, and provoked excitement and a sense of movement. The two *together* spelled Golden Age music.

Sparta put this blending of instrumental moods into practice. She was the first to make lyre music part of her civic training (Lycurgus believed it encouraged respect for the gods and for the laws); at the same time her soldiers marched into battle to music composed for the aulos. In music theory we have additional evidence of passion-and-control. The two basic scales upon which Greek music relied during the Golden Age were the Doric, running roughly E D C B A G F E (the order is a descending one) connoting serenity and restraint; and the Phrygian, running roughly D C G A B F E D (in descending order) connoting excitement often bordering on frenzy.

Figure 2.5 ICTINUS AND CALLICRATES. Model of the Parthenon in Athens. (447–442 B.C.). [Metropolitan Museum of Art, Purchase, 1890, Levi Hale Willard Bequest].

Figure 2.6 CALLICRATES. Temple of Athena Nike, East Façade. (c. 426 B.C.). Athens. [Alinari: Art Reference Bureau].

Figure 2.7   PRAXITELES.   *Hermes Holding the Infant Dionysus.*   (c. 350 B.C.).
Museum, Olympia.   [Dr. Franz Stoedtner].

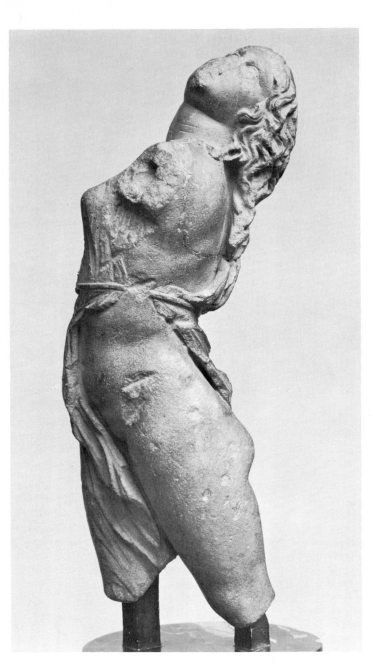

Figure 2.8 SKOPAS (?). *Raving Maenad.* (c. 349 B.C.). Dresden, Staatliche Kunstsammlungen.

Figure 2.9   OLTOS.   *Red-figure Amphora.*   (c. 520 B.C.). Louvre, Paris.   [Hirmer Foto-archiv Munchen].

Almost a corollary to the trait of passion-and-control is BALANCE, a term especially favored by art critics when discussing the Greek Golden Age. Balance as serene harmony is not in any profound sense a Greek trait. But balance as passion-and-control-under-hasty-scrutiny offers an approach to Greek culture just independent enough to qualify as an aspect, although a sketchy one, of Greek temper and to merit a separate humanities approach.

Balance gives form to the most famous of all Greek ethical concepts— the Golden Mean. Set forth by Aristotle in his *Nicomachean Ethics,* the Golden Mean holds that each virtue is a virtue only if practiced in the right proportion: that is, in a perfect balance between excess and deficiency of that virtue. For example, the excess of courage is foolhardiness; its deficiency, cowardice; true courage is balanced somewhere between the two extremes in, as Aristotle puts it, "a mean relative to us."

Spiritual life in the Golden Age achieved this kind of Golden Mean balance, between life here and life hereafter. The fear-based earlier myths gave way to a new sense of serenity in the contemplation of God, and Socrates' prayer at the close of Plato's *Phaedrus* reflects a balanced harmony between the two worlds. "Beloved Pan," he prays, "and all you other gods who haunt this place: give me beauty in the inward soul, and may the outer and inner man be one." In the Greek polis everyday life depended upon a particular kind of balance. The polis was sustained by the voluntary political activity of its citizens who were rewarded in turn with freedom to do what they pleased in almost every other area of activity. The Greek citizen was therefore free in proportion as he was bound up with his government: the amounts might vary; the balance remained the same.

LITERATURE.   The epics of Homer reflect the same balance as in Greek spiritual life. The *Iliad* and *Odyssey* take place on both earthly and heavenly levels: events on earth are matched by events in heaven; quarrels between mortals equate with quarrels between gods, and earthly councils are smaller versions of heavenly ones. In the *Oresteia* of Aeschylus, Orestes' struggle with the Furies parallels Zeus' struggle with the Titans, and change on earth from a law of vengeance to a law of love is balanced by a benevolent cosmic evolution. In the dramas of Sophocles his protagonists often strike a balance between ideal and everyday human beings: Oedipus and Antigone suggest the same balance between sublime nobility and all too human passion that one finds in the sculpture of Pheidias (Figure 2.14) and Praxiteles.

ARCHITECTURE.   The even-numbered columns of Greek temples and their frontal triangles point up the perfect symmetry of the buildings and convey an initial sense of balance (Figures 2.5 and 2.6). Greek theaters achieve the same symmetrical effect by the balance—akin to the Aeschylean relationship of earth to heaven—between the horizontal orchestra circle and the vertical tiers of carved marble seats that rise in concentric circles above it as in the theaters at Athens and at Epidaurus (Figure 2.10).

SCULPTURE.   Writers on Greek sculpture often talk about "balance of movement" to describe the way a figure's shift of weight onto one foot is counterbalanced by the backward thrust of the opposite arm and shoulder, as in the *Spearbearer* of Polyclitus (Figure 2.11). The thrust of the head away from the backthrust shoulder provides additional counterbalance. The famous "S" curve of Praxiteles may be said to set up the same kind of balance, only between greater extremes. One also finds *a balance in time* in these works; the movement caught in bronze or stone hangs midway between stillness and the peak of action, as in the *Spearbearer* and even more strikingly in the poised readiness of the *Discus Thrower* of Myron (Figure 2.12).

PAINTING.   Vase painting offers a variety of examples of balanced composition. One example of the practice of harmonic grouping is in the red-figure vase of *Thetis Bathing* by the Marsyas Painter. An even more common and obvious example of balance is the frequent use of pairs of figures, as in the *Mistress and Servant* lekythos (a slender vase to hold scents or oil) probably by the Achilles Painter (Figure 2.13). On this lekythos the figures stand in near perfect balance at either extreme of the setting, the lekythos offered by the servant pointing up the symmetry of the design. The figures are tidily balanced by height, by physique, and by virtue of their similarly reserved expression.

MUSIC.   Music historians often speak of the balance between the meter of Greek verses and their musical notation when set to music, and some writers theorize that the balanced symmetry of temple architecture is echoed in the structure of much, if not all, of Golden Age music.

The Greeks of the Golden Age had a special way of looking both with eye and mind. By looking at particular things they could discover almost by instinct universal implications in them. No other aspect of Greek temper would produce such profound results as this trait of MOVING FROM THE PARTICULAR TO THE UNIVERSAL. The earliest Greek philosophers developed their whole mode of thinking out of this process. Thales took a particular element—water—and universalized that it was primary matter from which all else was created. His successor, Anaximenes, claimed that air was the "true cause of everything," the key to universal truth. Pythagoras and his followers held that number lay at the base of everything: "All bodies consist of points in space, which taken together constitute a number." By means of number the Pythagoreans built up a science of astronomy, geometry, and music and used those disciplines mainly as evidence of the universal quality of number. Aristotle, whose Chain of Being theory links all particular creatures to a universal prototype, summed up this special Greek way of looking by saying in his *Posterior Analytics* that knowledge begins in sense impressions (particulars) and ascends to the general or universal.

Anaxagoras used the trait of particular-to-universal to convert philosophy to metaphysics. He achieved this by declaring that "idea" was not only a particular thing but a universal abstraction. Plato's *Republic* uses the particular-to-universal for political theory; in the second book Socrates inquires into the nature of justice for the individual and then moves on to consider the State, where one finds the same explanations "written larger and on a larger scale." The great Golden Age historian Thucydides, in his account of the Peloponnesian War, explained how his work is a study of particulars in order to point up universals: "But if he who desires to have before his eyes a true picture of the events which have happened, and of the like events which may be expected to happen hereafter in the order of human things, shall pronounce what I have written to be useful, then I shall be satisfied." In this same vein Hippocrates, the father of medicine, wrote: "The human being is a part of the whole of nature and cannot be understood without it. What we need is a satisfactory general view of the process of the universe. Having this, we shall have the key to open the most secret recesses of the art of medicine."

LITERATURE.   The heroes of Homer are at once individuals and universal types. The passionate and high-strung individual who is Achilles also stands for all that is best of the Heroic Age; he has honor, courage, greatness of soul, contempt for death. The *Iliad* goes beyond the story of a small war to include the implications universal in all wars; the *Odyssey* makes of the adventures of a single hero a universal drama of homecoming. In another liter-

Figure 2.10 (above) Theater. (c. 350 B.C.). Epidaurus. [Dr. Franz Stoedtner].

Figure 2.11 (left) *Doryphorus* (*Spearbearer*). Roman copy after a bronze by POLYCLITUS. (Original c. 440 B.C.). National Museum, Naples. [Alinari: Art Reference Bureau].

Figure 2.12 (right) MYRON. *Discus Thrower*. (c. 450 B.C.). Vatican Museum, Rome. [Dr. Franz Stoedtner].

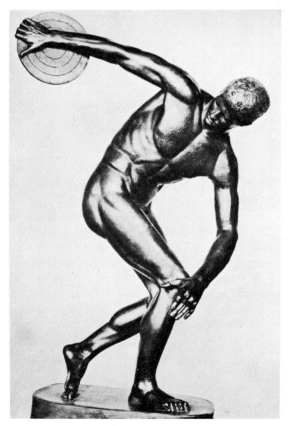

Figure 2.13   THE ACHILLES PAINTER.   *White-ground Lekythos of Mistress and Servant.* (c. 450 B.C.).   [The Metropolitan Museum of Art, Rogers Fund, 1908].

ary genre, the ode, Pindar makes festivals and games stepping-stones to universal commentaries. This bears out Aristotle's later dictum that poetry "is something more philosophic and of graver import than history, since its statements are of the nature rather of universals."

Greek tragedy moves from particular to universal everywhere, as is superlatively shown in the character drawings of Sophocles. All of his protagonists are at once people enmeshed in tragic situations and compendiums of Greek virtues. The best known example is probably Oedipus, whose towering nobility sums up all of the attributes of Greek greatness. By watching Oedipus the Greeks could see themselves not as they were, but raised to a lofty universal plane. How real these universals were to them may be seen in this Oedipuslike fragment from a eulogy on Pericles by Protagoras:

His sons perished within a week in the beauty of their youth and he bore it without repining. For he clung to his attitude of serene repose which permitted him every day to enjoy welfare, tranquillity and popular fame; for every man who saw him bear his own sorrow with strength would recognize that Pericles was noble and manly and much better than himself, seeing that he would be found lacking in a similar trial.

ARCHITECTURE.   The Greeks concentrated on only two kinds of structures, temples and theaters. Every structure they built used the same elements in the same relationships so as to mirror the universal "Idea" of temple or theater. From the imposing Parthenon to the delicate Temple of Athena Nike and including the full range of temples in between, stylobates, columns, capitals, architraves, and cornices follow a single, universal, ordered relationship. The same particular-to-universal construction principle holds true for all Greek theaters. It might also be observed that the temples represented man in relation to his god or gods (particular to universal); and the theaters housed man-made festivals for the gods in which particular events provided the springboard for universal commentary.

SCULPTURE.   Like literature sculpture uses particular-to-universal as a principal means of achieving towering nobility. Since Greek gods were man-shaped, all Greek statues, of men or gods, started with particular human beings or human features. In the case of gods the sculptor generally used the features not of one person but a sum total of all of the beautiful features to be found. The head of *Athena Lemnia* after Pheidias (Figure 2.14) is at once sweet and powerful, human and divine. Composed of the most perfect features of particular individuals, it compellingly conveys the ideal beauty of divinity. The noble face and form of Praxiteles' *Hermes* achieves a similar effect. Golden Age statues of particular types such as the *Spearbearer* of Polyclitus and the *Discus Thrower* of Myron become, by being summaries of the noblest features of that type, the universal example of spearbearer and discus thrower. Statues of particular men are ennobled beyond the normal reach of their subject, as in the statue of Pericles after Kresilas (Figure 2.15), which resembles Pericles but in so idealized a way as to convey the idea of universal greatness. The youthful freshness of the features and the sublime expression around the mouth make this work a model of grandeur for any age.

PAINTING.   "Painters," writes Plato in the *Republic*, "must fix their eyes on perfect truth as an eternal standard of reference to be contemplated with the minutest care before they go on to deal with earthly canons about things beautiful." This rule suggests that Greek painting idealized its subjects in much the same way as did Greek sculpture and that the vast murals of Polygnotus and Mikon must have achieved the same particular-to-universal quality as did the statues of Pheidias, Praxiteles, Myron, Polyclitus, and Kresilas.

MUSIC.   For the Pythagoreans music in particular formed a part of their vast universal pattern of numbers. The four-stringed lyre fitted in with their theory that all matter expressed the number four; the eight-tone scale led to their generalization that eight symbolizes love and perfect harmony. Plato, who reflects most clearly the temper of the Golden Age, tells us in *The Laws* that music has "truth of imitation"; that is, it particularizes and leads up to a general truth. He saw in the music of men a sampling of the universal music of the spheres.

Figure 2.14 *Head of Athena Lemnia.* Roman copy after an original by Pheidias (?).
(Original c. 450 B.C.). Civic Museum, Bologna. [Alinari: Art Reference Bureau].

44

Figure 2.15   KRESILAS (?).   *Pericles.*   (c. 440 B.C.).   [Courtesy the Trustees of the British Museum].

The Greeks relied upon REASON as their chief prop and authority. It was what distinguished them most sharply from their predecessors; it was also the trait that their most earnest imitators, the seventeenth- and eighteenth-century rationalists, would chiefly admire. Greek reason had its basis in logic. The precise analyses and definitions of logic whetted Greek philosophy from its inception and carried over into all other areas as well. It affected Greek life in the guise of common sense, the side of reason that later rationalists would find most congenial. And it affected the arts by restricting them to tested and logical constructions—to rules.

The philosopher Xenophanes early cut through the fancies of myth with sharp and pointed logic: "If oxen and horses or lions had hands and could paint with their hands and produce works of art as men do, horses would paint the forms of the gods like horses, and oxen like oxen, and make their bodies in the image of their several kinds." Aristotle made logic a separate and intact science. The following argument of Parmenides for the permanence of Being is typical of the reason-anchored logic that Greek writers customarily used: "How should the thing that is ever be unmade; how should it ever come into being? If it came into being there must have been a time when it was not, and the same holds good if its beginning is still in the future."

Greek reason points toward a scientific temper, and Greek science did emerge early and make use from the start of logical, common sense observation. To cite a few examples, Anaximander deduced that life originally came from the sea and that all present creatures evolved by means of adaptation to their environment. Empedocles worked out the theory of conservation of matter and of primary elements which in combination would produce other elements (the start of modern chemistry). Leucippus, who speculated early upon atomic theory, fused scientific observation and Greek reason together in his famous law of conservation: "Nothing happens without a cause, but everything with a cause and by necessity."

LITERATURE.   Although the Homeric epics mainly reflect the surging enthusiasm of the Heroic Age, reason penetrates parts of them. The counsel of Nestor in the *Iliad* is grounded in common sense. And in the opening book of the *Odyssey* Telemachus, inspired by Athena in the guise of Odysseus' friend Mentes, changes from a wistful stripling into a sharp-minded adult who chides his mother "with good sense" for her sentimental reaction to a minstrel's song. The *Oresteia* of Aeschylus culminates in a rational, legalistic debate between Orestes and the Furies at the law court of Athens. Earlier parts of this trilogy are shot through with the same firm logic: Clytemnestra reasons Agamemnon into treading upon the royal purple; Electra reasons Orestes into murdering Clytemnestra. In the *Oedipus Rex* of Sophocles the terror builds from Oedipus' relentlessly logical inquiry into the identity of the murderer of Laius.

ARCHITECTURE.   The whole aim of Greek architecture, the perfection of just two types of buildings—temple and theater—became an exercise in the application of rules of construction. The "order of temples" prescribed the exact size and shape of the columns, and these in turn determined the details of the other parts of the building. In the Doric order, for example, the height of a column was five to six times its base diameter; in the Ionic order the proportion of column to base diameter was one to eight or ten, thus supplying a kind of prefabricated logic for building.

SCULPTURE.   Similar logical "rules for beauty" existed in sculpture. The *Canon* of Polyclitus, his handbook for sculptors, required, for example, that the head be one-seventh the height of the body, as in his own *Spearbearer* and in the *Discus Thrower* of Myron. When a later sculptor like Praxiteles broke that rule it was only to adopt another one, of a head-to-body relationship of one to eight, as in his *Hermes*.

PAINTING.   Whatever rules governed painting have since been lost, but by analogy with the other arts we may assume that some of them dealt with proportions. We know that Greek artists also practiced perspective, and rules must have existed for this too.

MUSIC.   This most emotional of the arts was also subject to rules in the Golden Age in two ways. Its forms obeyed rules or laws, known as *nomes,* which determined in advance the structure of composition logical to a particular subject. Its elements, too, were subject to rules: sedate music used the Dorian scale, sensuous music the Phrygian, trivial and effeminate music the Lydian. Add to these rules the scientific speculations on music by Aristoxenus and we have reason-dominated music not only in practice but also in theory.

Finally, a trait corollary to Greek faith in reason, which may at first seem unlikely. Greek temper is in one aspect COLD, VERGING ON CRUELTY. This coldness hardened the laws of Sparta and the punishments meted out to defeated city-states. It can be observed in the unwillingness of any polis to let its neighbors thrive (witness how Athens turned on Thebes when Thebes became powerful); in the casual acceptance of slaves; in the treatment of women (which will be discussed later) and of popular heroes (witness the Athenian treatment of Miltiades, hero of Marathon; even Pericles, the most popular figure in Golden Age Athens, was forced to beg publicly for the life of his mistress Aspasia simply to satisfy a popular whim).

The bare literary style of all Golden Age writers reflects this coldness. Sophocles' chorus in *Oedipus Rex* receives the news of Jocasta's death by saying merely: "Unhappy woman. How came death to her?" And his Oedipus announces his approaching death by saying, "My path slopes downward." In architecture the Greek temple with its spare frontal triangle surmounting unadorned columns conveys a sense of cold impersonality. The first sight of any of the great Greek buildings, even of the comparatively intimate Temple of Athena Nike, is an experience largely devoid of emotion. In sculpture the impersonal calm on the faces of statues by Praxiteles and Pheidias conveys a similar coldness. In vase painting the stylized female faces of Oltos and of the Achilles Painter convey the same detached calm. In music the tendency toward small intervals must have seemed and sounded similarly antiemotional.

This trait of coldness is carved less deeply into Greek temper than, say, that of passion-and-control, but like the trait of balance it has the outline accuracy of a sweeping view, and even a beginner in Greek studies will notice it at once.

In contrast to the fatalism of the Orient, the Greeks believed in FREE WILL. The idea of free will seems to have originated with them and is certainly the idea that sets them farthest apart from their predecessors. Its effect, self-determination, became a potent part of the Greek legacy. Heraclitus sounds the idea early in Greek philosophy when he writes that "Man's will is his destiny," that is, a man becomes what he wills to become. Plato applied Heraclitus' doctrine to metaphysics by implying throughout his canon that one *elects* to find God, by means of philosophy, and Socrates, the philosopher in action, elected to die.

Even Homer tinged as he is with the fatalism of the earlier Heroic Age sounds the new Greek concept early in the *Odyssey* when he has Zeus say: "What a lamentable thing it is that men should blame the gods and consider us the source of their troubles, when their own wickedness brings them sufferings worse than any which destiny causes them." Homer's Achilles elects to kill Hector even though it means his own death will follow soon after. Sophocles' Oedipus is allowed to determine on four separate occasions whether to continue the investigation or to stop it; his Antigone brings tragedy to herself and to those around her through an act of free choice.

It needs only a little imagination to find this same independence of will in the *Spearbearer* of Polyclitus, the *Athena Lemnia,* and the portrait statue of Pericles.

The Greek idea of NATURE AS SOMETHING ETERNAL AND IMMORTAL, AS SOMETHING DIVINE AND THEREFORE CREATIVE is rooted in primitive tribal traditions of place gods, nature spots believed to be divine. The Greeks, however, made more profound use of this idea than any of their predecessors, and that use has helped to shape concepts of nature ever since. The physical fact of Olympus, home of the gods, being an actual mountain in north-central Thessaly, and of Parnassus, home of the Muses, existing in the central region of Phocis, influenced the Greek mind to view those mountains and the nature spots surrounding them as divine habitats. The next logical and inevitable step was to view nature in general as a kind of Eden. Such a view led the sixth-century B.C. Orphics, followers of the legendary Thracian musician Orpheus, into a belief in Pantheism. And all of the early Ionian philosophers viewed the universe as Pantheistic. Thales proposed water as the universal primary element that formed the universe; for Anaximines it was air; for Heraclitus, fire. Plato, following Heraclitus in part in *The Republic* equated God with "the sun itself which represents the Idea of the Good." Xenophanes equated God with "universal nature."

In the *Politics,* Aristotle used the Greek concept of nature to give divine sanction to the state and to politics as well. "It is evident that the state is a creature of nature and that man is by nature a political animal." In the *Poetics* Aristotle sets forth his famous doctrine that art aims to imitate nature, meaning in one sense at least that creativity imitates the work of the divine creator: the word poet, after all, comes from the Greek *poietes,* meaning creator.

In literature Homer's Odysseus is imprisoned by the divine love of Calypso in a cave "sheltered by a green thicket of alders, aspens, and fragrant cypresses . . . while from four separate neighboring springs four crystal rivulets were trained to run this way and that; and in soft meadows on either side the iris and the parsley flourished." After his escape from drowning, Odysseus is sustained and protected by a mysteriously symbolic "pair of bushes, one an olive, the other a wild olive which grew from the same stem." In the *Oresteia* of Aeschylus, Orestes fleeing the Furies finds sanctuary in the nature spot at Delphi. The infant Oedipus, cast out into the forest to die, is sustained by it and kept alive.

In architecture nature settings determined the erection of temples and theaters to the gods. The Erechtheum in Athens was built where Athena made an olive tree spring up and thereby became patron goddess of the city. Dipylon vases (funeral urns) often depict votive pastoral processionals as God-brushed as that of the Parthenon frieze. The music of the lyre is profoundly associated with the holy cult of Apollo in the nature spot at Delphi, and the pipes of Pan (the syrinx) used for pastoral songs and dances had significant religious connotations.

The Greek concept of ARETE—highest worthiness and competence— fits no single definition, but is adaptable to every subject. There is an *arete* of hero and an *arete* for everyman, an *arete* of physician, and an *arete* of blacksmith, tyrant, athlete, even politician. In each case the standards vary to define the highest level of competence of the particular personality or profession. The tyrant with *arete* would be the perfect ruler; the physician with *arete* would be the best in his field; the sculptor with *arete* would create the head of *Athena Lemnia.* The Renaissance will later take this concept and call it *virtù;* Machiavelli's Prince exemplifies the *virtù* of Renaissance ruler, of which our own word "virtue" is a pale and feeble echo.

The *arete* of citizen in the Greek polis meant someone who contributed to his government and society in every possible way and at the same time freely cultivated his own individuality. Thales of Miletus, the first major philosopher, could boast this type of *arete*, being a statesman, merchant, and civic engineer as well as mathematician, astronomer, and philosopher. The Greek games displayed the *arete* of the athlete, and Pindar whose poems likened each athletic triumph to a religious myth shows the high regard the Greeks held for any type of *arete*. Odysseus displays the *arete* of athlete by effortlessly defeating the Phaeacians at discus throwing. In the same epic Homer sets forth the *arete* of woman, at least for the Heroic Age, in this description of Penelope: ". . . her skill in fine handicraft, her excellent brain, and that genius she has for getting her own way. In that respect, I grant she has no equal, not even in legend." And the central quarrel in the *Iliad* stems from the need of both Achilles and Agamemnon to be conceded the *arete* of general. Oedipus exemplifies the *arete* of the hero of the Golden Age. The statues of the *Spearbearer* and *Pericles* summarize the *arete* of mortal beauty, which is tinged with divine beauty. The *arete* of Greek temples is seen in the Parthenon. The *arete* of the musician was exemplified by the mythical Orpheus.

During the Golden Age the Greeks believed that LAW, not destiny or chance, GOVERNED THE UNIVERSE. This concept suited their reason-prone temper and their idea of free will. Free will in a law-governed universe meant that man could develop his potentialities unimpeded, which made for the most positive view of life ever known. Starting from the concept of a macrocosm—the big world or universe—ruled by law, the Greeks went on to work out a microcosm—the little world, the earth—similarly ruled. Heraclitus articulates the connection between the two worlds when he writes: "All human laws are nourished by divine law." Aristotle's Chain of Being, which fixes the rank of each creature on a universal scale, puts divine law into philosophical practice. In the microcosm the *nomoi*, the laws, of each polis regulated the social, ethical, and political conduct of every citizen. Architecture, sculpture, and music had their own especial *nomoi*, and the concept of a law-governed universe encouraged science to produce discoveries like Leucippus' law of causation and Parmenides' law of conservation of matter.

The climax of the *Oresteia* of Aeschylus takes place in and is shaped by a court of law. The punishment of Oedipus, monstrously unfair as it seems, is inevitable according to divine law. In architecture there were Doric, Ionic, and Corinthian *nomoi*, each rigidly followed. In sculpture the *Canon* of Polyclitus provided in effect the *nomoi* for sculptors. In a similar vein architectural *nomoi* went so far as to decree construction according to unit sizes of bricks. Whatever *nomoi* there may have been for painting have been lost, but Greek artists did use perspective and there must have been laws to govern it.

Nomoi were basic to music starting with those introduced by the Phrygian Olympos around 900 B.C., and composers of the Golden Age adhered as literally to musical nomes as builders did to the three architectural nomes. Besides these laws from within, music was subject to laws from without. Both Lycurgus of Sparta and Solon of Athens decreed its study as useful to the polis; in line with such decrees even the Greek modes became subject to law and took their names from the regions that promulgated them: there were among others Dorian, Phrygian, Lydian, Aeolian, and Ionian modes.

Lastly, the Golden Age Greeks generally considered WOMEN INFERIOR TO MEN, a concept that would later color Medieval and Renaissance thinking. The concept may well have been a backlash reaction to the overpowering feminism of Crete, with its worship of a Mother Goddess and its lushly decorative, impractical civilization. The shift to antifeminism seems to have begun sometime between the end of the Heroic Age and the beginning of the Golden Age and is reflected in contrasts between the *Iliad* and the *Odyssey*. In the earlier work (perhaps a reworking of older poems almost contemporary with the Trojan War) the hero, Achilles, is ridden by emotion, sentimentality, even tears; his chief concern is status among and friendship with his fellows. In the *Odyssey*, Odysseus is dauntless, masterful, athletic, and manly, attracting the love of goddess and princess alike. The principal wife in the *Iliad*, Andromache, is a potent force. She climbs the great Tower of Ilium upon hearing that her husband, Hector, is in danger. When he joins her there she urges him in the language of an equal to give up the fighting. And it is through her eyes that we see the mutilation of Hector's corpse. Penelope, the principal wife of the *Odyssey*, is a far more shadowy figure with nothing of the force and energy of Andromache. One could never imagine her dictating terms to Odysseus. In *Oedipus Rex* Jocasta commits suicide as a means of escaping the bitter truth, while Oedipus endures the full and protracted measure of suffering fit for their crime. It is Aeschylus who earlier shows the pendulum of antifeminism at its topmost swing in *Eumenides* where he has Apollo say: "The mother is not the true parent of the child which is called hers. She is the nurse who cultivates the young seed planted by its real parent, the father."

In Golden Age sculpture men and gods radiate sensual as well as spiritual beauty. Goddesses on the other hand are carved with chaste indifference to their sex. The *Athena Lemnia* is depicted with such dispassionate objectivity that she seems almost as masculine as she is feminine.

A few important scholars have questioned whether the Greeks were actually antifeminist and have cited an absence of overwhelming evidence and some counterevidence to challenge this idea. Most of the evidence, however, is based on the Greek idealistic attitude toward, not actual treatment of, women. Socrates in the *Symposium* discourses on true love by quoting what he says he learned from the prophetess Diotima; such love extends to objects, ideas, and God, but never to woman, and in real life there was Socrates' relationship to Xantippe. In Plato's Athens women were not even citizens. Once we recognize that these idealistic views of woman are only compensations for actual mistreatment, what seems to be counterevidence turns out to reinforce rather than to challenge the Golden Age concept of anti-feminism.

FORMS AND TECHNIQUES

For anyone with imagination and insight, finding similarities of form and technique among the works of any period can be an almost endless process. The "form and technique" sections throughout the text, therefore, will offer only a part of the similarities, leaving the student free to exercise his own humanities insights upon the other works he studies as well as those he encounters on his own.

FIVE-PART FORM: The Pythic Nome, written in 586 B.C. by the aulist Sakada, is the oldest known work of program music. It describes Apollo's battle with a dragon and consists of the following parts: (1) Making Ready; (2) The Challenge; (3) The Battle; (4) Hymn of Praise; (5) Dance of Triumph. It parallels the five-part scheme of classical tragedy, also begun in the sixth century B.C., whose four choral interludes divide the drama into a prologue, three episodes, and an exode. (Note that the plot structure of the Pythic Nome also parallels the exposition-climax-resolution structure of drama.) The Doric column, highly influential in this period, often fixed its height at five times its widest diameter.

EIGHT-PART FORM: Transitional sculpture such as the *Delphi Charioteer*, the Aegina statues, and the Temple of Zeus statues at Olympia used a head-to-body relationship of one to eight, as Praxiteles later was to do. Ionic columns frequently fixed their height at eight times their widest diameter. Pythagorean music theory evolved the eight-tone scale.

TRIANGLES: Triangles formed the pediment of Greek temples, where the most significant sculpture was placed, and the heads and bodies of early Greek vase paintings. Even later vase paintings like the red-figure amphora of Oltos are compositionally exercises in triangles. The triangle may have had some special significance because it was three-pointed. The Pythagoreans held the number three sacred because it had a beginning, middle, and end; Homer addresses a trinity of gods—Zeus, Athena, and Apollo—and Plato held that there were three levels of soul.

CIRCLES: Plato also held that souls were circular in shape, and the circle is the guiding form of the Greek theater. Golden Age sculpture held the viewer's interest from a circle of vantage points, as did vase paintings and friezes, notably that of the Parthenon.

CLASSICAL FORM: Greek style at its most sophisticated achieved a stripped simplicity which we now call classical. Doric architecture, statues by Polyclitus, Pheidias, and Kresilas, Greek prose style, poetic metaphor, musical intervals, and white-ground *lekythoi,* all partake of this same "classical simplicity."

THE ANTHROPOCENTRIC MOTIF: Man as the measure of all things made the entire world of Golden Age culture kin. Man-forms held sway from their first appearance on ninth-century B.C. dipylon vases. Homer's gods looked and acted like men, as did those of Aeschylus and Sophocles. And while philosophers from Anaximander on viewed God as an abstract infinite, human-shaped gods continued to be used by artists and philosophers as a means of making abstract ideas concrete. Socrates' Diotima is a woman, and Plato's demiurge, the artisan who built this world, is man-shaped. Golden Age sculpture was entirely anthropocentric, and architecture turned to reliefs made up of human-shaped figures in order to communicate its views. The philosopher Protagoras, who announced that "Man is the measure of all things," followed those famous words by: "of those that are that they are"; (that is, what does not reflect mankind cannot exist).

SYMBOL AND ALLEGORY: These techniques were used by many earlier civilizations, but the Greeks made such broad and searching use of them that they became a special feature of the arts of the Golden Age. Like all primitive peoples the early Greeks used myths to decorate deeper truths, such as the Orphic myth of man's creation (p. 31). Later philosophers used myth for a similar allegorical purpose; Plato's myth of Er in *The Republic* was a magnificent allegory of man's ultimate fate. Symbol and allegory were basic to literature as early as Homer, whose epics as a whole may be viewed as vast allegorical structures. H. D. F. Kitto (*The Greeks*) sees the *Iliad* as allegorizing "the tragic conception that a quarrel between two men should bring suffering, death and dishonour to so many others." From another viewpoint the beauteous *Helena* may well be a symbol for the identity of the *Hellenoi* (the Greeks' name for themselves), and winning her away from Troy may symbolize the formal beginning of Greek civilization.[3] The *Oresteia* of Aeschylus symbolizes the establishment of justice in the microcosm, earth, and its parallel establishment in the macrocosm, heaven. Francis Fergusson (*The Idea of a Theater*) brilliantly interprets *Oedipus Rex* as an allegory of the royal scapegoat who must sacrifice himself so the many may be saved.

Symbol penetrates even into architecture where the Corinthian capital is composed of acanthus leaves, a perennial plant connoting timelessness.

---

[3] While Homer calls the Greeks Danaans, Achaeans, and Argives, and in only one debatable instance Hellenes, the Golden Age Hellenes who used his epics as a bible certainly regarded Helen as symbolic of their essential selves.

Golden Age sculpture furnished repeated allegories of man's divinity, and its use of drapery, at least from Pheidias on, is an exercise in symbolism. In the Parthenon statues of the three goddesses attending the birth of Athena, for example, the folds and masses of drapery vary from slight to dense, from open to mysterious, according to the parts of the body they cover. Painting, like philosophy and literature, makes allegorical use of myth, as vase paintings attest, and even Greek music is touched by the universal wand of symbolism. Aristotle in the *Poetics* calls music a form of "dramatic imitation," which we may interpret to mean that melodies are symbols of ethical concepts.

THE HELLENISTIC AGE

The Hellenistic period begins about the time of Alexander the Great (c. 340 B.C.) and extends to the Battle of Actium in 31 B.C. Art historians occasionally subdivide the period into a Hellenistic and a Graeco-Roman phase, the latter beginning around 212 B.C. when Rome overran Syracuse, but the two phases form a part of a single cultural arc, as the humanities approach will verify. Their central impulse remains Greek but the center of Hellenistic activity is no longer merely Athens, Sparta, or Corinth; it is the whole of the civilized world.

The idea of city-state fell into discard after Alexander and that of empire became the new way. With the idea of empire Hellenism became international, flourishing as much in Alexandria and Pergamum as in Athens, belonging to a new elite of culturally superior people all distinguished by their ability to speak Greek. In philosophy, literature, and the arts Hellenism falls short of the peaks of the Golden Age, but its variety of forms is richer and its achievements in such areas as biography, philology, mathematics, astronomy, geography, and rhetoric certainly are superior. In all Hellenism is not a decline in the wake of the Golden Age, but rather a vital launching forth into new directions.

TRAITS AND IDEAS

Where the Golden Age achieved a balance between macrocosm and microcosm, the Hellenistic Age sought solace and truth, as well as pleasure, in the things of this world. The Stoic philosopher Diogenes Laertes summed up this CONCERN FOR THE THINGS OF THIS WORLD when he wrote: "Virtue is a quality that conforms to reason, desirable for itself and not because of hope or fear or any other-worldly motive." Hellenism conceived of God or the gods as a force remote from the affairs of this world, leaving man free to cultivate self-interest. The gods inhabit "the spaces between the worlds and care for no man," wrote the philosopher Epicurus, thus explaining how the apparent irreligion of Hellenism was, in actuality, worldliness. The Sophists, the philosopher-educators of the Hellenistic period, taught mainly rhetoric, the art of persuasion, which insured greater success in this world (and they taught only those who could pay). The philosopher-historian Euhemerus re-wrote mythology as a kind of world history which treated the gods as real life kings and noblemen, and thereby funneled even the hereafter into the here and now.

LITERATURE.   Euripides, whose avant-garde Golden Age dramas were shaded with Hellenistic influences, turned from the cosmic concerns of Aeschylus and Sophocles to psychological probing. His Trojan women, his Phaedra in *Hippolytus,* and even the demigod Hercules in *Hercules Furens* are all measured alongside a human scale of psychological values. Each of the comedies of Aristophanes points a worldly moral: *Knights* demonstrates the shrewd common sense of the average man; *Clouds* takes a dim view of new fads and of their proponent Socrates (*sic*); *Lysistrata* spotlights the ab-surdity of war and of its causes. In *Characters* Theophrastus explores the realistic, everyday world of Hellenism from the standpoint of its foibles. The Priapic poems of Sotades and his followers are pungently worldly, if not edifying.

ARCHITECTURE.   Hellenism took a new interest in other kinds of buildings besides temples or theaters. The Tower of the Winds (a clocktower) in Athens and private structures like the monument Lysicrates, the Athenian chorus writer, erected to himself (Figure 2.16) were constructed with lavish care. Lysicrates' monument, essentially a mammoth column circled by engaged columns, is the first known structure to make exterior use of Corinthian capitals. These produced a showier effect than Doric or Ionic capitals. The monument has no entranceway, although it is hollow inside, and so is con-spicuously useless, an act of worldly vainglory. Traditional types of buildings were also redesigned with an eye to worldly magnificence. The Artemisium (Temple of Artemis) at Ephesus and the Temple of Apollo at Miletus were so immense as to call attention to this world's achievements—the Temple of Apollo (Figure 2.17) was a colossal 366 by 163 feet, and its intricately orna-mented bases and scroll carvings were richly distracting.

SCULPTURE.   The 400-foot frieze encircling the Great Altar of Zeus at Pergamum and the 100-foot-high statue of Apollo at Rhodes (The Colossus) joined with the Temple of Apollo to furnish examples of materialism magni-fied. Moreover, at this time the purpose of sculpture changed from a wish to idealize to a drive to humanize. Even sculpted gods now belonged essentially

Figure 2.16 LYSICRATES. *Monument to Himself.* (c. 334 B.C.). Athens. [Dr. Herbert Kreft, Bavaria].

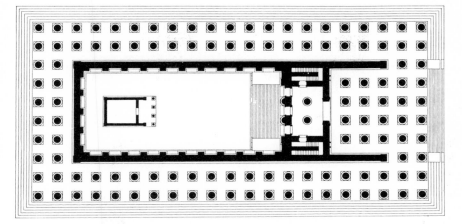

Figure 2.17   Paeonius of Ephesus and Daphnis of Miletus.   Temple of Apollo at Miletus.   Begun 313 b.c. (unfinished).   Projected version of ground plan.   [Hirmer Verlag Munchen].

to this world, the best known example being the *Aphrodite of Melos* or *Venus of Milo* (Figure 2.18) with her portraitlike face and spiral stance, the Praxitelian "S" curve made supremely feminine. Stone takes on the sensual impression of flesh in this statue, and the use of semidrapery, particularly the band of horizontal folds about the hips, enhances its allure. The popular belief that *Venus of Milo* is the classic example of Golden Age sculpture pays unconscious tribute to her timeless humanity. Hellenistic sculpture also turned to worldly subjects done with a wealth of realistic detail. The bronze *Boxer* by Apollonius (Figure 2.19) with its gouged cheek and cauliflower ear never rises above the level of the ground on which the boxer is seated. Such realistic details as the boxer's fingers, the hair on his chest, the precisely articulated muscles of his arms and legs, and his foggy, brutalized expression make for a cumulative effect of gross worldliness. The famous *Dying Gaul* and the equally impressive companion statue of a Gaul in the act of suicide while supporting the body of his dead wife offer poses momentarily held which lock the viewer in a world of time as well as space.

Painting.   Painting too exchanged this world's present moment for the eternity of the next. Hellenistic vases depict comic scenes like a gorilla chasing a traveler and parodies of ancient heroes (one crater portrays a pudgy, silly looking Hercules gorging himself at a banquet). The *Battle between Alexander and Darius,* possibly by Philoxenos (Figure 2.20), preserved in a mosaic version on the floor of a villa in Pompeii, captures the world-of-time moment when Alexander is smashing toward Darius who is cut off from his army by a wall of Greek spears. Alexander, his expression grim and possessed, fixes his gaze on the enemy king, while from his chariot Darius stretches an

Figure 2.18   *Aphrodite of Melos* (*Venus of Milo*).   (c. 150 B.C.).
Louvre, Paris.   [Archives Photographiques].

arm toward a dying companion. Determination clashes with compassion in this thoroughly human psychological study matched by the human predicament of the dying men and horses that clutter the center of the scene. Worldly overtones also surround *The Three Graces* (Figure 2.21), which even more than the *Venus of Milo* is an illustration of gods humanized. Originally a statuary group, now lost, the Hellenistic painted copy shown here uses the Praxitelian "S" curve to endow the Graces with chorus-girl movements and qualities. The purpose of this painting is emphatically worldly and copies of it served as bordello signs during the Renaissance.

Music.   Music too turned to momentarily pleasing flourishes, as we may deduce from the new nomes of Timotheus of Miletus and of Philoxenus. Long melismatic passages, sensual uses of chromaticism, and hushed, intimate settings for popular lyrics seem to have been these composers' stock in trade. Timotheus and Philoxenus predate Hellenism by a generation or so, and even their early excesses must have seemed mild alongside the musical formats of Hellenism proper: variety shows, comic pantomimes, acrobatics set to music, all of which brought music into the sphere of worldly entertainment.

The worldliness of Hellenism included a practical, empirical outlook that forms the basis for another trait of Hellenistic temper: scientism. Hellenistic scientism was not the total worship of science that the term generally implies, but the worship of a special kind of science. Science had flourished in the Golden Age too, but where Anaximander theorized that the universe was formed by flinging matter into the sky and Leucippus speculated on the nature of atoms, Hellenistic scientists measured the earth (Eratosthenes), classified plants (Theophrastus), described the physical world (Strabo), and codified mathematical knowledge (Euclid). In sum, the scientism of the Hellenistic Age meant *observing the world around one* or *converting observation to practical use.* As such it was a double-edged tool that would serve all branches of Hellenistic culture. "Do you not see the little plants, the little birds, the ants, the spiders, the bees working together to put in order their separate parts of the universe?" observed Epictetus, and then went on to recommend that man too do the work "which is according to [his] nature." The Skeptics observed how the same object appears differently to the different senses, how mountains at a distance look smooth yet seen up close are rough, how whatever we observe changes quality with changing climate or as it combines with air, light, heat, moisture, or motion.

Literature.   A favorite dramatic method of Euripides is to examine empirically the dimensions of human nature by placing protagonists close to a breaking point and then standing back and observing what they do. Medea, Phaedra in *Hippolytus,* and, as extreme examples, Orestes and Electra in

Figure 2.19 APOLLONIUS. *Boxer.* (First century B.C.). Terme Museum, Rome. [Alinari: Art Reference Bureau].

Figure 2.20 PHILOXENOS (?). *Battle between Alexander and Darius*, from the *Battle of Issus.* (Fourth century B.C.). Mosiac copy after a Hellenistic painting. National Museum, Naples.

Figure 2.21 *The Three Graces.* (First century B.C.). National Museum, Naples. Alinari: Art Reference Bureau].

Figure 2.22   NIKIAS (?).   *Perseus Frees Andromeda.*   (Fourth century B.C.).   National Museum, Naples.   [André Held].

Electra are all so handled. The average man of good sense, who is Aristophanes' hero, mirrors the scientism of this period by empirically observing the world around him, and by seeking to convert it to practical use: Demos in *Knights* makes politics serviceable; Strepsiades in *Clouds* destroys Sophism because it is impractical; the women in *Lysistrata* observe nature and convert it to a practical use that is timeless. Menander too is a practical observer and his comedies of manners itemize and classify the society of his day.

ARCHITECTURE.   Hellenistic architects converted the world of nature to practical use by cutting up building sites so that they conformed to plans for cities laid out as practically and efficiently as possible, rather than bending with the terrain as Golden Age architects used to do. The Hellenistic city of Priene was constructed with parallel crisscrossing streets at the total expense of natural slopes and turnings. The Acropolis at Pergamum, unlike that at Athens, manipulated nature into a patterned series of tiers that made for the most practical layout possible.

SCULPTURE.   Where Golden Age sculpture had blended realism with idealism, Hellenistic sculpture observes the world around it with a clinical detachment. Statues like the *Venus of Milo* and the *Boxer* achieve a new precision of observation. They are not only anatomically accurate but even observe and communicate differences of texture. Compare, for example, the sensuality of Venus with the flat musculature of the boxer and the different sense impressions conveyed by the leather and metal on the boxer's hands and arms.

PAINTING.   Hellenistic painting too profits from anatomy precisely observed. The figure of Perseus in the *Perseus Frees Andromeda* possibly by Nikias (Figure 2.22) is so physically accurate that there is no room left for idealism and hence for any suggestion of divinity. His arm and leg are raised in a staged pose to show off his muscles drawn with the same careful detail as in the *Boxer*. Comparison with the *Hermes* of Praxiteles will make clear the wide difference between Hellenic idealism and Hellenistic scientific observation.

Hellenistic observation of the phenomena of light and dark made possible studies of nature which achieved new dimensions of depth and roundness. This is seen to some extent in the *Perseus Frees Andromeda* where light, coming implausibly from two points behind the protagonists, highlights the semidraped Andromeda and sets off the posed Perseus in sculptured three dimensionality. Gradations of light and color are used with even sharper observation in the *Heracles and Telephos* (Figure 2.23), the extant copy of which is probably Roman. The rounded arms, for example, set off as they are by light-bathed space, are as lifelike as reality itself.

MUSIC.   Scientism probably did little to affect Hellenistic musical performance, but it did affect music theory. Music commentary begins in this period starting with Aristoxenus, who investigated not only the components of music but also their psychological effects. Though the greatest, Aristoxenus was only one of many Hellenistic music analysts. Other "scientific" observers of musical effects included the famous astronomer Ptolemy, who wrote three books on music theory and Marcus Terentius Varro, who narrowed his treatment of music to observations on harmonic effects.

Along with scientism the Hellenistic temper leaned toward EMOTIONAL-
ISM, and vital signs of it characterize much of Hellenistic thought and art. This
trait complicates the Hellenistic picture, and rightly so, for a society as richly
innovating as this one would inevitably be more intricate than straight-line
scientism would allow. Hellenistic emotionalism ranges all the way from
gentle sentiment as in the romance of *Daphnis and Chloe*, to frenzied violence as in the death throes in *Laocoön* (Figure 2.24).

Figure 2.23   *Heracles and Telephos.*   (Second century B.C.).   National Museum,
Naples.   [Alinari: Art Reference Bureau].

In philosophy the strongest evidence we have of the full tide of emotionalism in Hellenistic society is the Stoics' emphatic rejection of it. By dismissing all emotions as irrational and by urging their complete eradication the Stoics sounded the view of scientism against a patently pervasive force. Their contemporaries, the Epicureans, on the other hand, coddled the emotions, and were in fact the first philosophers to make emotion an adjunct to thought. The placid emotion of pleasure was the intellectual goal of Epicurus, who described it thus: "Pleasure is the beginning and end of living happily . . . to this we come as if we judged passion to be the standard of all good." The popular philosophers, the Sophists, catered upon many occasions to the emotional temper of the times. Where rhapsodists used to sing passages from Homer during Golden Age religious festivals, Sophists replaced them in the Hellenistic period and (wearing the same symbolic purple robes) delivered passionate harangues and panegyrics.

LITERATURE.   Euripides offers the most pungent examples of emotion sprung from violence. The murder of the children in *Medea* is one of the most frenzied scenes in all dramatic literature. Also, there is the agonizing shame of Hercules after his god-driven madness in *Hercules Furens,* and the hysterical repentence of Orestes and Electra after they murder their mother in *Electra.* Euripides also explores the other end of the scale in *Iphigenia in Tauris,* sweetly sentimental in its depiction of the gentle life and the happy destiny of its heroine. The late Hellenistic romances like the *Daphnis and Chloe,* already mentioned, and the romance of *Ninos and Semiramis,* king and queen of Assyria, are written in a similar vein.

ARCHITECTURE.   The effects sought in Hellenistic buildings were often more emotional than esthetic. One feels the impact of size in the Temple of Apollo at Miletus and of enthusiastic display in Lysicrates' Monument whose columns and crowning statue give fillips of pleasure instead of a sense of organic inevitability.

SCULPTURE.   The size of the Colossus of Rhodes and of the frieze figures of the Great Altar of Zeus at Pergamum parallel the emotional impact of size in Hellenistic architecture. And the drapery used in the Golden Age to convey idea is now used to suggest mood or emotion, as in the *Winged Victory* (Nike) of Samothrace (Figure 2.25) whose swirling dress echoes the excitement of victory. The subject matter of sculpture also conveys emotional impact sometimes sprung from violence, as in the *Laocoön* (Figure 2.24) with its twisted limbs and agonized faces. The facial expressions of the priest and his two sons run a gamut from agony to fear. The boy on Laocoön's right who is in the act of succumbing is very moving. The priest himself, thick-muscled and in pain, is an object of lively pity. The scene is essentially theatrical and catches at the viewer's emotions with dramatic impact.

Figure 2.24 (left) AGESANDER, ATHENODORUS, AND POLYDORUS OF RHODES. *Laocoön.* (c. 100 B.C.). Vatican Museum, Rome. [Archives Photographiques].

Figure 2.25 (right) *Winged Victory (Nike) of Samothrace.* (c. 200 B.C.). Louvre, Paris. [Archives Photographiques].

Figure 2.26 (below) Theater. (c. third–second century B.C.). Reconstruction of Priene. [Hirmer Verlag Munchen].

PAINTING.   Here, too, subject matter ranged from violent emotional impact, as in *The Battle between Alexander and Darius* where the grimness of Alexander and the despair of Darius help to charge this painting with feeling, to sentimentality, as in *Heracles and Telephos* which shows the infant Telephos being nursed by a deer.

MUSIC.   In music the new nomes introduced by the dithyrambist Timotheus contained embellishments and chromaticisms designed to appeal to the emotions rather than to purify the soul. The aulos of the reveling Dionysus now took undisputed precedence over the lyre of contemplative Apollo. Ensembles using aulos, syrinx, cithara, cymbals, and other instruments played together added a new dimension of excitement to Hellenistic music.

Hellenism achieved its own special way of viewing the world, which determined the nature of its knowledge, just as the tendency to go from the specific to the universal molded that of the Golden Age. The Hellenistic temper tended to view things in depth and detail, but with the breadth of its view limited to the boundaries of the subject at hand. It therefore tended toward SPECIALIZATION.

In philosophy Aristotle advocated specialization in his *Categories*, by classifying all conditions of things under ten headings or "predicaments" (he later reduced the list to eight). Zeno further divided philosophy into three categories: physical, ethical, logical. The Sophists no longer concerned themselves with universal truth but with special subjects such as science, doctrine, interpretation of poetry, grammar, and rhetoric.

LITERATURE.   The tragedies of Euripides each offered a special approach to a central problem: in *Medea* the problem was psychological; in *Hippolytus* it was one of conscience; in *Hercules Furens* it was the cruelty of the gods. Similarly, each of the comedies of Aristophanes approached a problem inherent in a special situation: in *Knights,* the problem of democratic politics in an unlearned society; in *Clouds,* the problem of the effect of Sophist teaching upon the young; in *Lysistrata,* the problem of women left at home while men went off to war.

Minor Hellenistic literature abounds in examples of the specialist temper. Alexandrian poetry divided itself into two schools, the Kallimacheian, which specialized in shorter poems, and the Apollonian, which specialized in poems of epic proportions. Epigram specialists appeared in clusters, and their collected products, the *Palatine Anthology* (named after a manuscript copy owned by the Elector Palatine at Heidelberg) runs to fifteen volumes. Specialist scholars arrived on the scene, men like Aristarchus, who edited the definitive text of Homer. Along with scholars came literary critics, including Didymus, the Homer critic nicknamed Bronze Intestines because of the way he could churn out work. Didymus gave a new finite meaning to the term specialization.

ARCHITECTURE.   New building specialties arose to claim a place alongside Golden Age temples and theaters. Hellenistic architecture lavished care upon private dwellings, market places, hotels, music halls, monuments, libraries, and other kinds of public buildings, and each type evolved its own special style and plan of construction.

SCULPTURE.   In sculpture a new variety of subject matter paralleled architecture and hardened into the fixed style that specialized in precise and perfect observation. Examples include the *Venus of Milo* and the *Boxer* with their specialized exercises in texture (the *Boxer* also made a special study of wounds), *Winged Victory* with its specialized handling of line and drapery, and *Laocoön*, which was a specialized exercise in varieties of contortions.

PAINTING.   We are told that the legendary Apelles, court painter of Alexander the Great, specialized mainly in portraits and in Aphrodites (all of them lost). The Hellenistic shift from large murals to smaller wall paintings adapted to houses—*Heracles and Telephos* and *Perseus Frees Andromeda* were wall paintings—created the new specialist function of the painter as wall ornamenter.

MUSIC.   Like ethics, philology, and literary criticism, music emerges as an independent study in the Hellenistic period. Festival notices of the time frequently list the name of the aulist ahead of the playwright. Divorced from religious ritual, music became pure entertainment and, like the Alexandrian mime dramas of Herodas (drama divorced from ritual), became more popular and trivial in the process. Along with its new specialized function as pure entertainment, music began to develop specialized aspects. From the fourth century B.C. on, instrumentalist and composer were no longer the same person; each belonged to a separate craft, with the inevitable decline in status of the former.

Finally, Hellenism is generally characterized as an age of INDIVIDUALISM. By using the balanced interaction between individual and polis of the Golden Age as a point of departure we may describe Hellenistic individualism as an impulse to reject social and civic *nomoi* in favor of private interests. This kind of individualism showed itself in the Cynics' custom of wearing beards and coarse clothing when more humdrum citizens shaved and favored elegant robes; in Diogenes' attitude of ignoring the world around him while he sat in his tub; in a tendency among philosophers to reject abstract ideas and general types in favor of individual entities existing in and for the sensible world. The Cynic Antisthenes expressed this viewpoint earliest and most pungently when he commented in answer to Plato's doctrine of Ideas: "O Plato, I see a horse, but I do not see horseness."

LITERATURE.   The conservative Aristophanes attacked the tendency to cling to private opinions and interests in such plays as *Knights, Clouds,* and

Wasps. Euripides on the other hand found it the perfect vehicle for his special voice; Medea and Phaedra transcend conventions in order to assert themselves as individuals. Individualism is reflected too in Hellenistic literary styles. The cult of Asianism practiced by deservedly minor writers like Hegesias and Antiochus stressed sound effects and precious diction so as to call more attention to the writer than to his content.

ARCHITECTURE.   The outlandish size of the Temple of Apollo at Miletus challenged architectural *nomoi*. Esthetic styles were deliberately mixed to defy the laws even further. An example of this is the theater at Priene (Figure 2.26) with its horseshoe, not circular, stage and its irrelevant statues perched everywhere. It is instructive to compare the organic unity of the theater at Epidaurus with the distracting variety of ornaments in the theater at Priene.

SCULPTURE.   As in architecture outlandish size (the Colossus of Rhodes) challenged the *nomoi*. The *Boxer*, the figures of *Laocoön*, and to a certain extent the *Venus of Milo* are individuals rather than universal types.

PAINTING.   Too little painting has survived to assess fairly the impact of individualism, but the burlesque vase paintings from the Paestum studios suggest the presence of individualistic forces in painting.

MUSIC.   The rise of the virtuoso soloist feted and applauded by the public marked a wholly new surge of individualism in musical performance. In addition, we may assume that popular music hall composers broke with the *nomoi* constantly.

The most distinctive and far-reaching of the Hellenistic ideas is that ALL VALUES ARE RELATIVE—especially moral values. Such a concept is the logical outcome of a worldly temper, since worldly standards and appearances constantly change. The Stoic philosopher Zeno writes as follows of the relative value of justice: "There is something that is just even according to nature, yet it is also changeable . . . similarly, things which are not just according to nature but to human laws are not everywhere the same." Epicurus too subscribes to the relativity of values, although his philosophy opposes Stoicism. "Every pleasure, then," he writes, "is good because of its natural kinship to us, but not every pleasure is to be chosen, even as every pain is also evil, yet not all are always to be avoided." The Skeptics were also concerned with relativity of values, and Skeptics like Sextus Empiricus denied the existence of absolute truth, holding instead that all truths were relative to custom, to country, to climate, and to the momentary moods and conditions of men.

Euripides makes significant use of moral relativism. In *Medea* the heroine is goaded into action by Jason's intention to dispose of her and then to marry someone else. She has been a loyal wife and has a strong sense of self-respect, and monstrous as her revenge is it is counterbalanced by the provocation, so that good and evil shift according to each protagonist's point of view.

The superb *Hercules Furens* makes morality relative depending upon how it is viewed—from man's standpoint or from the gods': Hercules' murder of his wife and children seems like insanity to him, but like justice to the gods. This same relativism recurs in Hellenistic architecture with its deliberate mixing of styles which makes it equally acceptable to build a house or a music hall like a temple or to build a temple as a showcase for worldly display.

Another Hellenistic concept was that NATURE COULD INSTILL REASON. Where the Golden Age saw nature as a divine, creative force Hellenism equated it with its own *summum bonum,* the measurable, sensible world around it. "Life in accordance with nature is rightly understood to mean life in accordance with reason," proclaimed the Stoic Diogenes Laertes. Zeno defined "natural" as "that which has the same force everywhere and does not depend upon a person's thinking this or that." By this statement he meant that nature was impartially reasonable, like common sense.

Euripides deals with this idea centrally in *Iphigenia in Tauris* where the heroine's life in the nature spot of Tauris endows her with a daily beauty and virtue that serves its purpose *in this world.* The idea shines through most clearly in pastoral literature, however, especially in the serious pastorals of Theocritus: a prime example is the fifteenth idyll in which Alexandrian women visit the palace for the festival of Adonis and there, surrounded by nature, they hear a hymn of praise; they return home pleased, their daily lives somehow endowed with a reason for being. Architecture, by making nature adapt to building sites and even to city layouts, seeks to impose a reasonable pattern upon nature, thus applying the Hellenistic concept of nature in reverse.

Finally the Hellenistic concept of TWO AUDIENCES, ONE LEARNED AND THE OTHER VULGAR, affects not only its own culture but reverberates right down to the present time. Like the other Hellenistic ideas this one emerged as reaction to the Golden Age. Hellenistic life was varied and cosmopolitan in contrast to the monochromatic isolation of the Golden Age polis. Its citizens owed allegiance mainly to themselves and hence they evolved their own cliques in the form of classes. (Classes existed in the Golden Age, of course, but polis considerations and democratic governments tended to blur their boundaries.) The Hellenistic elite spoke Greek, which set it apart the way speaking French set apart the elite in Czarist Russia. The teacher-philosopher Sophists taught Greek and other learned subjects for considerable fees, which widened the gap between rich and poor.

In literature the Alexandrian poets wrote self-consciously for the learned few. The short poems of Kallimachos and the narratives of Apollonius of Rhodes bristled with erudition. Literary critics and scholars wrote for yet a smaller audience. On the other hand a mass of popular verse, mainly satiric and sensual, captured the second audience while losing the first. In sculpture miniature novelties like *Two Girls Playing Knucklebones* and comical, beak-nosed heads certainly appealed to more popular tastes than did *Winged*

Victory or the *Venus of Milo*. Comparing the *Venus* with *The Three Graces*, suggests the breadth of the gap at this time between the learned and the general public. Music, freed from its dependence upon ritual drama, became pure entertainment that found its way into the popular music halls. It was at this point that the learned class turned away from actual performance and developed an interest in abstruse theories of harmonics instead. Practicing musicians lost all status, as did the study of music in the universities. Hellenistic music belonged to the mob.

FORMS AND TECHNIQUES

COLOSSAL SIZE: Size for its own sake inflated works like the Apollonian epics, statues like the Colossus of Rhodes, and buildings like the Temple of Apollo at Miletus.

EMBELLISHMENTS: Ornate and irrelevant, embellishments provide the nonfunctional decor of the theater at Priene, the background decoration in vase painting, and the musical nomes introduced by Timotheus and his followers.

TECHNICAL VIRTUOSITY: The Hellenistic period introduced fireworks of form at the expense of content, as in the epigram, the rhythms of Asianism, and the riddle poetry (the *Alexandra* of Lycophron [of the original Pleiade] was a riddle poem 1474 lines long). Technical virtuosity marked the varieties of decor in structures like the theater of Priene, the detail work in statues like the *Boxer*, the handling of light and dark in such paintings as *Heracles and Telephos*, the rise of virtuoso soloists and of musical compositions suited to their talents.

EXPERIMENTATION: A characteristic of Hellenistic art was its tendency to violate existing rules of form. Literature was constantly developing forms, and then moving on to newer ones. Hellenistic literature saw the emergence of satire, comedy of manners, dramatic pantomime, pastoral, epigram, diatribe, didactic poetry, riddle poetry, prose romance, historical novel, and biography. Architecture mixed Doric, Ionic, and Corinthian modes in countless ways. And the new musical nomes kept giving way to ever newer, more experimental ones.

USE OF GROTESQUE: Distortions were used for special effects, as in the murder of the children in *Medea*, in statues like *Laocoön*, in vase painting parodies like those from the studios of Paestum.

SENSUAL APPEAL: A product of Hellenistic worldliness, sensual appeal permeates the poetry of Sotades, statues like the *Venus of Milo*, paintings like *The Three Graces*, and presumably the new music starting with Timotheus.

REALISM: Realism accounts for the psychology of Euripides' dramas and the topicality of those of Aristophanes, the technique in statues like the *Boxer*, and the treatment of reality in *Battle between Alexander and Darius*.

SELECTED BIBLIOGRAPHY

History

Boardman, John. *The Greeks Overseas*. Baltimore: Penguin, 1965.

Botsford, George W., and Charles A. Robinson. *Hellenic History*. New York: Macmillan, 1956.

Burn, A. R. *The Pelican History of Greece*. Baltimore: Penguin, 1966.

Bury, John B. *A History of Greece to the Death of Alexander the Great*. New York: Macmillan, 1951.

Cary, Max. *A History of the Greek World from 323 to 146 B.C.* London: Methuen, 1951.

_____. *The Legacy of Alexander*. London: Methuen, 1932.

Durant, Will. *The Life of Greece*. New York: Simon and Schuster, 1939.

Finley, M. I. *The Ancient Greeks*. New York: Viking, 1963.

Robinson, C. E. *A History of Greece*. London: Methuen, 1929.

Tarn, William W. *Hellenistic Civilization*. London: Longmans, Green, 1930.

Social and Intellectual Background

Agard, Walter. *The Greek Mind*. Princeton, N.J.: Anvil, 1957.

Armstrong, A. H. *An Introduction to Ancient Philosophy*. Boston: Beacon, 1964.

Bonnard, André. *Greek Civilization*. 3 vols. New York: Macmillan, 1957–1963.

Bowra, C. M. *Classical Greece*. New York: *Time*, Inc., 1965.

_____. *The Greek Experience*. New York: Mentor, 1958.

Burnet, John. *Early Greek Philosophy*. New York: Meridian, 1963.

Cornford, F. M. *Before and After Socrates*. New York: Cambridge University Press, 1960.

Dickinson, G. L. *The Greek View of Life*. New York: Doubleday, 1928.

Freeman, K. *The Pre-Socratic Philosophers*. Oxford: Clarendon, 1946.

Glotz, Gustave. *Ancient Greece at Work*. New York: Knopf, 1926.

Graves, Robert. *The Greek Myths*. 2 vols. Baltimore: Penguin, 1955.

Grube, George M. *Plato's Thought*. London: Methuen, 1935.

Hale, W. H., *et al. The Horizon Book of Ancient Greece*. New York: American Heritage, 1965.

Hamilton, Edith. *The Greek Way*. New York: Norton, 1948.

Harrison, Jane Ellen. *Prolegomena to the Study of Greek Religion*. New York: Meridian, 1964.

_____. *Themis*. New York: Meridian, 1964.

Jaeger, Werner. *Paideia: Ideas of Greek Culture*. 3 vols. New York: Oxford University Press, 1939.

Kitto, H. D. F. *The Greeks*. Baltimore: Penguin, 1954.

Livingstone, R. W. (Ed.) *The Legacy of Greece*. Oxford: Clarendon, 1928.

More, Paul E. *Hellenistic Philosophies*. Princeton, N.J.: Princeton University Press, 1923.

Oates, W. J. (Ed.) *The Stoic and Epicurean Philosophers.* New York: Random House, 1940.

Rose, H. J. *Gods and Heroes of the Greeks.* New York: Meridian, 1963.

Ross, William D. *Aristotle.* London: Methuen, 1949.

Taylor, Alfred E. *Plato, the Man and His Work.* New York: Dial, 1929.

Toynbee, Arnold J. (Ed.) *Greek Civilization and Character.* New York: Mentor, 1950.

Warner, Rex. *The Greek Philosophers.* New York: Mentor, 1958.

Zeller, Eduard. *Outlines of the History of Greek Philosophy.* New York: Meridian, 1955.

_____. *The Stoics, Epicureans and Sceptics.* London: Longmans, Green, 1880.

Literature

Bowra, C. M. *Ancient Greek Literature.* New York: Oxford Galaxy, 1960.

_____. *Landmarks in Greek Literature.* New York: World Publishing, 1965.

Finley, M. I. *The World of Odysseus.* New York: Meridian, 1954.

Flickinger, Roy C. *The Greek Theater and Its Drama.* Chicago: University of Chicago Press, 1960.

Hadas, Moses. *A History of Greek Literature.* New York: Columbia University Press, 1950.

Harsh, P. W. *A Handbook of Classical Drama.* Stanford, Calif.: Stanford University Press, 1944.

Kitto, H. D. F. *Greek Tragedy.* Garden City, N.Y.: Anchor, 1961.

Norwood, Gilbert. *Greek Comedy.* New York: Hill and Wang, 1963.

Rose, H. J. *A Handbook of Greek Literature.* New York: Dutton, 1960.

Sinclair, T. A. *History of Classical Greek Literature: Homer to Aristotle.* New York: Crowell-Collier-Macmillan, 1965.

Wright, F. A. *A History of Later Greek Literature.* London: Routledge, 1932.

Architecture, Sculpture, Painting

Arias, Paolo, and Max Hirmer. *A History of 1000 Years of Greek Vase Painting.* New York: Abrams, 1963.

Beasley, J. D., and Bernard Ashmole. *Greek Sculpture and Painting.* New York: Macmillan, 1932.

Bieber, Margaret. *The Sculpture of the Hellenistic Age.* New York: Columbia University Press, 1961.

Boardman, John. *Greek Art.* London: Thames and Hudson, 1964.

Corbett, P. E. *The Sculpture of the Parthenon.* Baltimore: Penguin, 1959.

Dinsmoor, William B. *The Architecture of Ancient Greece.* London: Batsford, 1950.

Lamb, Winifred. *Greek and Roman Bronzes.* New York: Dial, 1929.

Lawrence, Arnold W. *Classical Sculpture.* London: Cape, 1929.

_____. *Greek Architecture.* Baltimore: Penguin, 1957.

Lullies, Reinhard, and Max Hirmer. *Greek Sculpture.* New York: Abrams, 1960.

Richter, Gisela. *A Handbook of Greek Art.* New York: Phaidon, 1959.

_____. *The Sculpture and Sculptors of the Greeks.* New Haven, Conn.: Yale University Press, 1950.

Robertson, Donald S. *A Handbook of Greek and Roman Architecture.* Cambridge: Cambridge University Press, 1954.

Robertson, Martin. *Greek Painting*. New York: Skira, 1959.

Scranton, R. L. *Greek Architecture*. New York: Braziller, 1965.

Swindler, Mary H. *Ancient Painting*. New Haven, Conn.: Yale University Press, 1934.

Music

Sachs, Curt. *The Rise of Music in the Ancient World, East and West*. New York: Norton, 1943.

Schlesinger, Kathleen. *The Greek Aulos*. London: Methuen, 1939.

Stevens, Denis, and Alec Robertson. (Eds.) *Pelican History of Music*. (Vol. I. *Ancient Forms to Polyphony*). Baltimore: Penguin, 1963.

Wellesz, Egon. (Ed.) *Ancient and Oriental Music*. (Vol. I of the *New Oxford History of Music*). New York: Oxford University Press, 1957.

EVENTS

ORIGINS

Tradition fixes the founding date of Rome as April 21, 753 B.C. The legend surrounding its founding is as follows: Romulus at birth was flung into the river Tiber, but Destiny saw him safely to shore and provided a wolf to suckle him. When he grew up he founded a community on the Palatine hill and got wives for his followers by kidnapping women from the Sabine settlement on nearby Quirinal hill. Behind this legend lie some relevant facts.

From 2000 to 1500 B.C. Indo-European invaders moved southward across the Balkans and assimilated with peoples who had been in south-central Italy since the Stone Age (10,000 B.C.) to establish fortified hilltop villages. These were tribal units and the more prominent were named Sabini, Umbri, and Lucani. Greek colonies to the south had taught them to write, to fight in closed ranks, and to cultivate grapevines and olive trees. To the north of them, in what is now Tuscany, Etruscans—a race of uncertain origin, probably a Greek-influenced mixture of native Italians and Asian migrants— taught them their own highly ceremonial ritual worship of the anthropomorphic deities Jupiter, Juno, and Minerva; the practical value of paved and drained cities; and the concept of monarchy.

About 600 B.C. a priest-king, traditionally Romulus in 753 B.C., performed the Etruscan religious rite of *pomerium*, the plowing of a holy furrow around an area, thus ritually forging it into a single kingdom. The Romulan, or Roman, *pomerium* encircled an area of some 450 acres and included the Palatine, Quirinal, Esquiline, and probably Capitoline hills. A line of seven kings governed the new kingdom until, traditionally, 509 B.C. Of the seven kings—Romulus, Numa Pompilius, Tullus Hostilius, Ancus Marcius, Tarquinius Priscus, Servius Tullius, Tarquinius Superbus—the first is mythical and probably the second; the fifth and the seventh are Etruscan. Stories about them are mainly hero tales mingling history and legend, but it seems certain that Tarquinius Superbus abdicated to a coalition of aristocratic families.

As early as the sixth century B.C. patricians and plebeians were sharply divided, and patrician family groups called *gentes, the* people, controlled the government of Rome. The king's legislative powers were turned over to a Senate made up of the aristocracy; his executive powers fell to two patrician magistrates, called at first *praetors* (heads), then consuls; the king's religious function was taken over by a patrician *pontifex maximus* (chief pontiff).

About 450 B.C. pressure from the plebeians, mainly in the form of threats to secede from Rome, brought about the famous Code of the Twelve Tables. This provided slight protection of the rights of all Roman citizens. The code remained in force throughout the whole history of Rome, and while it did little to cure existing inequities, it provided a core of law-based justice that would expand into one of the abiding glories of Roman civilization.

ROME CONQUERS THE ITALIAN PENINSULA

Legislation, however, ranked second in this community of sixty square miles. Its main concern was conquest, and while neighbor cities viewed war as something to do in between farming, the Romans from the first regarded war as their primary business. During this century they persistently attacked the Latin (after Latium, the name of Rome's surrounding region) tribes around them, reserving their all-out efforts for their most powerful neighbors, the Etruscans. By 405 B.C. they marched against the Etruscans in force, their first decisive move toward world conquest, and by 396 B.C. they had subdued the chief Etruscan city of Veii; by 391 B.C. they had conquered all of Etruria.

In that same year the Celts (whom the Romans called Gauls) invaded Etruria from the north, and the following year met the full Roman army at the Allia River, a few miles north of Rome. In the bitterest defeat of its early years the Roman army was overwhelmed and forced to run away—the Gauls occupied Rome until a ransom in gold bought their departure. Rome learned from this defeat to surround its infantry with a cordon of spears and slings and returned to war with more supple and versatile legions. She defeated the individual cities of Latium by 360 B.C., then created and assumed military control of the Latin League. In 343 B.C. she declared war on the Sammites to the southeast of her, pausing in 338 B.C. to crush a rebellion of the Latin League. She effectively conquered the Sammites in 304 B.C., and in the Third Sammite War, 290 B.C., her army of 40,000 men wiped out all Sammite resistance in the largest military action yet seen in Italy.

Rome now controlled the whole south-central strip of the Italian peninsula, while on the domestic front her growing plebeian population obtained new concessions. A Plebeian Council was appointed, and after 341 B.C. one consul was regularly a plebeian. Less hostile Latin allies were granted Roman citizenship, and all allies were held liable for Roman military service. With this increased manpower Roman technology got under way with the building of the massive highway from Rome to Capua in 312 B.C. under the direction of the *censor* (a magistrate who ranked and classified all citizens) Appius Claudius Caecus, and named for him the Appian Way.

THE GROWTH OF THE ROMAN EMPIRE

By the third century B.C. Roman civilization began to advance with the growth of its empire. Rome started to mint coinage around 300 B.C.; plebeians were admitted even into the priesthood by 292 B.C.; and by mid-century local and civil law gave way to a more international outlook, and a *praetor* was appointed to deal with all cases involving Romans and foreigners.

Despite this broadened outlook Rome fixed her gaze more firmly than ever on war, and when in 279 B.C. the city of Thuria asked protection against the southern Greek city of Tarentum she at once took up the challenge of fighting a Greek city in the shadow of the Carthaginian empire. For its defense Tarentum hired King Pyrrhus of Epirus, the finest Greek general of his day, who advanced into Italy with an army of 50,000 men and a cohort of elephants. Rome fought him time and again until, with the tide turning against him, Pyrrhus returned home in 264 B.C. Now Rome dominated the entire Italian peninsula. Her nation covered 52,000 square miles and numbered 4 million people; its southern edge bore directly upon Carthage.

THE PUNIC WARS: THE SPREAD OF THE ROMAN EMPIRE

Carthage had at this time the most imposing empire in the west, comprising north Africa, southern Spain, and western Sicily. Its rich and luxurious citizenry used mercenary armies under trained and dedicated Carthaginian generals to do its fighting. When in 263 B.C. its Sicilian city of Messana offered itself to Rome in order to shake off Carthaginian rule, Rome accepted the challenge. Needing a fleet, Rome built one which defeated the Carthaginian navy in 260 B.C. A Roman invasion of Africa was turned back in 256 B.C., but in 255 B.C. the Roman navy again destroyed the Carthaginian fleet, and Carthage surrendered all of Sicily, Sardinia, and Corsica. Thus ended the First Punic War (so named because the Carthaginians were Phoenicians, in Latin *Poeni*). From this campaign Rome gained her first overseas province, western Sicily, annexed in 241 B.C.

In 225 B.C. the Gauls again invaded Etruria, but this time the mobile Roman legions wiped them out almost to the last man, and in three swift campaigns conquered all of northern Italy.

When the Carthaginian general Hamilcar died in Spain in 221 B.C., his son Hannibal, a sworn enemy of Rome, succeeded him. Rome demanded Hannibal's arrest, Carthage refused, and the Second Punic War began. In 218 B.C. Hannibal crossed the Alps into Italy with 50,000 men—only half of whom survived—and with this small force he harassed Rome for two years.

Only the delaying guerrilla tactics of Roman General Q. Fabius Maximus could contain him.

Plebeian-patrician political squabbles at home resulted in Fabius being replaced by two inept consuls who met Hannibal's army at a plain near the Apulian city of Cannae. Hannibal was outnumbered 50,000 to 40,000, but he was the greatest strategist Rome had yet encountered. He trapped the Roman army in a circle and wiped it out. Rome at once raised another army, sent it back into the field that same year under Q. Fabius Maximus, and turned over full control of the government to the patrician Senate. Fabius' delaying tactics held Hannibal off for five years, while Rome fought a diversionary battle in Spain. In 210 B.C. she produced in Spain her first great general, P. Cornelius Scipio. By 206 B.C. Scipio drove Carthage out of Spain and then invaded Africa. Hannibal was recalled to defend Carthage, and in 201 B.C. Scipio defeated him with the same tactics Hannibal had used at Cannae. Carthage surrendered to Scipio Africanus, as he was now dubbed in tribute to his victory, and agreed never to fight again without Rome's permission. Rome had now become a world power.

The Senate retained full control of Rome throughout the second century B.C. The Roman republic was one in name only, and senatorial decrees and even whims became official Roman policy. In the sphere of conquest the Senate managed well. It turned its sights eastward where three great kingdoms held sway: that of the Antigonids in Macedonia; of the Seleucids in southern Asia Minor; and of the Ptolemies in Egypt. After a series of wars, Rome took over the Macedonian empire by 148 B.C.; when Corinth revolted in 146 B.C. it was instantly destroyed and all of its inhabitants sold into slavery. Rome forced an unwilling Seleucian king, Antiochus III, into war and by 188 B.C. wiped out his entire army; Hannibal, Antiochus' hostage, committed suicide rather than be brought to Rome. By virtue of an ancient treaty Rome supervised Egyptian affairs, passively in this century at least.

The Roman policy of stern control during this period was typified by the senator M. Porcius Cato, who for personal reasons drove the great Scipio Africanus out of public life and even out of Rome. When Carthage, goaded by an African neighbor, declared war on it in 150 B.C., Cato persuaded the Senate to declare war on Carthage by hammering incessantly that "Carthage must be destroyed." Rome crushed a brave but weakened Carthage in 147 B.C., razed the city, sold its citizens into slavery, and made Africa a Roman province.

REPUBLICAN EFFORTS AND ROMAN AFFLUENCE

In 133 B.C. the Senate became embroiled in a different kind of war. Tiberius Gracchus, himself a patrician, proposed a revolutionary scheme of land distribution to the growing number of underprivileged plebeians. Despite Senate disapproval popular pressure carried his proposal through, but the nobles beat him to death in 133 B.C. while his supporters were busy with the harvest. A decade later his brother Caius proposed similar and broader land reforms, including the establishment of new overseas colonies. The Senate offered proposals outbidding his, and turned commoners as well as nobles against him. He was attacked as an enemy of the state and committed suicide in 122 B.C.

Besides revealing the might of the Senate the Gracchus' attempts at reform cut the ties between plebeians and nobles and led to the civil wars and military takeovers of the following century. But in the second century B.C. Rome rode a crest of power and success. Her genius for organization made her the world leader in banking and money lending. Her standard of living reached new heights as the influx of slave labor after her conquests gave rise to huge estates and to the creation of a new and wealthy middle class.

Roman literature began in this century with the tragedies of Ennius and the comedies of Plautus and Terence. Imposing buildings like the Basilica Aemilia and luxurious private villas were built and stacked with art objects from all of Rome's conquered territories. Rome now even housed an important philosopher—Panaetius of Rhodes.

ROME CIVILIZED: ROMAN CIVIL WARS

With her capital city grown to 1 million inhabitants Rome was becoming civilized, perhaps too soon. Her citizens began to evade military service, although the need to patrol her expanded frontiers was vital. Her upper class began to divert itself with new-found luxuries, leaving a municipal type of government to cope with a growing empire. The way to easy power lay open for the politically minded general, whose archetype appeared in Caius Marius, a tough, efficient, ruthless leader. When the Northmen, Cimbri, and Teutons invaded Italy in 102 B.C. after a successful preliminary raid, his new-style army slaughtered them. These were hardened professional soldiers instead of citizen conscripts, superbly equipped and polished fighters. They fought in cohorts of 360 to 500 men, took great pride in their units, and owed their chief loyalty to their commanding general. Marius' men, nicknamed "Marius' mules," could march forty miles a day with eighty pounds on their backs. When in 89 B.C. the Senate bypassed Marius and appointed other generals to put down the Italian rebellion, Marius bided his time, entered Rome with his troops in 87 B.C. and declared himself and L. Cornelius Cinna co-consuls of Rome—in effect, military dictators.

Marius methodically killed those patricians hostile to him, but he himself died soon after. Cinna's position was challenged by L. Cornelius Sulla, a successful general in the Italian campaign, and in 83 B.C. the first of a series of civil wars broke out—this is doubly ironic in retrospect, since in 89 B.C. all Italians had been made Roman citizens, marking the end of city-state government in Italy and the beginning of a "united" nation.

In 80 B.C. Sulla defeated Cinna and owned the Roman Empire. Like Marius he murdered all his enemies and then took 10,000 of their slaves to form his private bodyguard. By 79 B.C., his power weakening, he withdrew from politics to his country estate, and control of Rome passed again into the hands of the politicians of the Senate. New domestic problems were further complicated by the persistent guerrilla warfare of Mithridates VI, king of Pontus in the eastern Mediterranean, and the wiliest general Rome had faced since Hannibal.

Mithridates harassed Rome's eastern flank from 90 B.C. to 63 B.C. when a rebellion led by his own son forced him to commit suicide. At home a slave revolt led by a gladiator named Spartacus was crushed in 71 B.C. by Marcus Crassus, one of Sulla's chief lieutenants and the wealthiest man of his day. His chief rival for power was another of Sulla's lieutenants, Gnaeus Pompeius Magnus, Pompey the Great; the two men formed an alliance in 70 B.C. Pompey campaigned in the Near East where he made Syria a Roman province in 64 B.C. In 63 B.C. a conspiracy in Rome under Lucius Sergius Catiline to take over the government was unmasked by a brilliant new statesman, Marcus Tullius Cicero, and when Pompey, another potential Catiline, returned to Rome in 62 B.C. he faced a wary and hostile Senate. He had made the mistake of disbanding his army, so that when a newly successful Roman commander in Spain, Gaius Julius Caesar, proposed that Pompey join with Crassus and himself in a triple alliance, Pompey agreed. In 60 B.C. the first triumvirate— Pompey, Crassus, and Caesar—took unofficial control of Rome.

Pompey took command of the two provinces of Spain, but administered them from Rome. Crassus left Rome to govern the rich province of Syria. Caesar took over Transalpine Gaul, and he undertook to conquer all of Gaul (58–49 B.C.). In 53 B.C. Crassus was killed and a Roman army wiped out by the Parthian cavalry. This left Pompey and Caesar, and when in 49 B.C. Caesar closed out his brilliant campaign against Gaul, the Senate for obvious motives turned the republic over to Pompey. Caesar crossed the little river Rubicon that divided Gaul and Italy and invaded Italy, precipitating a second civil war. Caesar took over Italy in less than two months, humbled Pompey's army in Spain, then defeated Pompey himself at Pharsalia, in Thessaly. Pompey fled to Egypt where he was killed by the ministers of Ptolemy XII. Caesar's army marched into Egypt, killed Ptolemy XII and established young Ptolemy XIII on the throne—the actual ruler of Egypt, however, was Cleopatra, a learned and resourceful Macedonian princess.

In 45 B.C. Caesar was master of the Roman Empire, and he ran it efficiently. He made the first reliable gold coins, established soldiers' pensions, created overseas settlements, and set right the Roman calendar. But he made himself perpetual dictator, accepted an official cult of himself, and had his lieutenant Marcus Antonius appointed its priest. A number of Caesar's former officers led by Marcus Brutus and Gaius Cassius, friends of Pompey, assassinated Caesar on March 15, 44 B.C.

In his will Caesar had chosen his grand-nephew Gaius Octavius to be his heir. Octavius was eighteen, and Cicero expressed the judgment of the Senate when he wrote that the boy was to be used, then shoved aside. Cicero was at that time verbally attacking Marcus Antonius while Brutus and Cassius were raising an army against him in the East. Octavius took the name of Gaius Julius Caesar Octavianus, let the Senate use him briefly against Antonius, then in 43 B.C. formed a second triumvirate composed of himself, Antonius, and Marcus Aemilius Lepidus, another of Caesar's lieutenants. Their purge of political enemies, including Cicero, equaled Sulla's for thoroughness, and left the second triumvirate in full control of Rome. That same year they crushed the armies of Brutus and Cassius at Philippi in Macedonia, and this civil war ended when both losing generals committed suicide.

In 40 B.C. Antonius married Octavia, sister of Octavian, as he was then called, and the alliance seemed secure. But Antonius fell under the spell of Queen Cleopatra in Egypt and in 33 B.C. became her prince consort. In 31 B.C. Octavian declared war on Cleopatra. Antonius added his forces to those of Cleopatra, creating another civil war. In the Bay of Actium off the Adriatic coast Octavian scored a swift decisive triumph, and a year later, after land defeats in Egypt, Antonius and Cleopatra committed suicide. Octavian made Egypt a Roman province and confiscated its treasury.

THE AGE OF AUGUSTUS

Rome had known little else but civil war for more than fifty years. Glutted with territory, wealth, and battle fatigue she longed to settle down to an expansive peace. To her great good fortune the leader who could best accomplish this survived. Octavian was a shrewd practical politician who took over complete control of everything under the guise of constitutional reform and in his capacity as merely *princeps*, first citizen. He started a vast civil service network and kept his own household army of accountants, who lifted the actual business of government out of the hands of the Senate. He set up a police force to keep the peace and a model army of 9000 men, the Praetorian Guard, as a standard for his other armies to follow. He converted Rome from a nominal republic run by an elected Senate to an empire with a mammoth centralized organization. All decisions were now made in secret. In 27 B.C. the Senate was pleased to confer upon Octavian the title of Augustus, and fifteen years later that of *pontifex maximus*. The Senate had deified Julius Caesar; therefore Augustus too trailed clouds of divinity, thus justifying the Roman conviction, religious in its intensity, of its divinely appointed destiny. The Age of Augustus was the Golden Age of Roman culture, bringing forth in literature, Virgil, Horace, and Livy; in sculpture and architecture, the Altar of Peace, the Temple of Julia, the Temple of Apollo on the Palatine hill, and innumerable public buildings. As Augustus said of himself, he found Rome a city of brick and left her a city of marble. The master key to his success was that he, more than any leader before or after, was typically Roman: he loved power and organization and managed to keep them without seeming to usurp the rights of others; he was practical and therefore undertook only what was reasonably possible, shunning foolhardy exploits; and he was moral and lived respectably in a modest villa (known today as the House of Livia). He controlled an empire that included France, Spain, Britain, Egypt, Syria, Palestine, and Asia Minor. He clamped upon it a single system and a single code of law that lasted for two centuries and produced the *pax romana*, the Roman Peace.

THE *PAX ROMANA*

The dynasty of Augustus (called the Julio-Claudian dynasty) lasted through four more emperors, longer than any succeeding dynasty. Augustus had consolidated the empire so well that virtually nothing could shake it, although two of his heirs did their violent best. His stepson Tiberius (A.D. 14–37) followed along his lines with cold efficiency. He diminished the role of the Senate to that of a criminal court and abolished the popular election of magistrates. Caligula (37–41) was irresponsible and probably mad. His excesses led to his murder by a palace guard. Claudius (41–54) took the name of "Caesar," a practice adopted by all later emperors. He increased and improved the civil service, dividing it into three vast sections dealing with correspondence, budget and taxes, and law. His last two wives were Messalina, whose immorality is legend, and Agrippina, whose lust for power probably led her to poison Claudius so that her son Nero could be emperor. Nero (54–68) offset a talent for civil administration—when Rome burned he planned its rebuilding intelligently—by an insane and ruthless egomania. He killed his mother and, to please his mistress, his wife; he was deposed by the Senate after a string of cruelties rivaling Caligula's and was ordered to commit suicide.

In spite of Nero and Caligula, Rome prospered. Commerce thrived as never before. Since the Romans disliked business details, slaves were released to do this work, which built up the clerk and merchant classes. The treatment of slaves on the huge estates also improved. A network of Roman roads connected up even the farthest of the forty-three provinces Rome now possessed, and their social and cultural life began to rival that of Rome.

After the death of Nero the army produced several successors and finally Vespasian (70–79), a tight-fisted, practical administrator. He raised taxes to make good Nero's deficits and set the empire back on an even keel of prosperity. His sons Titus (79–81) and Domitian (81–96) formed the Flavian dynasty. Titus seemed promising but died young. Domitian was a hard and capable tyrant who handled the empire well and gave Rome magnificent new public buildings, until his last years when he assassinated enemies as freely as Nero had done. He was killed on orders from his wife, and Rome again had to cast about for another imperial line.

For the first time in its history the Senate was free to choose an emperor, and it selected Nerva, a shrewd, conservative old man. Nerva (96–98) accomplished little himself but established a succession policy of great merit. He "adopted" a man of proven capability to be his successor, and the next three emperors did the same. Nerva adopted Trajan (98–117), a socially conscious administrator who set up a program of welfare for the children of the poor. Trajan also added an imposing new forum and other key public buildings to Rome. An even more dedicated and visionary builder was his successor Hadrian (117–138), whose steady administration and frequent tours of the provinces kept the empire running smoothly. Hadrian adopted Antonius (138–161), probably the most popular of all Roman emperors and the most humane lawgiver Rome had yet seen. Marcus Aurelius (161–180), the philosopher, succeeded him, and while the empire was shaken at that time by the Black Death and by an invasion of barbarians along the Danube, the leadership held steady.

The reign of those four emperors brought Augustus' foundations to full development. The empire reached its maximum size and stability, and the *pax romana* remained essentially in force for almost two centuries. But hindsight shows us signs of impending decline even then. The empire was getting too big, becoming top heavy. The city of Rome, whose main business had become the taking of tribute and the manipulation of money, was turning into a parasite feeding on its healthier provinces. At this juncture Marcus Aurelius broke the skein of adoptions and appointed his son Commodus to succeed him. Commodus (180–192) was as corrupt, vicious, and profligate as Nero, and after his assassination there was, as in Nero's case, no heir. Civil war raged briefly and then the empire was restored to order under Severus—but at a price.

DECLINE OF THE ROMAN EMPIRE

With Lucius Septimius Severus (193–211) begins the first overt phase in the decline of the Roman Empire. Severus established a government wholly dependent upon the good will of the army. From this time on Rome was committed to support of, and domination by, its military force. To pay for this ever growing army Severus' son Caracalla (211–217) proclaimed all free men in the empire Roman citizens and thus made them liable to taxation—and once prized Roman citizenship now became commonplace. When Caracalla was murdered by a clique of officers, he was succeeded by a series of minor emperors until under Alexander Severus (222–235) Rome enjoyed a respite of stability. Severus, a mere youth, turned over full control of the government to his mother, Julia Mamaea, and Rome under its first empress was run uncommonly well. The next fifty years (235–285) saw a turnover of eighteen emperors while army factions quarreled among themselves and barbarian invasions punctured the frontiers along the Danube and in the East. The best of these eighteen emperors, whose career at the same time typified them all, was Aurelian (270–275). He retook Roman territories up to the Danube, defeated and captured Zenobia, queen of the now menacing north Arabian city of Palmyra, and fortified Rome with a massive wall (much of it still standing). As he was preparing Rome for defense against another foreign enemy, his officers assassinated him.

By the end of the third century the Roman army consisted largely of frontier barbarians and was almost double the size of the army of Augustus. The cost of its maintenance was so enormous that wealth as well as power began to filter from Rome to the provinces. In 284 Diocletian, a praetorian prefect, emerged the winner in yet another civil war and brought about a new stability, but for a new and higher price.

Diocletian (284–305) made bureaucracy and administration so all-engulfing that there was little room left for civil war, or for much else for that matter. He fixed prices, devised an annual tax rate that everyone had to pay, divided the empire into 120 administrative units all functioning alike, even opposed Christianity—forbade Christians to hold Roman citizenship—because its independent views challenged standardization. Unlike most of his predecessors he was not assassinated but instead retired to a magnificent palace in Split in Yugoslavia after turning the empire over to a corporate body consisting of two *augusti* and two caesars. This division of power set off yet another civil war, but by 312 Constantine, one of the *augusti*, managed to assume sole control and to restore peace.

Constantine (312–337) relied upon the same choking bureaucracy as had Diocletian, but he accepted Christianity. In 313 he published the Edict of Milan (or only redacted in more popular language the proposals it contained), guaranteeing religious freedom to all. At the same time he announced that he was a Christian. To cope with the drift of wealth and power he moved the capital of the empire from Rome to Byzantium, which he renamed Constantinople, in 330. These measures were only surface patches for a system in the final stages of decay. The death of Constantine was the signal for fresh civil wars, and in 364 the brothers Valens and Valentinian divided the empire into eastern and western districts. In 378 a combined army of German Goths and Mongol Huns crossed the Balkans into Thrace, and when an army under Valens came up to meet them wiped it out and killed the emperor. The Goths and Huns remained in the Balkan peninsula, and became a permanent barbarian wedge between the two halves of the empire.

Theodosius I (379–395) made a last gallant attempt to reunite the empire—he even tried to use Christianity as a binding force by declaring it the official religion of the empire and by banning paganism—but it was beyond saving. His sons partitioned the empire into two subempires with

Arcadius ruling the eastern half and Honorius ruling the western half. Neither ruler was in any way distinguished.

The eastern or Byzantine empire shrank in size, but its core remained intact until 1453. That core had long ceased to be Roman however, was instead "a Hellenistic kingdom with a Christian church and a Roman law book." The western or Roman half was less fortunate. Northern invasions lacerated it until in 410 the Goths under Alaric sacked Rome itself. In 451 Rome showed a flicker of her former greatness when she joined with the Gallic tribes to beat back an invasion into France by the Mongol Huns under Attila. But then in 455 the Vandals under Gaiseric sailed over from North Africa, where, ironically, their capital was Carthage, looted Rome, and left it in ruins.

The end came quietly, almost as an anticlimax, when in 476 the barbarian general Odoacer, linked with the Goths who had killed the emperor Orestes, casually deposed his son Romulus Augustulus (little Augustus), the last of the western Roman emperors.

THE HUMANITIES APPROACH

Two special situations seem to complicate the humanities approach to the study of Rome. (1) The Roman grand passion was politics. So great was this interest that they tended to undervalue the arts. In their early days of greatness they looted whatever art works they desired from the Greeks, and later when these became depleted they often simply imitated Greek models. Many critics therefore dismiss Roman art as second hand or with words like the following by the Greek scholar Arnold Gomme: "In Greek archeology any object you turn up is beautiful; in Roman, you are delighted if you can argue that it is second rate." (2) The Romans shrugged off abstract ideas. What there is of Roman philosophy consists mainly of adaptations of Greek philosophy and the popularized wisdom of Seneca and Cicero.

Since the humanities approach is built upon the study of the arts and ideas, its application to Rome will require a few special considerations. During the discussion of traits we shall see that in Rome all of the arts did not always reflect each trait, which is not surprising in view of the lesser role the arts play. And instead of defining Roman traits with philosophical statements, we shall emphasize Roman philosophies of action—the philosophy of life best suited to its temper. Other than these slight variants the humanities approach to Roman traits will follow the same pattern as for the other periods.

TRAITS AND IDEAS

First and foremost, the Roman temper was PRACTICAL. "Practical Roman" becomes a kind of Homeric epithet for historians of this period. Where other nations conquered, the Romans made alliances; where other nations imposed creeds on conquered peoples, the Romans rarely interfered with local customs: the fact of mastery was enough. "Even the wise man is a fool," said Horace dryly, "if he seeks virtue beyond what is enough." The Roman attitude toward religion was the same as its attitude toward commerce or farming: specific rituals for specific gains.

Roman philosophy totally adapted itself to this trait of practicality. The philosophers focused upon problems of conduct which were solved by practical advice or illustration. When Panaetius of Rhodes preached Stoicism to the Roman republic he wisely substituted Scipio Africanus for the Stoic ideal of the "Man of Wisdom." Cicero wrote as follows on patriotism: "Nor is it sufficient to possess this virtue as if it were some kind of art unless we put it into practice. An art indeed, though not exercised, may still be a part of knowledge, but virtue consists wholly in its proper use and action." Marcus Aurelius gave practical if eloquent advice on how to die: "Serenely take your leave; serene as He who gives you leave to go."

LITERATURE.   Rome brought one form of literature to a higher level of perfection than had the Greeks: the didactic poem, the aim of which is to teach. Lucretius' *De Rerum Natura*, the greatest of the Roman didactic poems, simply translates into Latin poetry the ideas of the Greek philosopher Epicurus, but at the same time its choice reveals the translator's bent. For Epicurus and Lucretius all things, even ideas, consist of matter, thus there are no abstractions; there is only the solid world around us. Other major didactic poems include Ovid, *Ars Amatoria*, a handbook for lovers; Horace, *Ars Poetica*, a handbook on poetry; and Virgil, *Georgics*, a handbook on farming that advises on the growing of crops, the cultivation of the vine and olive, the breeding of cattle and beekeeping. Rome also favored prose literature on practical topics, such as *De Agricultura*, Cato's jottings on farming, Vegetius on warfare, and Frontinus on the Roman water supply.

Much of Roman writing was history—Caesar, Sallust, Livy, Tacitus are a few great names from among many. History as written by the Romans was never a mere record of events, but rather a means of illustrating practical rules of conduct. Virgil's *Aeneid* too was practical in its reason for being: to propagandize the empire of Augustus. When Cicero adapted Plato's *Republic* as *De Republica* he wrote not about an ideal state as Plato had done, but about the most practical constitution and government a state could have.

ARCHITECTURE.   The Romans did their best and most original building on constructions that were wholly practical: aqueducts, roads, bridges, walls, forums, baths, amphitheaters, circuses. Giant aqueducts like the *Pont du Gard* at Nîmes (Figure 3.1) are still standing, and their ingenuity is impressive. The *Pont du Gard* is 900 feet long and its triple tier of arches reaches a height of 180 feet. Fluid and precise, the arches have no adornment whatsoever. Their beauty is purely functional. The double tier of arches in the aqueduct at Segovia stretches an incredible 825 yards, and its state of preservation after close to twenty centuries calls to mind the Renaissance architects' aim of "building for eternity." One can still drive on the Appian Way, and sections of Aurelian's wall are still standing; the arched bridges at Rimini and Alcantara seem indestructible.

More characteristic Roman havens of solace than its temples—for the most part copies of Greek temples elevated on stairways and frequently squared off in the Etruscan manner—were its baths. The Baths of Caracalla (Figure 3.2) combined public and private pools, steam rooms, refrigeration rooms, gymnasiums, club rooms, library, salons, art galleries, and gardens in its vast and ornate structure. It could accommodate some 3500 bathers at the same time. The central, principal salon shown in Figure 3.2 in its restored version suggests why these baths were one of the chief glories of Roman architecture. This vast and spacious salon with its flawless marble

Figure 3.1   Pont du Gard.   (c. 14 A.D.).   Nîmes, France.   [Marburg: Art Reference Bureau].

Figure 3.2   Baths of Caracalla.   (211–217).
Drawing of Roman reconstruction by Spiers.
[Dr. Franz Stoedtner].

floors, its giant columns, and its richly coffered ceiling must have been awesome in its magnificence.

The Romans, who saw material value in places of amusement, built them on a scale that rivaled their aqueducts and baths. For their games they virtually invented the amphitheater, a huge ellipse with encircling tiers of seats, of which the Colosseum (Figure 3.3) in Rome is the best known example. Not time, but earthquakes in the fifth and fourteenth centuries cut it down. Built to house 50,000 people, its interior contained a beehive of staircases to keep the crowds flowing while the ring of arches on the ground floor permitted the same mass movement in and out of the building. These arches recall those of another practical Roman structure, the *Pont du Gard*.

The Roman practical bent influenced architectural techniques as well as types of buildings. Roman builders developed a mixture of lime and *pozzolana* (volcanic earth) that formed an almost indestructible concrete. With it they could build quickly and cheaply, and achieve enormous size, as in the Colosseum and the Baths of Caracalla. Roman builders also developed the arch, known to the Greeks and Etruscans but never really exploited by them, as a means of making interior space greater and more usable than ever before. By extending arches to form vaults, by intersecting them to form groined vaults, by modifying vaulted heights to form a dome the Romans achieved

Figure 3.3   Colosseum.   (70–82 A.D.).   Rome.   [Institute of Italian Culture].

enormous interiors. The main salon of the Baths of Caracalla is an example of intersecting vaults modified to form a series of partial domes.

Roman practicality shows even in what its architecture did *not* do. For Roman architects the function of a building came first, and when it fulfilled that function they were satisfied. Useless ornamentation left them at a loss. As a result most Roman ornamentation is ponderous and irrelevant, like the use of unnecessary columns outside the Colosseum, with each story representing a different Greek order. In a similar vein ornaments of glory like the monumental arches of Titus and Constantine conspicuously serve no function whatsoever. Since function is performed inside a building, Roman architects lavished their efforts on interiors and frequently did nothing whatsoever to exteriors. The interior of the Pantheon (Figure 3.4) is breathtaking. Its hemispherical dome is higher and broader than any previous dome, connoting the spaciousness of empire. The rich Corinthian columns and pilasters, the tinted marble walls, and the coffered ceiling lighted solely by the oculus or circled eye above suggest that heaven itself served the sumptuous Roman world. In contrast is the bare exterior of the Pantheon, where beauty would have no practical value.

SCULPTURE.   The Romans devised one original decoration in stone, and it suited their practical nature: the horn of plenty. But the basic Roman contribution to sculpture is realistic portraiture. The busts of Emperors Caracalla (Figure 3.5) and Commodus (Figure 3.6) both illustrate blunt and honest portraiture despite their contrasting use of ornament. Nothing diverts us

Figure 3.4 GIOVANNI PANINI. Painting of the interior of the Pantheon in Rome.
(c. 1750). National Gallery of Art, Washington D.C., Samuel H. Kress Collection.

from the portrait of Caracalla with its heavy brows, squinting eyes, and brutish, determined expression. Commodus on the other hand is shown with the club and lion skin of Hercules, but these only serve to set in sharper focus the willful, foppish, self-indulgent face. Moreover, the emperor's skinny arms provide literal denial of the adornments he wears.

Roman practicality also determined what sculpture could *not* do. Heavy contact with idealistic Greek sculpture (Livy writes that Lucius Aemilius Paulus brought home 250 wagon loads of Greek art from conquered Macedonia) led to Roman imitation, and nothing was more lifeless and insincere than the Roman's efforts to idealize. One successful compromise between Greek idealism and Roman practicality might be the statue of *Augustus Addressing His Troops* (Figure 3.7). The "Roman" part of this statue, its portraiture, is quite successful in its depiction of a nobly serious Augustus, his expression lofty even in repose. His breastplate, despite its symbols of the harmony of his reign, is appropriately realistic. The "Greek" lower half of the statue is less impressive. The horizontal drapery seems feminine, the bare feet done in the manner of Greek statues of gods seem out of place. The Cupid nudging Augustus' thigh makes him seem uneasy (it symbolizes Augustus' supposed descent from Aeneas, half-brother of Cupid) and itself seems almost ludicrous.

Figure 3.5   (left)   *Caracalla.*   (c. 215).   Staatliche Museen, Berlin.

Figure 3.6   (right)   *Commodus.*   (c. 190).   Palazzo dei Conservatori, Rome. [Deutschen Archaeological Institute].

Figure 3.7 *Augustus Addressing His Troops.*   (c. 20 B.C.).   Vatican Museum.
[Vatican Photographic Archives].

PAINTING.   Here we must descend to the shakier footing of minor and inadequate examples. We may read about Roman painting in the thirty-fifth book of Pliny's *Natural History,* but all of its major works are lost and we must assess Roman painting on the basis of house and tomb decorations at Rome and Pompeii. Roman practicality probably made for realistic portraiture in painting as well as in sculpture: as evidence we do have the *Achilles Revealed by Diomedes and Odysseus in Scyros* (Figure 3.8), whose fat, dissipated looking Achilles was probably a well-known contemporary personage.

Practicality is more surely in evidence in Roman still lifes like that of the *Kingfisher, Vase, Trident, and Sea-fish* at Naples or of the *Fruit Bowl and Vases* (Figure 3.9). In the latter work the clay bowl is disproportionately large and the tilted glass jar at the right makes for imbalance. There is some interest in form, as the different shapes of the vases and the central cluster of fruit attest, but the main concern is with tricks of literal representation at the expense, if need be, of unified composition.

Painting techniques offer more solid evidence of Roman practicality. Roman fresco technique apparently produced more brilliant and lustrous results than any frescoes before or since. Vitruvius in *De Architectura* describes the preparation of their ground; it called for six successive coats of plaster, the last three made with increasingly powdery marble, and produced a surface capable of brilliant luster. Easel paintings too achieved a new brilliance and subtlety of shading through a method, now lost, of blending colors with encaustic.

MUSIC.   Roman music offers little for a chronological survey to deal with and not much more for the humanities approach. It consisted mainly of popular tunes composed for shows, spectacles, and pantomimes, and none of it survives. Literature and the visual arts furnish us with some knowledge of Roman music, but it is at best secondhand knowledge. In consequence writers like Alfred Einstein (*A Short History of Music*) and the editors of the *Pelican History of Music* omit Roman music entirely. So vital, however, was Roman practicality that we can even find traces of it in the inkling we have of Roman music. Roman music was essentially *Gebrauchsmusik,* music for use, and served to assist at a variety of functions. Some of them were vast in scope, and the Roman practical genius invented new instruments like oversized trumpets and water organs to accompany, say, the races at the Circus Maximus whose arena measured some 480,000 square feet. For all events large or small music served not for esthetic delectation but for use. It abetted the dancing, skits, and acrobatics of pantomimes; it added to the pleasures of dining and shipboard cruises; and it keyed up the Roman legions at the brink of battle. The cithara served as ally to the courtesan, and brass horns and trumpets punctuated funeral processions. In the Trimalchio banquet episode from the *Satyricon* of Petronius Arbiter the slaves sing and do musical turns incessantly, and often badly. This is satiric commentary on the wholesale use of music for every occasion.

Figure 3.8   *Achilles Revealed by Diomedes and Odysseus in Scyros.*   (Before 79 A.D.).
National Museum, Naples.   [Alinari: Art Reference Bureau].

Figure 3.9   *Fruit Bowl and Vases.*   (Before 79 A.D.).   National Museum, Naples. [Soprintendenza Alle Antichità della Campania, Napoli; Art Reference Bureau].

The following two aspects of Roman temper are offshoots of Roman practicality, but sturdy enough to claim a separate existence. The first of these is a strong bent toward ORGANIZATION, that is, toward the administration of group enterprises. The Romans, in fact, *created* administration— committees, boards, study teams, civil service—and practiced it everywhere. The Greeks taught them the custom of regular bathing, and they organized public baths; the Greeks taught them medicine, and they organized hospitals. Early in their history they replaced their king with *praetors* and consuls functioning as boards. Later under the emperors they transferred their knack for organization to their provinces and administered an empire 3000 miles wide under a single system.

This knack for organization stemmed from the deep-rooted Roman habit of subordination to outside authority. The early Roman worshiped *numina,* hazy impersonal forces which controlled his life and the world around him. In time he subordinated himself to the state and then to the emperor: these shifts of allegiance differed in object but not in nature. It was his nature to prefer order and organization to individual liberty. The philosopher Panaetius taught subordination for the good of the state in the name of Stoicism; Cicero in his dialogue on *Old Age* has Cato say: "to those who seek perfect good nothing can seem evil that the laws of nature [reason] impose."

LITERATURE.   The Roman tendency to organize shows most clearly in the field of oratory. Cicero in *De Oratore* set up his now classic five points for a well-organized speech: choose the right material; arrange it well; write it vividly; remember it exactly; deliver it well. Quintilian lays similar emphasis on organization in his *Education of an Orator*. The *De Re Rustica* of Varro is a series of dialogues on how to administer a farm, a ranch, an orchard. Virgil presents in the *Aeneid* an underworld properly administered like a Roman colony or municipality, with regions for all classes: the Fields of Mourning for Dido; the depths of Tartarus for the Titans; the Homes of the Blessed for Orpheus. The result is a more vivid and logical afterworld than that described by any of Virgil's predecessors, including Homer.

ARCHITECTURE.   The Roman system of construction reflects its organizational temper. All building methods were standardized so that teams of soldiers and natives could set up Roman-type buildings everywhere; decorative details were similarly standardized so that technicians anywhere could duplicate them. The result was the spread of Graeco-Roman architecture over the entire world.

Roman placement of buildings also emphasizes organization. Where the Greeks saw a building as something complete in itself, the Romans saw it as part of an organized whole. In the Roman fora like those of Augustus and Trajan colonnades, porticoes, gateways, temples, basilicas, and triumphal arches were all subordinate to a symmetrical pattern of organization. Roman organizational temper even produced a building to meet its needs: the basilica. Basilicas provided centers for the administration of private and public business. They were huge to accommodate large gatherings—the Basilica of Maxentius (Figures 3.10 and 3.11) had interior dimensions of 265 by 195 feet. As its plan shows it consisted of a large center aisle or nave ending in a protruding semicircular apse and flanked by two side aisles. The nave was covered with a groined vault to allow maximum space, and barrel vaults at right angles to it ceilinged the side aisles and linked the entire building as a single organized unit. Hemispherical windows on the second story provided ample light. Basilicas became attached to private villas to permit the administration of business to flow uninterrupted at all hours. In time they also came to be used as places of worship, an eloquent testimony to the Roman attitude toward administration. (This latter development will have a strong bearing on Medieval church architecture.)

SCULPTURE.   The creators of the portrait statues of Caracalla, Commodus, and Augustus, and indeed of any Roman statues of importance all remain unknown, their works a product of the organization that was Rome. And in contrast to the individualized workmanship of Greek vases, the production of Arretine ware, the most popular Roman pottery, became the work of management, not art. Ornamental figures were carved into terra cotta molds and then impressed upon the outer surface of each bowl in true assembly-line fashion.

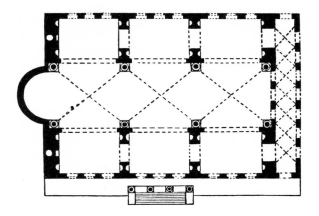

Figure 3.10   Basilica of Maxentius.   (c. 310–313).   Rome.   Reconstruction of ground plan.   [Marburg: Art Reference Bureau].

Figure 3.11   Basilica of Maxentius.   (c. 310–313).   Rome.   Reconstruction of cross-section.   [Marburg: Art Reference Bureau].

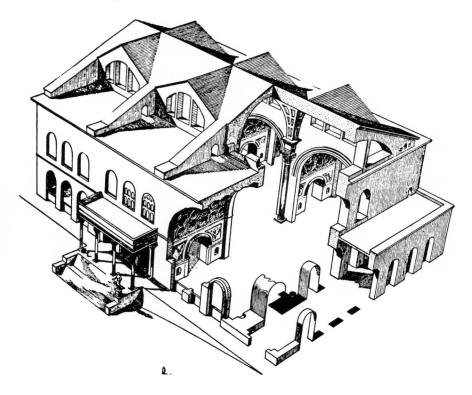

PAINTING AND MUSIC.   Neither painting nor music reveals any organizational influence beyond conjecture, in part as stated earlier because Rome tended to undervalue the arts, and possibly in greater part because of our lack of materials to examine.

The other Roman trait stemming from its basic practicality is RESPECT FOR AND RELIANCE UPON LAW. The trait of organization grew out of a need for order; law maintained that order. The second king of Rome was Numa Pompilius, the lawgiver, legendary like Romulus, revealing how profound a part of Roman temper respect for law had always been. From Numa to the Twelve Tables to the great codifications of Hadrian and Justinian (in 533) Rome had 1000 years of law to underwrite its 1000 years of history. Even where there should have been mystery there was law, for in ancient Roman religion—which became by law the religion of the state—the worshiper made vows to the *numina* who presumably granted his requests *after* he had completed his part of the contract. The Emperor Augustus in his famous prayer hoped to "be known as the author of the best possible constitution." Panaetius "proved" in the name of Stoicism the perfection of Roman constitutional law. And Cicero, the voice of Rome, said in *De Republica:* "That citizen therefore who requires men to do virtuous actions by the authority of laws and penalties, to which philosophers can scarcely persuade a few by the force of their eloquence, is certainly preferable to the wisest of scholars who spend their lives in such [philosophical] pursuits."

LITERATURE.   It is law, not love, that governs the next world in Virgil's *Aeneid.* Of the shades of the dead waiting near the entrance to the underworld Virgil says: "Here their places are always justly assigned by a jury chosen by lot; Minos, as president of the court, shakes the urn, convenes a gathering of the silent, and gives a hearing to the accounts of lives lived and charges made." Terence in *Phormio* shows how potent a force Roman law can be by using it to entangle the lives of his characters and by safeguarding even a parasite under its protection.

ARCHITECTURE.   The *De Architectura* of Vitruvius codifies, like the code of Justinian, all of the laws of building. It takes account of everything, from temples to aqueducts, and even includes methods of dealing with contractors. Vitruvius closes out the humanities approach to Roman law. Its bedrock practicality is too far removed from the Roman view of the decorative function of sculpture, painting, and music to permit any significant interpenetration, although several tentative linkings can suggest themselves.

The Roman moral sense combines with practicality to form the twin peaks of Roman temperament. The two are bridged by the fact that Roman MORALITY upholds such homely practical virtues as *gravitas, pietas* (duty as well as piety), *frugalitas, industria, constantia,* and *disciplina.* Qualities like these bred such statements as "A sound mind in a sound body" (Juvenal) and "Virtue is its own reward" (Seneca) whereby Roman morality took on a distinctly puritanical cast.

Morality lay at the base of most Roman activity and of all Roman thought. The republic sustained itself with ringing moral tales (practical substitutes for Greek myths) of its own heroes, like Horatius at the bridge fending off an army single-handed, and Gaius Mucius who put his hand in fire and held it there to show his captors that torture could not make him betray his fellow Romans. The one Roman goddess whom the influx of Greek gods never endowed with human form was Vesta, symbol of virginity, whose sacred flame protected the security of Rome. The Roman matron, symbol of respectability, exercised rights equal to her husband's within the household. The empire was launched by a deeply moral man: Augustus' family life was exemplary, and at one juncture he even attempted to legislate model family lives for all Roman citizens. He marked the anniversary of ten years' rule with "games" consisting of seventy-two hours of continuous prayers and sacrifices. If the moral fiber slackened in the later days of empire, historians and satirists were there in plenty to criticize and to preach the old morality.

Roman philosophy was suffused with moral precepts. The ethics of Panaetius were the virtues of old Roman morality, and Roman moral tenets were the chief concerns of Epictetus, Marcus Aurelius, and Seneca. Epictetus wrote: "What then is man's nature? To bite, to kick, to imprison, to decapitate? No, rather to do good, to cooperate with his fellows, and to wish them well." Marcus Aurelius stated: "We realize that men are our brothers, that sin is ignorance and unintentional." Seneca continues this theme: "A holy spirit dwells within us, one who records our good and bad deeds and is our guardian. As we treat the spirit, so are we treated by it."

LITERATURE.   Moral precepts abound in the *Aeneid*. Dido is the Roman matron who has sinned and must be punished for it. The Roman matron rewarded is the spirit of Aeneas' first wife, Creusa, "her ghostly stature taller than life," who takes serene leave of her husband as he embarks upon his travels. Probably the best-known line of the epic is the one explaining to the Romans that their "art is to spare the meek and to conquer the proud," thus dressing up the Roman drive toward conquest in a cloak of moral righteousness.

Plautus in *buffo* comedies designed to appeal to the mob preaches the same morality as Virgil. His Alcmene in *Amphitruo* is a Roman matron impressive in her honesty and dignity; and all of the indecent projects in *Casina* are checked at the last minute by a proper and respectable marriage. Terence in *Mother-in-Law* similarly reveals at the last minute that virtue wins out over vice and that the honesty of the Roman matron is above reproach. Cicero climaxes the *First Oration Against Catiline* with these ringing sentiments: "Therefore let the wicked depart; let them separate themselves from

Figure 3.12   Temple of Vesta.   (First century B.C.).   Tivoli.   [G. E. Kidder Smith].

the good; let them assemble in one place. And finally, as I have often said, let them be separated from us by a wall." Apuleius in his legend of Cupid and Psyche from the *Golden Ass* preaches the value of the virtuous life to an empire at the height of its material prosperity.

ARCHITECTURE.   The circular temple which remains traditional throughout Roman history derives from the early, simple Italian peasant hut. Examples of it include the Temple of Augustus in Athens, the eloquently simple round temple at Baalbek, and the Temple of Vesta at Tivoli on the outskirts of Rome (Figure 3.12). Its Corinthian peristyle (row of surrounding columns) surrounding a circular framework recalls Lysicrates' Monument (Figure 2.16), but its wholly circular motif gives it a purity that the latter work lacks. It also stands in simple contrast to elaborate worldly buildings like the Baths of Caracalla and the Colosseum. It is worth noting that the finest work of Roman architecture is the Pantheon, a home for all the gods and therefore all the virtues. Notable too is the count of the buildings comprising the six principal Roman fora: three basilicas, eight triumphal arches, thirteen temples.

SCULPTURE.   Friezes were often designed as moral allegories, the Altar of Peace frieze, for example, symbolizing the good life enjoyed during the reign of Augustus. That early masterpiece (probably Etruscan), the bronze she-wolf suckling Romulus and Remus (Figure 3.13), symbolizes the benevolence of nature. As evidence of the puritanical side of Roman morality, the sculpted goddesses like the matrons were almost always discreetly clothed.

PAINTING.   The painting that remains mainly depicts Greek myths for no ulterior purpose (Pliny calls painting a "dying art") but we do hear hints that allegorical sequences like the Altar of Peace friezes existed, and the quietly reverent *Aldobrandini Marriage* (now in the Vatican library) is apparently one of a series of such pictures extolling matrimony.

Figure 3.13   *She-wolf Suckling Romulus and Remus.*   (c. 500 B.C.).   Capitoline Museum, Rome.   [Vatican Photographic Archives].

Coexisting with this hard core of morality overlaid with puritanism were immoral excesses so shocking that, blown up out of proportion, they have distorted many a history of Rome from Tacitus onward. The racy accounts by Edward Gibbon set down in his temperate prose have lent special conviction to the notion that Rome, especially during the empire, was the essence of corruption and debauchery. Gibbon's less astute borrowers have stung serious historians into extremes of rebuttal to the point where many of them gloss over Roman immorality or else deny that it was more virulent in Rome than anywhere else.

The truth falls somewhere in between these two extremes, with IMMORALITY decidedly a trait of Roman temper. It corroded not only the late empire but the republic and early empire as well, and its general cause is easily explained in the light of modern psychological theory. The Romans were Puritans at heart, repressing all license. At first they managed to restrain immoral flare-ups to fits and starts, but as Rome grew more powerful she could afford to act out her unconscious drives. The deadly gladiatorial games, the communal baths for men and women, the savored cruelty to slaves, the gluttony prolonged by emetics all characterize a society whose censor bar is lifted.

Such was the case even under the republic, where money was king. "Virtue, honor, fame, everything human and divine obeys lovely money," wrote Horace. A foreign prince shaken by republican corruption described Rome as a "City in which everything is for sale." Cicero in a letter to a friend wrote as follows about the Roman games: "Two wild beast hunts a day for five days—magnificent, of course. But what pleasure can it be to a cultured man when a puny human being is mangled by a peaceful beast or a splendid beast transfixed by a spear? And even though it is spectacular you have seen it all so often." Two centuries earlier Plautus taps this same vein of cruelty. In *Amphitruo* the slave Sosia finally concedes that Mercury, disguised like him, must in truth be Sosia because "his back is scarred." His master threatens to cut off his tongue and to crucify him—a common punishment for slaves— and even the matronly Alcmene urges her husband to whip Sosia and to hang him.

At the start of the empire the historian Titus Livy, alarmed at the license of women, put this puritanical caution in the mouth of the elder Cato: "Recollect all the institutions respecting women by which our forefathers restrained their undue freedom. . . . The moment they achieve equality with you they will have become your superiors." Juvenal surveys female immorality in his blistering sixth satire, while Tacitus sees the same corruption in the empire as a whole: "A black and shameful age. . . . Nothing but base servility and a deluge of blood."

In the face of this roiling immorality philosophers either closed their eyes and lauded virtue, or if they were Cynics, harangued against it as they wandered from town to town. Since many Cynics were themselves corrupt, not even moral ones like Dion Chrysostom were taken seriously. Seneca, who as a philosopher wrote "I point other men to the right path," wrote a series of closet dramas which turned erstwhile three dimensional mythical characters into immoral caricatures: his Medea was a raving murderess, Phaedra a trollop, and Atreus a sadist.

Roman immorality touched almost all of its writers, great and small. Plautus closed his career with *The Boor*, a sordid play about a prostitute. The epigrams of Martial are dirty jokes strung like pearls. The *Priapea*, a collection of eighty-six priapic poems, include Virgil and Ovid among their contributors. Architecture lavished its engineering skill on sybaritic baths and on stadiums where torture was a game. Sculptors turned out obscene statues of *Priapus* for the gardens and interiors of the typical Roman home. Artists served up enticing dancing girls like those in the ten mosaics in the villa of Maximian in Sicily. Music incited to lust, warfare, cruelty, and gluttony. And all, it must be understood, because the Romans were at heart a moral people!

Roman thought like Roman art ceded its place to the world of politics and action, and in the main it borrowed what ideas it needed from the same source it turned to for art—the Greeks. But Roman culture differs significantly in thought as well as temper from the Greeks: Virgil's concept of Helen of Troy is a world apart from Homer's, and the portraits of Caracalla and Commodus challenge in principle the Kresilas portrait of Pericles (Figure 2.15). The Romans admittedly borrowed Greek ideas, but like anthologists they borrowed what suited them and in the process they, like anthologists, revealed themselves. The use they made of the Golden Age ideas of free will, nature as divine and as a source of creativity, *arete*, a law-governed universe, and antifeminism was special to themselves. Similarly special and selective was the use they made of the Hellenistic concepts of the relativity of values, nature instilling reason, and the existence of two publics. By surveying Roman adaptations of Greek ideas, therefore, we can piece out a rather definite picture of the Roman mind, which is what the humanities approach that follows proposes to do.

FREE WILL.   The Romans occasionally accepted a limited version of the idea of free will. Seneca, Epictetus, and Marcus Aurelius saw mankind as prone to virtue, which could be achieved if it were so willed: Alcmene in Plautus' *Amphitruo* and, of course, Aeneas, exemplify this will to virtue. In the main, however, the Romans tended to reject the idea of free will. In government they preferred stable authority to free speech, and as their empire evolved its citizens functioned more and more like cogs in a wheel. In religion they worshiped *numen* (divine will) a force so hazy that, like bureaucracy, it could not be dealt with individually. Panaetius, Rome's most flexible philosopher, taught that man must subordinate his will to the state. The *Amphitruo* hangs upon the whims of Jupiter, and the shade of Aeneas' wife informs him, in one of the finest passages in Virgil, that his entire future is predetermined, "is part of the divine plan." The Romans modified the Greek temple in one essential way: they placed it upon a pedestal, as in the Temple of Vesta and the imposing *Maison Carrée* at Nîmes, so that the worshiper subordinated himself to the gods rather than confronting them face to face. Roman sculptors too handled the gods in gingerly fashion, either making tame copies of Greek divinities like the *Venus Genetrix* and *Mars Ultor,* or else avoiding such challenging subject matter entirely. The bold independence implicit in free will clashed with the Romans' organizational temper and made them for the most part reject it.

NATURE AS DIVINE AND AS A SOURCE OF CREATIVITY.   In the main the Romans bypassed this idea of nature as divine and as source of creativity as alien to their hard-bitten knowledge of farming. It did touch them at times, paradoxically not as idea but as ancient superstition: the she-wolf

Figure 3.14   *Woodland Fresco from the House of Livia.*   (c. 20 B.C.).   Terme Museum, Rome.   [Anderson: Art Reference Bureau].

that suckled Romulus and Remus and the mysterious golden bough that safeguards Aeneas in the underworld are magical symbols from a cob-webbed past. When the Romans *thought* about nature, however, it was in responsible and practical terms. Virgil in *Georgics* and Horace on his Sabine Farm are admiring but realistic; Varro in *De Re Rustica* bends even closer to the soil. Roman architects approached nature with no awe what-soever, shaped and molded it to fit their foundations, fora, and city plan-ning and would never have dreamed of adapting to its contours as the Golden Age Greeks had done. In the Altar of Peace frieze Tellus, the Earth Mother, looks exactly like a solid Roman matron. Roman landscapes are about the best Roman paintings that have come down to us, and their approach is realistic rather than reverent. Even the finest example of them, the delicate woodland fresco from the House of Livia (Figure 3.14), mainly holds a hard glass mirror up to nature.

ARETE.   The Romans accepted the idea of *arete,* but introduced two im-portant modifications. Their concept of highest competence and virtue did not vary from profession to profession: *gravitas,* frugality, industry, and dis-cipline applied equally to the farmer and general; and the virtues they acknowledged were always practical ones. In the *Aeneid* Virgil ascribes to Marcellus, Augustus' heir who died prematurely, the *arete* of nobleman and lauds him for these solid virtues: "O righteousness, and old-fashioned faith-fulness. O arm unconquerable in war." *Arete* appealed to the Romans so long as it conformed to their practical standards and so long as it was not relative but fixed, like their moral code.

UNIVERSE GOVERNED BY LAW.   A universe governed by law was too theo-retical a concept to suit Roman practicality. Even Lucretius whose scope was the widest of all Roman writer-philosophers modeled his thought on a Greek philosopher, Epicurus, whose universe was not wholly governed by law. The Romans far preferred Greek comedy with its world of surprises to Greek tragedy with its law-directed universe. The concept modified to a *world* governed by law was a different matter. This the Romans seized upon and fitted into their own pragmatic context: the *pax romana,* the codes of Hadrian and Justinian, the laws for ploughing and planting in the *Georgics* of Virgil, and the Vitruvian laws governing architecture concretize the law-governed Greek universe in the remarkable Roman world.

ANTIFEMINISM.   The Roman mind was at once attracted and repelled by antifeminism. Fomenting antifeminism were Juvenal, Livy, Seneca (as a dramatist), and the laws that made Roman matrons dependents in the early days; opposing it were Virgil (in the *Aeneid*), the worship of Vesta, and the later status of Roman matrons who in their households enjoyed rights equal to those of their husbands. In sum, Rome took sides on antifeminism according to whether it suited the immoral or moral aspect of her temper.

Since Roman immorality represented the shadow side of Roman temper, its antifeminism was in the main less flagrant than in Greece.

RELATIVITY OF VALUES.   Rome rejected the Hellenistic idea that values are relative as being too wispy for its practical nature and too wavering for its moral one. Vespasian's dictum, "Money doesn't smell," sums up the rigid, one-sided, Roman approach to values, and the *pax romana* kept values unchanged across the centuries. Relativity of values could play little part in a civilization solid enough to weather a thousand years of history.

NATURE INSTILLS REASON.   Rome nowhere opposed the idea that nature instills reason and in part even adopted it. Cicero states it in his dialogue on *Old Age* (p. 98), and Roman jurisprudents used it to equate international law with "the law of nature." Cicero made this same equation when he wrote in *Laws:* "Law and equity have not been established by opinion but by nature." That nature instills reason is suggested in the Sabine Farm poetry of Horace and in meticulous Roman landscape paintings like the House of Livia fresco. But despite such instances as these, the idea did not gain widespread acceptance. Mainly it suited legal and philosophical theory but was too cerebral a concept to appeal deeply to the Romans. They tolerated it in the same way that they tolerated other religions, but it did not greatly affect their lives.

TWO PUBLICS: LEARNED AND VULGAR.   Of the Hellenistic ideas, the idea of two publics most appealed to Rome, in part probably because early in her history Rome had segregated patricians and plebeians. Her literature spoke by and large to the cultured elite. The plays of Terence, the polished verse of Horace ("I hate the common herd and keep them at bay"), the teachings of Lucretius, the subtle allegories of the *Aeneid* (Dido as symbol of Carthage; Acestes' symbolic parentage), and the learned references in Propertius' passionate lyrics to Cynthia were all directed toward the happy few. Seneca wrote his plays as closet dramas so as to restrict their distribution, and the political works of Roman historians could never have been intended for plebeians. Moreover, two broadly different forms of Latin were in use: a richly inflected literary Latin (the Latin of Virgil) and a simpler spoken language for the other public. For that other public there was music that accompanied entertainments such as street shows, pantomimes, games, and circuses.

The pattern that emerges from this overview is that Rome in adapting Greek ideas tended to reject those with built-in adaptability like the Golden Age concept of *arete* and the Hellenistic relativity of values. Otherwise, as the humanities approach attests, the Roman mind was neither Hellenistic, as many claim, nor a carbon copy of the Golden Age of Greece, as others believe. Rome did borrow its ideas, but selectively, and the ones it took it reshaped around a snugly anchored temperament.

FORMS AND TECHNIQUES

The Romans did little that was special or characteristic with form in art. They did borrow such experimental Hellenistic forms as satire, epigram, elegy, and didactic poem, but they made no unique use of them. In the main something as intellectualized as form did not intrigue them. Techniques, being more like physical exercises, had greater appeal, and although these too were all borrowed the Romans worked vigorously enough with them to make them at least Roman by adoption. Following are a few favorite Roman techniques.

THE HISTORICAL METHOD: In addition to the historians, literary writers like Virgil used history for special purposes, as in the eighth book of the *Aeneid.* In sculpture the Column of Trajan tells the history of his Dacian campaigns in 215 yards of spiraling scenes; and the breastplate of the emperor in *Augustus Addressing His Troops* symbolically depicts the history of his reign. We hear of paintings depicting Roman victories as early as the third century B.C., and Vitruvius writes about long walls decorated with historical and epic cycles done in fresco.

ASIANISM: This technique used fancy flourishes to produce art for art's sake. In literature the cadenced style of Cicero mingled Asianism with Attic simplicity; the inflated rhetoric of Seneca's dramatic speeches was Asiatic. Architecture leaned toward Asianism in its use of the composite order for capitals (Corinthian blended with Ionic) and of great strings of egg-shaped modillions. In sculpture Asianism appeared in *rinceau* reliefs, long spiraling stems adorned with leaves and blossoms and with acanthus leaf motifs and grotesques scattered indiscriminately throughout.

REALISTIC PORTRAITURE: In literature it led the Romans to an interest and special ability in biography. Tacitus' *Life of Agrippa* is a fuller portrait than any work that had preceded it, and Suetonius' biographies of twelve Caesars subjected even emperors to realistic assessments. In drama the down-to-earth realism of Plautus' characters also marked a new stage in realistic portraiture: Alcmene and Sosia in *Amphitruo* and Pyrgopolynices in *Miles Gloriosus* remain vital and vivid today. In sculpture the portrait gallery of dictators and emperors matches the biographies of Suetonius with counterparts in stone.

SELECTED BIBLIOGRAPHY

History

Boak, A. E. R. *A History of Rome to 565* A.D. New York: Macmillan, 1965.
Cary, Max, and John Wilson. *A Shorter History of Rome.* New York: St. Martin's, 1965.

Dudley, Donald R. *The Civilization of Rome*. New York: Mentor, 1960.

Durant, Will. *Caesar and Christ*. New York: Simon and Schuster, 1944.

Ferrero, G., and C. Barbagallo. *Short History of Rome*. 2 vols. New York: Capricorn, 1964.

Gibbon, Edward. *The Decline and Fall of the Roman Empire* (1776–1778). (Available in numerous editions including Everyman, Modern Library, Viking, Harper Torchbooks.)

Hadas, Moses. *A History of Rome*. London: Bell, 1958.

Scullard, Howard H. *From the Gracchi to Nero: A History of Rome from 133* B.C. *to 68* A.D. New York: Barnes & Noble, 1965.

Social and Intellectual Background

Altheim, F. *A History of Roman Religion*. New York: Dutton, 1938.

Arnold, E. V. *Roman Stoicism*. London: Macmillan, 1911.

Bailey, Cyril. (Ed.) *The Legacy of Rome*. Oxford: Clarendon, 1924.

Barrow, R. H. *The Romans*. Baltimore: Penguin, 1949.

Dudley, Donald R. *A History of Cynicism*. London: Methuen, 1937.

Grant, Michael. *The World of Rome*. New York: Mentor, 1961.

Greene, W. C. *The Achievement of Rome*. Cambridge, Mass.: Harvard University Press, 1934.

Hadas, Moses, *et al. Imperial Rome*. New York: *Time*, Inc., 1965.

Hamilton, Edith. *The Roman Way*. New York: Norton, 1932.

MacKendrick, Paul L. *The Roman Mind at Work*. Princeton, N.J.: Anvil, 1958.

Mattingly, H. *Roman Imperial Civilization*. New York: St. Martin's, 1957.

Payne, Robert, *et al. The Horizon Book of Ancient Rome*. New York: American Heritage, 1966.

Stobart, J. C. *The Grandeur That Was Rome*. New York: Hawthorne, 1962.

Wenley, Robert M. *Stoicism and Its Influence*. London: Longmans, Green, 1927.

Literature

Cruttwell, Robert W. *Virgil's Mind at Work: the Symbolism of the* Aeneid. New York: Macmillan, 1947.

Dimsdale, Marcus Southwell. *A History of Latin Literature*. New York: Appleton, 1915.

Duff, J. W. *A Literary History of Rome*. 2 vols. London: Allen and Unwin, 1927.

Fraenkel, Eduard. *Horace*. Oxford: Clarendon, 1957.

Grant, Michael. *Roman Literature*. Cambridge: Cambridge University Press, 1954.

Hadas, Moses. *A History of Latin Literature*. New York: Columbia University Press, 1952.

Mackail, J. W. *Latin Literature*. New York: Scribner, 1904.

Otis, Brooks. *Virgil*. Oxford: Clarendon, 1964.

Rose, H. J. *A Handbook of Latin Literature*. New York: Dutton, 1960.

Sikes, E. E. *Roman Poetry*. London: Methuen, 1923.

Architecture, Sculpture, Painting

Anderson, W. J., and R. P. Spiers. *The Architecture of Ancient Rome*. Rev. by Thomas Ashby. New York: Scribner, 1927.

Brown, Frank E. *Roman Architecture.* New York: Braziller, 1961.

Hanfmann, George. *Roman Art.* New York: New York Graphic Society, 1964.

Kahler, Heinz. *The Art of Rome and Her Empire.* New York: Crown, 1963.

Lamb, Winifred. *Greek and Roman Bronzes.* New York: Dial, 1929.

MacKendrick, Paul L. *The Mute Stones Speak.* New York: St. Martin's, 1960.

Maiuri, Amedeo. *Roman Painting.* New York: Skira, 1953.

Rivoira, Giovanni T. *Roman Architecture.* New York: Oxford University Press, 1930.

Robertson, Donald S. *A Handbook of Greek and Roman Architecture.* Cambridge: Cambridge University Press, 1954.

Scherer, Margaret R. *Marvels of Ancient Rome.* New York: Phaidon, 1955.

Strong, Eugenie S. *Art in Ancient Rome.* 2 vols. New York: Scribner, 1928.

Walters, H. B. *The Art of the Romans.* London: Methuen, 1911.

Music

Sachs, Curt. *The Rise of Music in the Ancient World, East and West.* New York: Norton, 1943.

Stevens, Denis, and Alec Robertson. (Eds.) *Pelican History of Music.* Vol. I. *Ancient Forms to Polyphony.* Baltimore: Penguin, 1963.

Wellesz, Egon. (Ed.) Ancient and Oriental Music. (Vol. I of the *New Oxford History of Music*). New York: Oxford University Press, 1957.

CHAPTER 4
THE MIDDLE AGES

THE RISE OF CHRISTIANITY

Near the beginning of the third century the vigorous Christian pamphleteer Tertullian hit out at the Romans as follows: "We are but of yesterday, and we have filled every place belonging to you: cities, islands, fortresses, towns, assemblies, even your camps, tribes, districts, palaces, Senate, law courts—the only thing we have left you for yourselves is your temples." At the close of the fourth century when the Roman emperor Theodosius permitted wholesale murder in Thessalonica, Archbishop Ambrose of Milan ordered the emperor to do public penance before him, and Theodosius complied. By the fifth century the church was the greatest landowner in Europe, and as barbarian invasions hacked the empire to pieces, church organization solidified.

Pope Leo I (Leo the Great, 440–461) did much to establish Rome as the center of the church and to increase the powers of the papal office. His successful mission to persuade Attila not to attack Europe also set a precedent for papal involvement in political matters. In this same century the monastic movement started in Egypt and spread across western Europe; and the most potent and influential book of the time was *City of God* of St. Augustine. With its central capital, dioceses, and provincial bishops, the church alone continued the policy of universal empire—except for one last surge under Charlemagne—until the thirteenth-century rise of nation-states gave the death blow to all imperial structures.

Barbarian invasions had sliced up the Roman Empire and turned civilization backward. Economic life reverted to agriculture and, except for theology, all literature and art in western Europe were at a standstill until the tenth century. Until the ninth century only three kings countered Europe's tendency to shrink into ever smaller agrarian units: Clovis, the Frankish king, who at his death in 511 ruled nearly all of Gaul; Theodoric, king of the East Goths, whose capital at Ravenna became an artistic mecca for a brief time in the sixth century; and Justinian, a Byzantine emperor of the sixth century whose conquests extended across western Europe as far as Spain. At Clovis' death his kingdom was split into three parts, but he had planted the seeds of a national tradition in France. Theodoric had no successors worthy of him. Although Justinian, like Clovis, left a kingdom that fell to pieces, his career was impressive. He was regent of Byzantium from 518 to 527 and then ruled as emperor until 565. He endowed the role of emperor with oriental grandeur; men had to kiss his feet before addressing him. A devout Christian, he shut down the schools of philosophy at Athens; a devout politician, he controlled all church appointments and church affairs within his kingdom. He reconquered North Africa, the East Gothic kingdom, and a part of Spain. He had Roman law definitively codified and was one of the most opulent and knowledgeable art patrons of all time. Among the many notable buildings he had constructed was the Hagia Sophia (Church of the Holy Wisdom) in Constantinople. Three years after his death the Lombards descended upon the East Gothic kingdom, and soon all of his other acquisitions slipped away, but Constantinople remained a buffer between East and West until the end of the Middle Ages.

Meantime the church increased in organization and status, and the major figure to follow Justinian onto the European scene was Pope Gregory I (Gregory the Great, 590–604). Gregory, the first monk to become pope, established the rule of St. Benedict (regulations for an organized community) in all monasteries, and these became the only centers of organized education from the sixth to the eleventh century. He assumed temporal control of cities, made a treaty with the Lombards, fed the poor, and managed vast and far-flung estates. He approved the development of plainsong (named Gregorian chant in his honor) and wrote commentaries that established him, along with Ambrose, Augustine, and Jerome, as one of the four principal church writers of the Early Middle Ages. During his papacy St. Augustine of Canterbury and forty other monks established Christianity in England; their first church was St. Martin's at Canterbury, and that city became the Christian capital of England.

At this time the so-called Donation of Constantine appeared, which pictured Constantine as offering to transfer his empire to the East in order that the pope may rule over Rome and all of Italy: where "the head of the Christian religion has been established by a heavenly ruler, it is not right that an earthly ruler have jurisdiction." Although a forgery, this document seemed so logical in view of the development of the church at this time that it was widely believed throughout the Middle Ages.

THE FRANKS ASCENDANT: CHARLEMAGNE

Early in the eighth century Germanic invaders pressed down upon Gaul, Spain, Italy, and Britain. Mohammedan Arabs, who had overrun Carthage in 697, invaded Spain from North Africa, just as Hamilcar and Hannibal had done a thousand years earlier. The Mohammedans set up a capital at Cordova, and although the Franks under their great general Charles Martel blocked the Mohammedans' invasion of Gaul at the Pyrenees in 720, they dominated Spain and Sicily, hemming in Christian Europe from the south until the middle of the eleventh century.

Also in the eighth century Charles Martel, illegitimate son of the Frankish king Pepin II, took over military control of the three Frankish kingdoms—centered around the Rhine, Paris, and Burgundy—and at his death in 741 his son Pepin III was proclaimed king. Pepin added Aquitaine to the kingdom. In 768 he was succeeded by his son Charles the Great (Charlemagne), who brought the Frankish kingdom to full flower, made it, in fact, an empire. Charlemagne spent much of his long reign fighting, conquered the Lombards, Bavaria, Saxony, and assumed control of every western Christian territory except England. In 778 he crossed the Pyrenees to attack Cordova, but changed his mind and withdrew. In the mountain passes his rear guard was slaughtered by Christian Basques. It included Hroudland (Roland), and from this incident derives the famous *Song of Roland.*

In his empire Charlemagne established just laws, provided for the education of the clergy and for the construction of churches and other public buildings at Aachen (Aix-la-Chapelle), his capital. *City of God* was his favorite book, but like Justinian he controlled church policy and kept it subordinate to political ends. On Christmas Day in the year 800, however, as he knelt in prayer at St. Peter's Cathedral in Rome, Pope Leo III crowned him "great and pacific emperor of the Romans," thus inaugurating a tradition of Holy Roman Emperor, Germanic in dynasty and crowned in Rome, that would last until 1452. (*The coronation of Charlemagne is the event generally used by historians to date the beginning of the Middle Ages. The period preceding is considered transitional.*)

With Charlemagne's death in 814 his empire fell apart. His own power and personality had created it, and his heirs divided and subdivided it until the Carolingian dynasty died out or was deposed. Its rise and fall served to mark two things: that the hub of Europe had been transferred from south to north, from Greece and Italy to France and Germany, and that the days of empire were definitely past.

FEUDALISM AND THE PAPACY

With the breakup of Charlemagne's empire western Europe soon assembled itself into the system toward which it had tended ever since the fall of the Roman Empire: feudalism. Under the feudal system the king or duke was a tributary lord whose nobles served as his vassals—a service in the main formality, entailing little obligation. Under the vassal was the serf, who worked the former's estate and depended upon it for everything. The landed estates of the nobles became worlds in themselves. In time more powerful vassals made smaller vassals their dependents, and the feudal network became more tightly interwoven. Feudalism took hold first in northern and eastern France, but spread across Europe during the ninth to the thirteenth centuries. In the ninth and tenth centuries its growth was hastened by new waves of barbarian invasions. Asian nomads called Magyars attacked from the east, Saracens from the south, and Vikings (Northmen) from the north, sectioning western Europe into pockets of defense. The walled feudal castle became a place of refuge—the only such place for the artisan or yeoman.

The Northmen were the most savage of the three groups of invaders. Northmen from Sweden and Norway plundered France and Germany from river boats regularly for more than a century; by 855 they had besieged Paris four times. They voyaged west to Vinland (Nova Scotia) and east to Kiev where they wrought terrible destruction on the Slavs. Northmen from Denmark invaded England and wiped out northern monastic culture there. They were thrown back by southern Britons under Alfred the Great (871– c. 901) but remained a menace in the north for generations. But by the tenth century even they were absorbed by the universal force of the age, Christianity, and settled down peacefully in the countries they used to terrorize.

As the powers of kings became curtailed by feudalism, those of the papacy increased. The church was the largest feudal landowner, and many of its priests and monks in order to free themselves from the control of worldly, estate-owning bishops allied themselves directly with the papacy. The papal court at Rome became the supreme court of Christendom and set up uniform laws based upon earlier church decisions. These laws, known as Canon Laws, were codified in 1100 by the Bolognese monk Gratian.

In 910 the Abbey of Cluny was founded in Burgundy. Its ideals were lofty, it ran an excellent school, and it held itself immune from all except papal control. By the twelfth century over 300 new monasteries patterned after Cluny came into being. In 1059 Pope Nicholas II decreed that from then on the pope would be elected by cardinals (at that time the word designated certain clergy in Rome) rather than by outsiders like the Holy Roman Emperor or the Roman populace. Yet the most vigorous pope of the century, Gregory VII, was elected by popular acclaim in 1073.

Gregory VII did much to increase papal power. He challenged feudal lords in Spain, England, Denmark, and Hungary, excommunicating some and deposing others. His chief contest was with the newly appointed Holy Roman Emperor, Henry IV. While the Holy Roman emperors, including Henry IV, failed to unite their native Germany, their position as feudal lord of a vast territory including Poland, Bohemia, some German duchies, and parts of Italy gradually strengthened. At the time of Henry IV it was near its height, and when in 1076 he dabbled in church affairs Gregory withheld his coronation and excommunicated him. Henry was forced to cross the Alps and do public penance (legend has it that he stood barefoot in the snow for three days) at Canossa in Tuscany where Gregory was visiting. The result was a stalemate: Gregory won the appearance of victory but had to lift the ban of excommunication. He died "in exile" (his own words) in Salerno in 1085, but not before setting in motion a century-long struggle between popes and emperors for temporal supremacy.

A pope could nod and even a major order like Cluny could decline into luxury, but church prestige and papal supremacy rose steadily through the eleventh century. The monastic movement kept growing and two new orders continued the devout tradition of the early Cluniacs: the Carthusians who wore hairshirts and lived in solitude; and the Cistercians who stressed simplicity and a life of mystic devotion. St. Bernard of Clairvaux (1091–1153), a Cistercian monk, became the most influential churchman of his century. Also there were the crusades, touched off by Pope Urban II in 1095 in a speech at Clermont-Farrand in southern France. The Seljuk Turks, named after their legendary founder, had seized Syria and Asia Minor in the later half of the eleventh century. They had taken Jerusalem in 1078 and were mistreating Christian pilgrims who journeyed there. The church launched the crusades to recover the Holy Land from them.

CRUSADES AND THE GROWTH OF CITIES

Medieval writers list seven crusades as taking place from the eleventh to thirteenth centuries; in actuality there were more, but seven is a Medieval mystic number. The first crusade was the most successful. A feudal army under Godfrey of Bouillon captured Jerusalem in 1099 and set up a Christian kingdom there. Two new orders were created to protect the Holy Land: the Knights Templars and the Knights Hospitalers. In spite of their help the subsequent crusades were in the main disastrous, and many sincere and pious souls were cut to pieces in the wastes of Asia Minor. Conspicuous for its tragedy was the Children's Crusade in 1212, which resulted in death for most and slavery for the remainder. The crusade of 1202–1204 was a drawn out blunder in which in order to pay off a debt to Venetian financeers Christian knights captured the Christian city of Zara and then, inflamed by conquest, sacked Constantinople, doing far more damage to that city than the barbarian Turks were to do in 1453. In 1187 the Saracens under Saladin retook Jerusalem, and by 1291 the Christians lost their last stronghold in Syria.

The crusades marked a decline in feudalism, although earlier forces had already cracked its foundations. Growth in population throughout the tenth century was too rapid to be absorbed by feudal strongholds. There was only so much arable land on each estate, and poor farming methods caused much of that to lie fallow every year. As a result people moved to work centers, which grew into cities. Emphasis began to shift from agriculture to industry and commerce. The church schools, while mainly concerned with theology, bred literate inquiring minds not satisfied with feudal life. Many crusading nobles, ruined by the expense of the journey, either saw their estates dispersed or had to let their serfs buy their freedom in return for needed funds. As a partial result of all of this, the eleventh century saw a great flowering of Western culture: Romanesque architecture, Germanic sagas, French *chansons de geste*, troubadour poetry, and polyphonic music all got under way, and all soared beyond the constricting walls of the feudal castle.

The northern Italian cities emerged first. Bypassed in the eleventh century during the strife between pope and Holy Roman Emperor they flourished freely and tasted enough independence to form a Lombard League consisting of almost forty cities, including Milan, Venice, Verona, and Bologna. In 1176 they resisted the imperial effort of a Holy Roman Emperor by decisively defeating the army of Frederick I (Barbarossa) at Legnano. A Tuscan League was formed which included Florence, Pisa, and Siena among its members, and in France cities like Paris, Chartres, and Troyes became almost as independent as their Italian neighbors. Flemish towns like Bruges, Ghent, and Cambrai, thriving on textile industries, attained major importance by the thirteenth century—in 1300 the population of industrial Bruges was three times that of agricultural London. In the thirteenth century cities began to develop in England, and during a period of anarchy following the death of Emperor Frederick I in 1190, Germanic cities like Augsburg, Nuremberg, Bremen, and Lübeck were free to develop.

As Medieval cities found strength in unity, their citizens found it in guilds. First merchant guilds, then guilds of artisans (in hierarchies of master workmen, journeymen, apprentices) arose and contributed to municipal independence. Europe was on the brink of achieving a middle class.

THE CHURCH AND THE RISE OF NATION-STATES

Through the twelfth and thirteenth centuries cities and church prospered side by side. Under Innocent III (1198–1216) the papacy reached its Medieval apex of sacred and secular influence. During his pontificate Roman Christendom extended from Greenland to Syria. Two major orders of friars, Dominican and Franciscan, got under way in his lifetime to reinforce the existing Augustinian and Carmelite orders. The Dominicans as teachers and the Franciscans as examples of Christian humility took active and exemplary roles in the outside world, thus strengthening church ties with the secular. Innocent gained more control over the appointment

of church officers everywhere and in general strengthened church administration abroad. The church at this time came closest to reviving in its own
image the network control of the Roman Empire. Latin was its common
language; Canon Law obtained in all its dominions; Rome was at its center;
and uniformity was maintained at any price. Since heresy disturbed the
peace of Christian unity it was quickly rooted out. A sect known as the
Albigensians had been flourishing in the Provençal region of southern
France. They were heretical, although the exact nature of their heresy
is not known. Innocent III arranged for a crusading army of feudal lords to
march against them in 1208. The march resulted in their massacre and the
extinction of their beliefs. A generation later the Inquisition was founded,
its purpose to stamp out heresies by any means. In 1215, the year before
his death, Innocent held the largest and most important church council to
date at the Lateran in Rome. It resembled an imperial congress.

In political affairs Innocent had a more limited success. In 1201
he declared in favor of Otto of Brunswick as Holy Roman Emperor instead
of Frederick II, the rightful heir. Unable to install Otto, he created a stalemate by withholding the coronation of Frederick during his entire papal
tenure. When the shakily enthroned King John of England interfered with
local church administration, Innocent declared him deposed in 1213 and
offered the crown to King Philip II of France. John recanted, acknowledged
himself vassal of the pope, and Philip called off his invasion. Although he
had been used by Innocent on this occasion, Philip made it clear that
he was not, nor did he intend to be, a vassal of the pope. It was a sign of
things to come. Emperors may have lost their sting, but kings were stirring
and expanding nations soon would topple the walls of feudal castles and
challenge the authority of the Roman church.

After Frederick II was crowned Holy Roman Emperor at Rome in 1220,
he moved down to his kingdom in Sicily rather than remain in Germany as
his predecessors had done. A shrewd and learned man, he aimed to restore
the empire in fact and believed that the starting point had to be the
unification of Italy. In this he was blocked by the power of the papacy and
by the independent leagues of cities. His death in 1250 ended the last
imperial effort to unite Italy. England and France lay a discreet distance
away from Rome and had no jealous leagues of city-states with which
to contend. Their history through the twelfth and thirteenth centuries
marks the rise of nation-states.

England had never been a part of Charlemagne's empire and therefore
had not relapsed into fragments when that empire fell. Her estates were
interdependent enough to mobilize under Alfred and to repel the Danish
invaders. William the Conqueror did introduce feudalism in 1066, but he
remained a strong, centralizing force. In 1154 King Henry II curtailed
feudalism by establishing the English common law and by making the

Royal Courts supreme throughout the land. After King John yielded to Innocent, his nobles took advantage of his weakness and forced him to sign the *Magna Carta* in 1215, which righted their wrongs and set up a Great Council to help direct the government. This Great Council, which met to "talk things over," came to be called a "parlement," subsequently Parliament. Under Edward I (1272–1307), the first English king since the Norman conquest, the "model" Parliament—consisting of the House of Lords and the House of Commons—met for the first time in 1295, and an English nation ruled conjointly by king and parliament came to birth.

Until the twelfth century France had a feudal government loosely controlled by the dynasty of Hugh Capet, the Capetian dynasty, whose longevity alone—from 987 to 1328—gave it a certain hereditary status. The Capetian territories were smaller and poorer than those of many of their feudal vassals, but the late eleventh century ushered in a succession of powerful Capetian kings. Philip II (Philip Augustus, 1180–1223), a formidable king, built up the royal treasury, paved and rebuilt Paris to make it an important city—the original Capetian duchy was an area some twenty-five miles square with Paris at its southern tip—and appointed members of the rising *bourgeoisie* to his Council of Regency. Louis IX (St. Louis, 1226–1270), who wore a hairshirt in private but in public seemed a fearless knight, crushed a general uprising of nobles in 1241–1243 so decisively as to make it the last such aggression against a French king. Philip IV (Philip the Fair, 1285–1314) held the first meeting of the Estates General, the French equivalent of the English Parliament. Seeming concerned for the welfare of all, he retained in actuality near absolute power. This power blazed forth in his relations with Pope Boniface VIII.

Near the start of the fourteenth century church and nation-states found themselves facing one another across a peak. Their conflict on secular ground could have only one outcome, and from it dates the decline of the Catholic Church as a universal force and also the decline of the Middle Ages. Earlier events had set the course for such decline: contact with the opulent Eastern Empire of Genghis Khan; the rise of banking and commerce; the growth of secular universities like Salerno and Bologna. The fate of Boniface VIII transposed those subtle currents into the visible world of events.

The goal of Boniface VIII (1294–1303), to increase the prestige of the papacy as Innocent III had done a century before, was lofty enough, but the world had changed. Moreover, his methods were too blunt and he bickered constantly with cardinals and nobles in Rome. In 1296–1297 Boniface published a bull, *Clericis laicos,* ordering churchmen not to pay taxes to any secular government. In England Edward I declared that he would outlaw any clergyman who obeyed the bull, and few did so. In France, Philip the Fair blocked the shipment of all revenues to Rome and ordered all Italians, laymen as well as clergy, to leave France, and their properties there, at once. Boniface backed down and withdrew the bull, but in 1302 published another, *Unam sanctam*, pointed at Philip and declaring that the salvation of every man depended upon his subordinating himself to the papacy. Philip sent an armed force to seize Boniface and bring him to France for trial. They captured the pope at Agnani, his birthplace. Citizens there rescued him after a three days' imprisonment, but a month after his humiliation Boniface died.

THE BABYLONIAN CAPTIVITY: HERESY AND REVOLT

After a brief interregnum Philip's candidate, the Archbishop of Bordeaux, was elected Pope Clement V. In 1309 Clement transferred the papal seat to Avignon, an independent principality, under the shadow of France. He and his successors remained there until 1376. Rome was a turbulent city and a difficult place in which to live, but the attraction of Avignon was luxury, not peace and quiet. The humanist-writer Petrarch who lived nearby called Avignon "Babylon, the home of all vices and all misery," and this period is often termed the Babylonian Captivity of the church. Indicative of its outlook, in 1323 the Franciscan doctrine of poverty was officially condemned.

The Babylonian Captivity was a time of growing social unrest. Marsilius of Padua in a shaking document, the *Defensor Pacis* (c. 1335), challenged papal supremacy and its right of excommunication and claimed that the state alone had a voice in secular concerns. In 1348 the Black Death, an epidemic of bubonic plague, swept across Europe wiping out about one fourth of the entire population. The deadliest plague in history, it left the survivors in a mood to question everything. In Flanders peasant revolts had already broken out (1323–1345) against clerical and secular landowners. In France a frenzied peasant revolt, the *Jacquerie*, exploded in 1358. In England the Peasants' Rebellion of 1381 was the bloodiest and most violent of all. Heresy sprang up and spread in broader waves than ever before. John Wycliffe (c. 1328–1384) preached for the sufficiency of the Bible and against the ceremonies and hierarchical practices of the church. With the papal court in rival France and dominated by a French king, England had added incentive to listen to Wycliffe. His followers, called Lollards, spread his ideas across Europe. In Bohemia, where they were taken up by scholar-preacher John Huss, they led to the Bohemian wars of independence. Less violent but just as insistent were middle-class pressures on the German *Reichstage* (Parliament) in the mid-fourteenth century, and the middle-class pressures for power in France and England during the Hundred Years' War. There was also the Hundred Years' War itself.

THE HUNDRED YEARS' WAR

England and France had been at war before 1337, but now as nations their struggle became decisive. The apparent cause was a dispute over the succession to the French throne. Philip the Fair (d. 1314) was succeeded by his son and then by his brother; he had a daughter too, but the French preferred a male succession. His daughter was the mother of Edward III, king of England, who in 1337 claimed the French crown and declared war. Thus began the Hundred Years' War, which was to go on intermittently until 1453.

The war consisted of three phases. The first began with a succession of English victories. In 1346 after a series of small conquests marked by pillage, the English crushed a large French army at Crécy, near Flanders. This battle marked a signal victory for the English longbow over the French crossbow. In 1356 at Poitiers the English won a decisive victory and captured the French king, John II. The flight of the French nobles at that battle was a disgrace to their class and led to the Great Ordinance of 1356, which gave unprecedented influence to the rising middle class. Under the shrewd administration of Charles V (Charles the Wise, 1364–1380) the French fortunes turned. By 1369 his brilliant general, du Guesclin, had recaptured all French territory except Calais, Bordeaux, and Bayonne, and both nations, badly depleted, rested for forty-five years before resuming hostilities.

Meantime the church, the centripetal force of the Middle Ages, grew ever more divisive. Pope Gregory XI (1370–1378) left Avignon for Rome in October 1376, thus ending the Babylonian Captivity. In March 1378 he died in Rome and an immediate dispute arose concerning his successor. The Romans elected an Italian pope, the French a Frenchman who took office in Avignon, and thus the Great Schism, with rival popes in France and Italy, began. It lasted until 1417. Behind this ferment were thrusts toward something new, an age of inquiry and individualism that would flower as the Renaissance. Changes had long been under way: feudalism and agriculture were waning while cities, nation-states, and commerce grew; trade with the East confronted Medieval unity with variety; peasant and middle-class movements were challenging the rigid social hierarchy. By 1400 what remained Medieval lay mainly on the surface in the form of events.

In 1414 the Holy Roman Emperor Sigismund summoned together one of the largest of Medieval church councils, the Council of Constance, to resolve the Great Schism. After three years of effort the council deposed both rival claimants and elected Pope Martin V, a Roman. Indicative of coming pressures, the council also burned John Huss at the stake, despite his safe conduct from Sigismund to present his views before the council.

In 1415 the second phase of the Hundred Years' War began. England under Henry V invaded France, won a smashing victory against great odds at Agincourt, and by 1420, with the aid of the Duke of Burgundy, Henry V conquered France and arranged to succeed King Charles VI, now help-lessly senile. But Henry died in 1422 and his heir, Henry VI, was less than one year old. Charles VI also died in 1422, and phase two of the Hundred Years' War ended amid anarchy and confusion. (The year 1422 also marked the first wholesale use of gunpowder.)

The last phase of the war began like the first with a series of English victories. Over a course of seven years French provinces were besieged and taken and the French countryside was laid to waste. By 1429 only besieged Orléans had not fallen to England and to her ally Burgundy. The Dauphin and his court sat futilely at Chinon, a city of no military importance to the south of the Loire. There an illiterate peasant girl, Joan of Arc, came to him. She claimed to have heard saintly voices urging her to help her king. First the kitchen servants, then some of the lower nobles were inspired by her, and the Dauphin at last gave her a small force. Clad in armor but car-rying only a banner inscribed "Jhesus Maria" she advanced on Orléans, rallied the French there, and within three days lifted a seven months' Eng-lish siege. Joan, now dubbed the Maid of Orléans, persuaded the Dauphin to march to Reims, the city in which French coronations were traditionally held. It meant a 250-mile march northward through territories barricaded by English forts, and the Dauphin had not previously dared to risk it. This time he did, and almost all of the cities he passed through rallied to his cause as a wave of pent up nationalism swept across France. On July 17, 1429, with Joan at his side the Dauphin was crowned Charles VII at Reims. He then returned to the Loire Valley and to apathy. The following year the Maid of Orléans took a small force to help the northern town of Compiègne, now besieged by Burgundy. The Burgundians captured her and brought her to Rouens, the English headquarters in France. Charles VII, who could have ransomed her, did nothing. She was imprisoned and tried by a French ecclesiastical court anxious to please the English. She was judged to be a relapsed heretic and a sorceress, and on May 30, 1431, was burned at the stake. The words of an English soldier who witnessed it yoked church and state together again for a final moment—of mutual guilt: "God forgive us," he cried, "we have burned a saint!" After this the English won no more victories in France. By 1450 they had lost back all of Normandy, and by 1453 all of their territories in southern France. They retained only Calais, which they would lose in the following century, and thus the Hundred Years' War came to an end.

Triumph and defeat had forged both countries into nations, Medieval in the sense that the mystique of king, not of country, rallied them. But what would culminate in our modern idea of nationalism was under way. Exhausted and depleted England and France would have to give way for a while to the new ways and new culture of the thriving city-states of Italy, Flanders, and Germany, so that 1453, the end of the Hundred Years' War, marks a nominal end of the Middle Ages.

In 1452 Frederick III was crowned Holy Roman Emperor at Rome; he was the last Holy Roman Emperor so honored, thus closing out another Medieval tradition. (The Hapsburg family kept a shadow of the imperial tradition alive for Germany, until in 1806 Napoleon blotted out even that.) In 1453 the Turks under Mohammed II captured Constantinople and made it the capital of Turkey. The source of light for the Early Middle Ages was no more, but the Western world was fast changing and had no time to look back in sorrow.

THE HUMANITIES APPROACH

STRAINS OF INFLUENCE

The Middle Ages traditionally open with the papal coronation of Charlemagne as Holy Roman Emperor on Christmas Day of the year 800. Like most suspiciously neat landmarks this one has some basis in truth. The coronation does signify that something new was launched—fusion of Christian and classical influences. From that time forward a special culture evolved which is reflected in a new emergence of all of the arts. What marks it off most especially, of course, is that it is a Christian culture whose framework and art are now in the service of the church.

Events reveal, however, that Christianity had become a potent force by the fourth century. Events also reveal that Charlemagne, like the church, was not a new and unexpected ninth-century marvel: Justinian and Clovis among others had paved the way for his special brand of Christian Romanism. Therefore while Charlemagne's empire led to the flowering of new thought and culture the groundwork had been laid long before 800, during the period once vaguely defined as the Dark Ages (or hygienically labeled 300 years without a bath) and currently defined with staid precision as the Early Middle Ages.

For the humanities approach this period in western Europe offers a special problem. It *seems* dark by its dearth of major art works. Even Gregorian chant postdates it, according to the re-

searches of Willi Apel. The general humanities practice is to nod
respectfully at the Byzantine art of this period and to pass on
to the Middle Ages proper, and since no Medieval traits, ideas,
or forms are unique to the Early Middle Ages the practice is valid
enough. There is, however, another avenue of inquiry. By general consensus the Early Middle Ages incubate three strains of
influence which the Middle Ages proper bring to maturity:
classical, Christian, and Teutonic. While these, in special mixture, became the Middle Ages and can be dealt with in this
period, their value and influence can take on fuller dimensions
if traced from their origins and sampled separately. For that
reason the classical, Christian, and Teutonic strains of the Early
Middle Ages are presented below in a humanities profile.

THE CLASSICAL STRAIN.   The greatest of classical monuments, the Roman
Empire, survived Vandal, Visigoth, and its own death to reappear as the
structure and organization of the early Christian church. The Roman language, Latin, became the language of the church, and Frankish kings like
Clovis relied upon Roman law and administrative methods. St. Augustine
peppered his *City of God,* the most influential book of the fifth century,
with quotations from Virgil and saw his Christian God as the source of
Platonic Ideas. "There are," he wrote, "certain Ideas, forms, or reasons of
things which are changeless and constant, which are immaterial and contained in the Divine intellect." As the Early Medieval idea of immaterial
essence derives from Plato, Early Medieval cosmology, with its moveless
mover and its first cause, derives from Aristotle.

Boethius (c. 470–525), the most important secular writer up to the
eleventh century, was a translator of Aristotle and his own principal work,
The Consolation of Philosophy, written in Latin, adopts a Roman Stoic
view toward the quirks of Fortune and the true pleasure to be found in
wisdom. The meager literature of this period also includes *On the Arts and
Disciplines of the Liberal Letters* of Cassiodorus, a textbook on education
based upon Greek and Roman principles; and the *Etymologiae* of Isidore
of Seville, an encyclopedia in lesser imitation of the work of Pliny the Elder.

Early Medieval architecture was primarily church architecture, based
in a few cases on eastern designs but mainly modeled on the Roman
basilica (Figures 3.10 and 3.11). The central nave with an apse at the far
end, side aisles separated from the nave, and clerestory or windowed side
walls became the standard plan (with the later addition of a transept) of all
Medieval churches (see p. 100). Very early churches like the original St.
Peter's and St. Paul's Outside the Walls, both in Rome, added to this plan
a rectangular forecourt for penitents and for non-Christian worshipers, and

the style of that forecourt, or *atrium*, was copied from the Roman villa.

The best sculpture of this period was ivory carving in miniature, some of it masterful. The sculpture frequently continued the classical strain, as in the sixth-century carving of *Apollo and Daphne* and the ivory plaque contemporary with it in whose center is an enthroned Christ modeled on Apollo, both in Ravenna. The crisp-curled hair of the exquisite Archangel Michael (Figure 4.1) betrays his stylistic classical origin. Classical, too, in this work are the Roman imperial staff, the handling of draperies, and the still present echo of the shift of weight onto one foot.

The classical strain appears in such illuminated manuscript painting— the chief type of painting of this period—as *Joshua and the Angel of the Lord*, from the Rotulus of Joshua now in the Vatican Library, where a Greek-appearing Joshua is addressed by an angel-centurion complete with spear and helmet; in the athletic toga-clad St. Matthew of a seventh-century Gospel book at Aachen; and in the Genesis scenes from the Moutier-Grandval Bible at Tours showing a youthful, beardless, Apollolike God the Father.

Most Early Medieval music was church music, and like the Catholic liturgy it used Latin texts. The vocal music of this period was subordinate to the syllables of the text, as it was in Greek music. The first Eastern Christian hymns were written in Greek and their style was influenced in part by Greek chants. In 1918 a hymn to the Holy Trinity was found at Oxyrhynchus, written in the Greek alphabetic notation of the third century. The first Western Christian hymns, the fourth-century Ambrosian chants with Latin texts, almost certainly evolved from the Oxyrhynchus tradition, for example, such Ambrosian hymns as *Aeterne rerum conditor* and *Aeterna Christi munera.*[1] Greek influence also appears in music theory. The *De Musica* of St. Augustine and subsequent Early Medieval treatises on music make important use of the number symbolism of the Pythagoreans: one symbolizes completeness, three unity, eight universal harmony, and so forth. These number symbols came to determine in large part the form, rhythm, and intervals of the music of that time: that is, the eight ecclesiastical modes, the preference for one-step intervals in Ambrosian chant (*Eructavit*, for example).

[1]These examples may be found in the *Historical Anthology of Music*, ed. Archibald T. Davison and Willi Apel (Cambridge, Mass., 1950), Vol. I, the standard core anthology of Medieval and Renaissance music. For the sake of uniformity virtually all of the specific Medieval and Renaissance music examples cited in this text can be found in the Davison-Apel anthology.

The surge of research in early music during the past thirty years has uncovered stores of hitherto unavailable compositions which many humanities professors will also wish to use. The record companies too are discovering early music, noteworthy among them the low-priced Nonesuch label whose list is rich with Medieval and Renaissance examples.

Figure 4.1 *Archangel Michael.* (Sixth century). [Courtesy of the Trustees of the British Museum].

128

THE CHRISTIAN STRAIN.   While the Medieval church converted *all* materials to its own use (Platonism, basilica, saga, troll) there were also
certain purely Christian elements that fed a steady current of influence into
the Early as well as later Middle Ages. The city of men was Rome; the
"City of God" was the church. Tenets of faith such as God, the incarna-
tion, the trinity, and divine grace; ceremonies and symbols such as baptism,
the Eucharist, the halo, and the cross all remained aloof from the classical
world in which they flourished—landmarks of an abstract and immaterial
heavenly city. So opposed had the two worlds become by the later fourth
century that St. Jerome feared that his love of classical writers might cost
him his salvation. Christian faith, not classical wisdom, alone could bring
the soul to God. "The Authority of Scripture," wrote St. Augustine, "is
higher than all the efforts of human intelligence."

The only noteworthy history of the Early Middle Ages is Bede's
Ecclesiastical History of the English People, written in Latin and completed
in 831. His contemporary Caedmon wrote Anglo-Saxon poetry that rhapsodically paraphrased the Bible. Since those two, plus St. Augustine, and
the non-Christian Boethius were about the only original writers of this
period, the reason for the Christian emphasis in literature is plain.

The Christian basilica stems from a Roman prototype (Figures 3.10
and 3.11), but a single Early Medieval addition, the transept (an aisle perpendicular to the nave) transformed its plan into the shape of a cross.
Thus, the very form of the building became a Christian symbol. Two early
cruciform churches were built during the reign of Charlemagne: the Abbey
Church of St. Denis and the Abbey Church of Saint-Riquier, both completed before 800.

Early Medieval sculpture and painting developed a wide range of
symbols to connote Christian tenets and elements. The eagle as resurrection, the peacock as immortality, the fish and lamb as Christ, A-Ω (alpha-
omega, the first and last) as Christ, the circle as eternity, the triangle as the
trinity, are only a few of the more common examples. These symbols
abound in Early Medieval sculpture and painting. The *Archangel Michael*
and the *Story of Abraham* mosaic (Figure 4.2) exemplify, among many
other possible choices, the pervasive Early Medieval use of Christian symbolism. Above the head of Michael are the circle and cross, the latter resting on a tiny globe, symbolic of this world. The motif is reversed above
Michael's right hand. In the *Story of Abraham* mosaic the cross at the top
supports a pair of scales, symbolic of divine justice and commenting on the
theme of the work. The hemisphere section contains such Christian symbols as the lamb, crosses circumscribed by circles, and the tree, symbolic
of life or death (and thus offering additional comment on the theme).

In the fourth century, St. Basil revealed the unconscious symbolism of
early church music by writing: "God blended the delight of melody with
doctrines in order that through the pleasantness and softness of the sound

Figure 4.2 *Story of Abraham* (mosaic). (c. 535). San Vitale, Ravenna. [Dr. Franz Stoedtner].

we might unawares receive what was useful in words." Large amounts of such music were produced during the Early Middle Ages: canticles, musical settings for the liturgy, the serenely simple strophic hymns established in western Europe by St. Ambrose, and the equally serene responsorial settings of Psalms, like those in the fifth-century *Codex Alexandrinus*. Most of this music consisted of a single melodic line using small intervals to achieve a brooding and ethereal effect (for example, the Ambrosian hymns *Aeterne rerum conditor* and *Aeterna Christi munera*) and matches perfectly the enormous bare basilicas, the linear weightless carvings, and the illuminated manuscript figures of the time. Christian symbolism even carried over to musical instruments. Trumpets symbolized the power of God's message; the harp symbolized the Book of Psalms; the cymbal the thirst of the soul for Christ; and instrumental ensembles symbolized the praising of God.

THE TEUTONIC STRAIN. Potent as a catalyst for the Middle Ages proper, the Teutonic strain contributes a skein of violence, vigor, and dark superstition. It will later erupt in the poetry of François Villon, the gargoyle statues of Notre Dame, and the Mass of Guillaume Machaut, but in the Early Middle Ages the actual contributions of the Teutons are few and in many cases conjectural. Those Teutons who were Christians at this time were in the main Arian heretics who held that Christ was secondary to God. This view developed out of the all-embracing Pantheism of their

tribal days—still accepted at this time by many of them—wherein everything
was wonder and superstition. Such superstition may well have affected
Gregory the Great when he wrote in his *Dialogues* about demons perched
on lettuce leaves. It must also have given shape and substance to the early
Northern folk poems which a few centuries later turned into Scandinavian
prose sagas—the "lying" or fictional sagas—like *Beowulf*, filled with monsters and thralls and perilous journeys across unknown seas.

In architecture the stretched out, rectangular mead halls held up by
massive piers suggest the surge and power of the Teutonic strain. The interior of the Palace Chapel of Charlemagne at Aachen (Figure 4.3) designed

Figure 4.3   ODO OF METZ.   Palace Chapel of Charlemagne.   (792–805).   Aachen
(Aix-la-Chapelle).   [Deutscher Kunstverlag, Bavaria].

Figure 4.4   Psalm 88 of the *Utrecht Psalter*.   (c. 820).   [University Library, Utrecht].

by Odo of Metz reflected that strain in its heavy piers and somber tunnel vaults. In sculpture power, vigor, and mystery intensify works like the Sigwald Relief in the Baptistery of Cividale (c. 775) with its lively carved grotesques. In painting the rust-colored ink drawings of the Utrecht Psalter illustrate the Psalms with an energy of movement unlike anything in Christian or classical tradition. Psalm 88 (Figure 4.4) in which David proclaims his "soul is full of troubles" and that he is "counted with them that go down in the pit" illustrates pit, crucifixion, and a gratuitous murder in the right-hand section of the drawing. The foreground illustrates how the terrors of the Lord "come around me daily like water." These sudden and spontaneous sketches tremble with violence and zest.

TRAITS AND IDEAS

Medieval man lived in an ordered universe composed of neatly stepped levels. His universe, a Christian adaptation of Ptolemaic astronomy, had earth as the center, nine planets circling it in equidistant ascending order, and the Empyrean or highest heaven as the tenth or outermost circle. This pattern of steps leading upward molded his temperament. All aspects of his life adapted to a world tiered in HIERARCHICAL ORDER. His world of feudalism consisted of lord, vassal, serf; his Christian world of pope, archbishop,

bishop, priest; his political world of first, second, third, and sometimes fourth estates; his ideal or chivalric world of knight, squire, page; and in the macrocosm God, nine levels of angels in ordered degree, man, and then the animals, fishes, and plants, also in ordered degree.

Massive philosophical support for this ordered world came from Neoplatonism which viewed God as the One from Whom emanated a First Intelligence (the Word), which created a Second Intelligence (the World Soul), and so on downward through the planets to the last spiritual intelligence, the human soul. Under the influence of Neoplatonism St. Augustine defined virtue as "the setting of love in order" and Scotus Erigena viewed the universe as a hierarchy of blessedness based upon nearness to God. Saint Thomas Aquinas, whose *Summae* are inclusive Medieval summaries, posits a universe with God at the top; then His higher intelligences, the angels, pure form without matter; then mankind, composed of form and matter.

LITERATURE.   The Provençal troubadour poets set love in order in their own fashion. Their formal, artificial song poems came charged with four levels of sentiment in which the troubadour would be in turn a *fegnedor,* a feigner of love; a *precador,* whose imprecations implored the lady to love him; an *entendedor,* about to reach an entente or understanding with his lady; and a *drut,* accepted lover. Dante makes hierarchical order the design of his entire *Divine Comedy.* All who inhabit the afterlife fit into a tiered scheme: in the Inferno the guilt and punishment of the damned increase with each of the nine descending layers; in the Paradise merit and reward grow greater with each of the nine ascending spheres. Chaucer's motley company in his "Prologue" to the *Canterbury Tales* contains all of the elements for an ordered hierarchy despite its random presentation. From knight and prioress to reeve and miller one may reconstruct degrees of worth that embrace all of the Medieval society.

ARCHITECTURE.   Hierarchical order forms the very principle on which Medieval cathedrals are built. The huge structures fixed the Medieval beholder with a sense of his own littleness. Inside them he could behold St. Augustine's City of God on earth and then readily imagine the higher level of the "Heavenly City." The east façade of the twelfth-century Cathedral of Speyer (Figure 4.5), the earliest north European Romanesque cathedral, consists of three tiers (a trinity) of pointed upward thrusts whose hierarchy in stone suggests a macrocosmic hierarchy. Gothic cathedrals convey the same hierarchical order, but with greater richness of detail. Gothic interiors like that in the great Amiens Cathedral (Figure 4.6) are composed of three ascending levels: nave, triforial gallery (the story above the nave), and clerestory (a horizontal row of windows in the upper wall, in Gothic cathedrals generally above the triforium) which lead symbolically upward to illumination. Gothic façades tend to match this ascending order. The west façade of the Paris Cathedral, *the* Notre Dame (Figure 4.7), leads from portals whose relief statuary literally presents a "Bible in stone" to a rose window, an earthly image of the Empyrean like the Mystic Rose in Dante's paradise, to towers and spires that point the way toward the prime order of reality, heaven itself.

Finally, the method of cathedral construction reflects yet another hierarchy. A master planner, frequently an abbot, planned the general design of the building; the details were then worked out by specialist guilds in which the master craftsman planned, the journeyman executed, and the apprentices hewed wood and carried water, all of them links in a great chain of being.

Figure 4.5   Speyer Cathedral, East Façade.   (c. 1030–1130).   Speyer.   [Deutscher Kunstverlag, Bavaria].

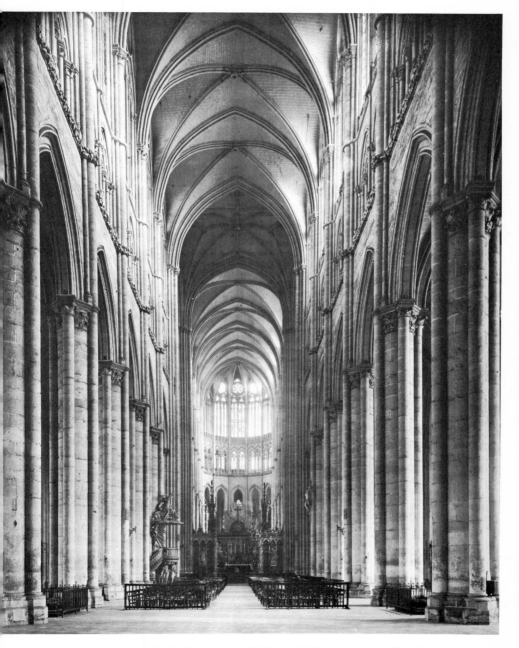

Figure 4.6   Amiens Cathedral, interior.   (1220–c. 1280).   Amiens.   [Marburg: Art Reference Bureau].

Figure 4.7   Notre Dame, West Façade.   (Twelfth–thirteenth centuries).   Paris.
[Alinari: Art Reference Bureau].

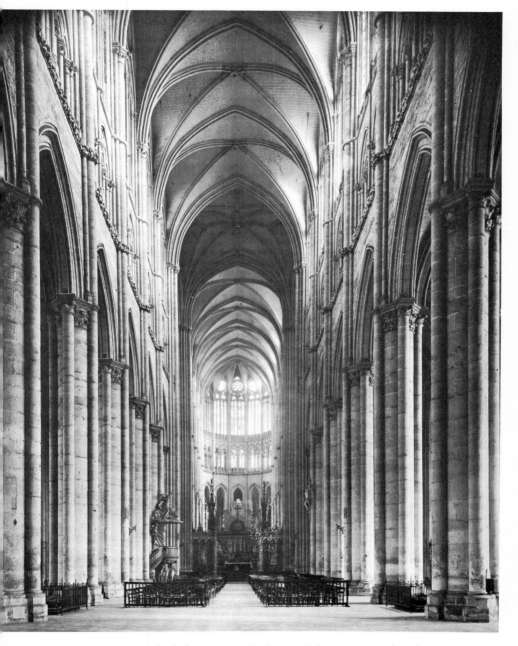

Figure 4.6   Amiens Cathedral, interior.   (1220–c. 1280).   Amiens.   [Marburg: Art Reference Bureau].

Figure 4.7   Notre Dame, West Façade.   (Twelfth–thirteenth centuries).   Paris. [Alinari: Art Reference Bureau].

SCULPTURE.   In cathedral building minor ornaments were almost always foliage, the lowest level of the chain of being. Façades, since they were significant, had more important subject matter, such as saints, biblical scenes, interpretations of Christ and the Virgin, and often these were further stratified. The Last Judgment of the arched relief above the central portal of Amiens Cathedral, for example (Figure 4.8), depicts the Judgment of Souls on the lowest band, then the Separation of the Damned from the Elect above, then at the highest level Christ as Judge.

Ivory carvings furnish the best examples of Medieval sculpture in isolation, and in them the same sense of ordered hierarchy obtains. The importance of the figures usually determined their size. In a sixth-century panel of the Adoration, now in the British Museum, the Virgin resembles an enormous sibyl; the archangel at her side is of lesser size; and the three wise men flanking them are made even smaller. Ivory carvings also convey a sense of order by setting their figures in ranks with the front and upper ranks containing the more important personages, as in the masterful Harbaville Triptych (Figure 4.9). Here Christ is seated in majesty in the upper central panel, the Virgin Mary and John the Baptist on either side of him on the same level, but standing. Below him but still central are five apostles; lesser figures, soldiers and patriarchs, occupy the flanking panels.

PAINTING.   Painting and mosaics make the same use as sculpture of size, ranks, and levels to convey the Medieval sense of hierarchical order. A mosaic in Hagia Sophia of *Christ and the Emperor Leo VI* (Figure 4.10) makes Christ the largest figure and sets him on a level higher than flanking medallions of the Virgin and of an angel who in turn are on a higher level than the kneeling emperor. A *Last Judgment* mosaic on the Venetian island of Torcello is done in five levels of ascending size corresponding to order of merit, with Christ on the top level again the largest figure (Figure 4.11). A painted icon of an *Assembly of the Apostles*, now in the Pushkin Museum at Moscow, is done in ranks with Matthew, John, James, and Peter largest and in the foremost rank.

MUSIC.   Polyphony began about the same time as Romanesque architecture and its structure too reflected the principle of hierarchical order. In its earliest form Medieval polyphony was strict or parallel organum, that is, a line of melody with one added part moving in parallel fourths or fifths or an octave below it: for example, the organa of the octave, of the fifth, and of the fourth of the *Scholia enchiriadis* whose lines of music form flowing parallels like the ribbed vaults or ceiling beams of a Romanesque cathedral (Figure 4.12). The finest examples of organa come from the School of Notre Dame in Paris headed by Léonin (fl. 1175) and Pérotin (fl. 1225). These composers and their school moved from strict to free organum, in which the lines of music instead of being parallel continually converged and diverged. Pérotin added a third and even fourth part to organa and clarified and intensified their rhythms, thus moving even farther away from a Romanesque toward a more Gothic type of composition, as in the *Hec dies organum* (c. 1200) "in Perotinus style."

Figure 4.8   Amiens Cathedral, exterior.   (Twelfth–thirteenth centuries).   [Jean Roubier].

Figure 4.9   Harbaville Triptych.   (Late tenth century).   Louvre, Paris.   [Alinari: Art Reference Bureau].

Figure 4.10   *Christ and the Emperor Leo VI* (mosaic).   (Tenth century).   Hagia Sophia, Istanbul.   [Courtesy of the Byzantine Institute].

Figure 4.11   *Last Judgment* (mosaic).   (Twelfth century).   Torcello Cathedral, Venice.   [Alinari: Art Reference Bureau].

From this development evolved the motet, a full-scale, tiered, Gothic unity. The motet in its developed form, polyphonic singing in three parts using different texts for each part, consisted of a lower part, the tenor, and two upper parts in rhythmic and harmonic relationship to it. The parts thus formed an ascending hierarchy, their lines converging and diverging like ribbed vault clusters in a Gothic cathedral. The Notre Dame School has left us a number of skillful motets, but the richest examples are those of Guillaume Machaut (c. 1300–1377). In such motets as *S'il estoit nulz* and in related compositions like polyphonic ballades (*Je puis trop bien*) and virelais (*Plus dure*) Machaut combined melody, melisma, rhythm, sonority, and syncopation to produce the same unity in diversity as the Gothic cathedral, thus mediating in the same way between the spectator and a higher order of things.

Figure 4.12   Church of Santa Sabina, interior looking east.   (c. 425).   Rome. [Alinari: Art Reference Bureau].

While classical and Teutonic elements helped to color the Middle Ages, the Christian strain gave it direction. The seven sacraments of baptism, the Mass, confirmation, ordination, marriage, penance, and extreme unction penetrated every phase of human life with symbolic ceremony. As a result, the Medieval mind tended to convert even secular acts into ceremony and *to find in them a parable*. This trait of FORMALISM, the ceremonious acting out of parable, ranged from the Eucharist to a social call, from marriages to witchcraft, from chivalry to handshakes, and saw in every act a deeper meaning. If, as the philosopher Plotinus said, every metaphor is an attempt to define God, then almost every Medieval act was Plotinian metaphor. When Guillaume Machaut arranged his first meeting with his lady love, she wore a blue hood, the conventional announcement of her fidelity. When Beatrice smiled at Dante it was formality: humans smiled, but not animals, and so Beatrice's smile served as a formal revelation of her *humanitas*.

The mystics achieved union with God through a fixed number of formal steps: for Hugh of St. Victor there were three, the number of the Trinity; for Richard of St. Victor there were nine, the number of the Trinity increased by its own power and consequently the miracle number; for St. Bonaventure the journey of the soul to God required six formal phases, symbolic of the six days God took to create the Universe. "There is, I hold, nothing visible or corporeal which does not signify the invisible and the incorporeal," wrote John the Scot about the world of nature. His statement applied to the world of men as well.

LITERATURE.   The troubadour poets like the mystics journey through formal phases of love, a simile that gained in force since the lady sung to was often likened to an angel and the poet's cycle often ended with a profession of worship symbolized by a kiss of the hand. The first section of the *Romance of the Rose*, the one written by Guillaume de Lorris, is an exercise in formal courtliness: the lover enters the garden of love where he encounters formal introductions, a courtly dance, and then a formal pageant. In the *Divine Comedy*, Dante in the Garden of Eden witnesses a formal pageant reminiscent of the Book of Revelation, and the formal seating order in the Mystic Rose is akin to that at a courtly joust. Chaucer's *Book of the Duchess* is steeped in the same courtly formality as *Romance of the Rose*. "The Parson's Tale" from *Canterbury Tales*, a sermon parable on the Seven Deadly Sins, is a tediously drawn out exercise in formal presentations. Morality plays like *Everyman* are in essence and purpose the ceremonious acting out of parable.

ARCHITECTURE.   The even-spaced flow of cathedral columns from entrance to apse along the nave provides a formal, deliberate approach to mystery. The steady repetition of clerestory windows conveys the same formalistic effect, and with the same symbolic connotation; so too does the ribbed vaulting of the ceiling, be it in parallel or in patterned clusters. Cathedrals as nominally unlike as the fifth-century basilicalike Santa Sabina in Rome (Figure 4.12) and the Gothic cathedral of Amiens both convey through columnar, clerestory, and ceiling beam repetition a similar formal, processional impression.

SCULPTURE. The custom of ornamenting churches with sculpture made it tend to reflect church ceremony. Frontal rows of figures like the ancestors of Christ (Figure 4.19) on the Cathedral of Chartres, and the apostles and prophets flanking the central portal of the Amiens Cathedral look like nothing so much as a ceremonial processional turning and formally addressing the beholder. The ivory Harbaville Triptych owes much of its serene elegance to its formal, courtly poses, especially in the center panel. The free-standing ivory statue of the *Virgin and Child* (Figure 4.13) has the stiff remoteness of a formal presentation. The Virgin seems remote and detached, and the prematurely aged, virtually lifeless Christ child seems to be little more than symbol.

PAINTING.   Medieval painting and mosaic, like sculpture, was a handmaiden of the church and stressed ceremonial scenes for formal symbolic effect. In a mosaic in the Hagia Sophia (Figure 4.14) the Emperor Constantine presents a model of his city to the Virgin and Child, while across from him the Emperor Justinian presents them with a model of the church. The effect suggests a formal audience at court except that, being symbolic of the power of the church over sacred and secular affairs, the figures are remote and two dimensional. The *Last Judgment* mosaic at Torcello has the same posed, two-dimensional quality as though to point up its ceremonious acting out of parable. Even when realism enters Medieval painting the trait of formalism persists, as in the fourteenth century *Maestà* of Duccio (Figure 4.15) where the Virgin seems remote enough to recall Figures 4.13 and 4.14. She is surrounded by a formal, courtly throng, many of whom look straight out as if to address the viewer, the way the apostles and prophets do in the central portal of Amiens Cathedral.

MUSIC.   The Byzantine hymns like those of St. Ephrem, with their introductory strophe, their procession of isorhythmic strophes like cathedral columns and their upsweep closing section were ponderous ceremony first and music second. Even more massively ceremonial were the Byzantine strophic canons built out of eight odes (sometimes nine) and lasting an interminable length of time. The hymns introduced into western Europe by St. Ambrose (for example, *Aeterne rerum conditor* and *Aeterna Christi munera*) also emphasized formality: eight strophes, each of four lines, each line in iambic dimeter, conveyed not sensuous sound but symbol. When that most formal of Christian ceremonies, the ordinary of the Mass, was set to music in the fourteenth century by Guillaume Machaut the effect was ponderously formal, an honoring of God as one honored a ruler at a coronation ceremony. (This seminal *Mass* of Machaut is not included in Davison-Apel: see footnote 1).

Figure 4.13   *Virgin and Child.*   (c. 950).   Victoria
and Albert Museum, London.

Figure 4.14   *Virgin and Child with Emperors Constantine and Justinian* (mosaic). (c. tenth century).   Hagia Sophia, Istanbul.   [Hirmer Fotoarchiv Munchen].

Figure 4.15   Duccio.   *Maestà*.   (1311).   Duoma, Siena.   [Anderson: Art Reference Bureau].

The power and influence of the Christian church infused the Medieval temper with a trait that reappeared instinctively in every walk of life: DUALISM. The church and church thinking were steeped in pairings: sacred and secular, essence and matter, finite and infinite, good and evil, venial and mortal, faith and reason—until in the fourteenth century William of Ockham hit upon a dualism so blunt and pungent as to anticipate the schism between this world and the next that would trouble the seventeenth century. For Ockham experience illuminated this world only; knowledge of God, the soul, and immortality belonged to a world apart.

One of the more striking effects of Medieval dualism was the Medieval attitude toward women. On the one hand women were considered weak, immoral, and untrustworthy. In England they could not even testify in courts of law "because of their frailty." On the other hand the Middle Ages developed a special office and elaborate ritual for the worship of the Virgin Mary. The great Medieval cathedrals were built in her honor (in France all of them were christened *Notre Dame*, Our Lady), and the ideal of womanhood that the Virgin represented became a part of the code of chivalry.

Medieval philosophy generally adhered to the Platonic dualism of material appearance versus essential reality, and to the Aristotelian dualism of God as Being at Rest and as the First Cause of all movement. For John the Scot God was in nature and beyond it. For St. Bernard of Clairvaux mystic communion with God involved the separation of soul from body. For St. Bonaventure the soul was divided into active and passive parts and mystic contemplation could be achieved only by rejecting the sensible world. Aquinas carefully separated faith from reason: "besides natural law and human law man must also be directed to his end by a divinely given law." Duns Scotus separated not only faith but all of theology from reason.

LITERATURE.   Troubadour poets sang idealizing songs of love and mystic adoration to stranger noblewomen who were for the most part uncouth and illiterate. The *Divine Comedy* contains the obvious dualism between heaven and hell and also dualistic contrasts between pagan Virgil and divine Beatrice, active Matelda and contemplative Eunoe. The introductory framework of Boccaccio's *Decameron* leads from death in plague-ridden Florence to life and creativity in the Edenlike nature spot where the hundred stories are told. In the *Troilus and Criseyde* of Chaucer the tale of lust of the plot proper is contradicted by the epilogue which damns "The blinde lust, the which that may not last," a conclusion that would not be understood without recalling the frailty-Mariolatry dualism in Medieval attitudes toward women.

ARCHITECTURE.   Cathedral architecture of the Early Middle Ages was frankly dualistic, the spare exteriors pointing to the world around us, the graceful, lighted interiors suggesting another world entirely. The Hagia Sophia in spite of its dome looks huddled and plain from the outside

(Figure 4.16). Within the Hagia Sophia (Figure 4.17) the lift of the dome, its drum windows, and the blaze of colored light from the windows in the apse and clerestory walls make it a setting of transcendent beauty. A subtler dualism appears in the Romanesque cathedrals of the eleventh to thirteenth centuries. These cathedrals exhibit a tug of forces between horizontal and vertical, a kind of *Troilus and Criseyde* in stone. The Romanesque interior of the dramatic Cathedral of Pisa (Figure 4.18) is long, massive, and comparatively low, and its rounded arches add to the total effect of horizontality; at the same time the upward thrusts of the columns and the ascending parallel arches from nave to clerestory contribute a clashing sense of verticality. The same conflict appears in the interior of the Hagia Sophia.

Figure 4.16   ANTHEMIUS OF TRALLES AND ISIDORUS OF MILETUS.   Hagia Sophia. (532–537).   Istanbul.   [Dr. Franz Stoedtner].

Figure 4.17 ANTHEMIUS OF TRAL-
LES AND ISIDORUS OF MILETUS.
Hagia Sophia (interior). (532–
537). Istanbul. [Maroon: Photo
Researchers].

Figure 4.18 Cathedral of Pisa (in-
rior). (Eleventh–thirteenth cen-
ries). Pisa. [Dr. Franz Stoedtne

SCULPTURE.   Early Medieval sculpture was sharply dualistic, growing less so by degrees until the end of the period. The flat linear early Byzantine style with its abstract, dematerialized figures served to separate symbol (essence) from body (matter), as in the ivory free-standing *Virgin and Child* and in the figures, especially the Christ, in the Harbaville Triptych. The Iconoclast period (726–843), when Byzantium banned the depiction of divine forms entirely, made the division between matter and spirit explicit and complete. By the tenth century this division showed up as tension of forces—as in Romanesque architecture—rather than as cleavage, and the realistic and abstract began to vie with one another: for example, in the contrast between the expressive faces and abstract bodies of the twelfth-century *Ancestors of Christ* on the west portal of the Cathedral of Chartres (Figure 4.19).

PAINTING.   In painting and mosaic an early cleavage followed by a Romanesque tug, as in sculpture, can be found. Two dimensional and separating symbol from matter are the *Story of Abraham* mosaic and the *Virgin Flanked by Constantine and Justinian* mosaic. The Byzantine Paleologue Revival (1260–1450) ushered in more realistic depictions like the vivid and detailed mosaics in the Church of Kariye Camii (c. 1310) in Constantinople where new dimensionality vied with, instead of turning its back on, symbol. This development sloped over into the Western world and appeared in paintings like the *Maestà* of Duccio.

MUSIC.   Medieval music was dualistic in construction from its very beginning. The early forms (all church forms; no secular music survived until the Late Middle Ages) divided their interest between words and music: hymns, psalms, canticles, plainsong, liturgy, sequences, tropes, canons, organa were not purely music for its own sake: for example, the Gregorian Chant settings of *Psalm 146* and of *Alleluia: Angelus Domini*. Another Medieval attitude toward music caused yet another dualism: the Christian interpretation of Pythagorean number symbolism—three as trinity, four as all of the elements, and so forth—as set forth by St. Augustine in his *De Musica*, forced church composers to keep one part of their minds on symbolic numbers while the other part was trying to create. The development of motets like the thirteenth-century *Hec dies* motets with their sharper rhythms and more sensuous over-all effects helped music to begin to dominate the text and effect a duality through tension rather than dichotomy.

The most salient trait of Medieval temper was FAITH, but of a special kind approachable only after surveying dualism. Medieval faith made dualism a unity and hierarchical order a unit pattern, these apparent inconsistencies resolved and explained by faith in God. It believed that all secular as well as sacred things were subsumed under God and sanctioned through His mediating agency, the Catholic Church. It achieved its fullest expressions toward the end of the Middle Ages when it transcended dualism not to complicate the Medieval temper, but to fulfill it, to bring it upward to

Figure 4.19   *Ancestor of Christ.*   Chartres
Cathedral (west portal).   (Twelfth century).
Chartres, France.   [Marburg: Art Reference
Bureau].

Oneness. It could absorb a hymn to the Virgin and a bedroom lament as texts of a single motet; a king's mistress painted as the Holy Virgin; gargoyle monsters in Gothic cathedrals. It was the highest achievement of the Middle Ages, and for a brief period of time it reached out and touched everything—even money—with its God-centered unity.

The first gold coin was the Florentine florin; it had the lily, emblem of Florence, on one side and John the Baptist, her patron saint, on the other. The florin was first minted in the thirteenth century, the time of the Gothic Cathedral, Gothic sculpture, the motet, and the emergence of Giotto in painting and Dante in literature. In the thirteenth century appeared the great *Summa Contra Gentiles* of Aquinas wherein the worlds of the senses, of reason, and of the spirit were all combined into a metaphysical Gothic edifice.

LITERATURE.   Virtually any topic literature touched could become grist for the mill of faith. A bawdy battle between Noah and his wife meshed appropriately into the Wakefield Cycle of mystery plays. In the Wakefield *Second Shepherds' Play* a lamb placed in a crib as a trick conjoins, in a moment of illumination, with the birth of the Savior to form a single theme. *Aucassin and Nicolette* blends love, war, pacifism, shepherds, and Saracen pirates into a unit affirmation of God's goodness. In the *Divine Comedy* Dante, following Aquinas, explains that souls combine matter and essence, that in effect all life is part of a unified structure. In his Paradise the literal and theological levels of meaning become one, for in reality earth and Empyrean are a single entity. Chaucer's "Man of Law's Tale" fuses paganism, murder, suicide, miracle, shipwrecks, and a world of time into a lyric hymn of Christian faith.

ARCHITECTURE.   Starting in the twelfth century the exteriors of churches take on a beauty worthy of their interiors, as in late Romanesque churches like Great St. Martin's and the Church of the Apostles, both in Cologne. This merging of external and interior worlds reaches sublime heights in Gothic cathedrals, conspicuously in those of northern France: Amiens, Notre Dame, Reims, Chartres. The lines of force in Gothic cathedrals flow in unified verticality, in contrast to the dualistic horizontal-vertical tug of Romanesque cathedrals. And where Romanesque architecture confined itself mainly to churches, the Gothic style reached out to absorb all sorts of secular edifices: private residences like that of Jacques Coeur at Bourges and the *Ca d'Oro* (house of gold) in Venice; castles like Marienburg in Prussia and Karlstein in Bohemia; town halls like the Flemish masterpieces in Bruges, Brussels, and Louvain; and council halls like the *Palazzo Vecchio* in Florence (Figure 4.20). Gothic architecture converted these words of the Cluniac monk Raoul Glaber from metaphor to truth: "It was as if the whole earth, having cast off the old by shaking itself, were clothing itself everywhere in the white robe of the church."

Figure 4.20 ARNOLFO DI CAMBIO. Palazzo Vecchio. (Begun 1298). Florence.
[Anderson: Art Reference Bureau].

SCULPTURE.   The thirteenth-century thrust toward realism brought body and spirit into a unity wherein both seemed touched by the same illumination. This unity is captured perfectly in the stirring life of the statues of the Amiens Cathedral, most notably in the *Beau Dieu* and in the *Vierge Dorée* (gilded Virgin), so named because her crown was originally painted gold (Figure 4.21). By gazing directly at the Christ child, in contrast to earlier works like the ivory *Virgin and Child,* she takes on sudden and immediate life. Her body beneath its comparatively simple drapery seems more real, and her comparative slimness, her smile, and the eloquence of her fingers all contribute to the divine aliveness of the total effect. Conversely, the tender statue of *Uta* on the façade of the Naumburg Cathedral (Figure 4.22) infuses a secular subject with the same spiritual loftiness as in the *Vierge Dorée* and transforms her into something like a saint.

Figure 4.21   *Vierge Dorée.*   Amiens Cathedral.   (c. 1270).   Amiens.   [Dr. Franz Stoedtner].

PAINTING.   Here as in sculpture world and spirit donned the single cloak
of faith. A superb early Byzantine example is the *Virgin of Vladimir*
(c. 1125), now in Russia, in which the face of the Virgin blends sorrow with
remote mystery in a way that makes present and future, world and universe
a single point. But it was Giotto, Dante's friend, who brought painting to
its Medieval culmination of faith and thus opened the way for the Renaissance fusion in painting between this world and next (see Chapter 5).
Like Dante's Beatrice who is at once a golden-haired girl and a symbol of
blessedness, Giotto's figures unify the here and hereafter within the single
span of Christian context. His *Madonna Enthroned* (Figure 4.23) shimmers
with *humanitas* and grace. Compared with the *Maestà* of Duccio, Giotto's
figures are more three dimensional and solid, particularly his Christ child,
and his Virgin's face is more expressive and sublime. Also, where Duccio's
composition is split between a centering on the Madonna and a direct
turning to the spectator, the *Madonna Enthroned* is compositionally a
circle with everything converging toward a central point.

MUSIC.   The motet served as the Gothic Cathedral of music, and its
development combined the same variety of elements into the same essentially reverent unity. Unity began with the "Romanesque" organa of

Figure 4.22   *Uta.*   (c. 1250).
Naumburg Cathedral, Naumburg.
[Dr. Franz Stoedtner].

Figure 4.23   (facing)   GIOTTO.
Madonna Enthroned.   (c. 1305).
Uffizi Gallery, Florence.   [Ali-
nari: Art Reference Bureau].

Pérotin whose rhythmic relationships gave his compositions a common base, as in the *Hec dies* organum "in Perotinus style." Then as the three-part motet evolved in twelfth-century France it turned to love songs for its texts, thus fusing Trinity and romance. Thirteenth- and fourteenth-century motets often used sacred and secular texts in the same compositions so that prayers and frank love songs became parts of a single structure, as in the *S'il estoit nulz* motet of Guillaume Machaut. The Ars Nova of the fourteenth century permitted binary divisions or double time, as well as ternary divisions, adding new rhythmic variety, much of it racy and intoxicating, to further complicate the motet. The entire mixture penetrated church music of the fourteenth century and reached its culmination in the *Mass* of Guillaume Machaut where every available musical device was poured into a single crucible.

A byway of sacred-secular unity in music also deserves mention, namely Nativity and Easter music dramas like the twelfth-century play of *Daniel*, using mostly secular performers and being presented in the market place as well as the church.

Far below the spire of faith lay the Medieval world itself, cut off from the world of spirit by dualism and infused with Christian pessimism and with the virulent superstition of the Teutonic North. "This world nys but a thurghfare ful of wo,/And we been pilgrymes passing to and fro."—thus Chaucer sounded the Medieval Christian attitude toward everyday life. This world was one that nature visited with brutal punishments. Gregory the Great painted the following picture of the famine-ridden North: "Cities are destroyed; strong places toppled; the fields are empty; and the land is become desert. No inhabitants remain on the land, and scarce any in the towns." The famines that struck in the twelfth century had men eating the barks of trees, and the Black Plague of 1348, one of a long series of such plagues, wiped out one fourth of Europe's population; and the tortures of criminal courts and of the Medieval Inquisition took over where nature left off.

In 1260 flagellants "by thousands, by tens of thousands" marched half-naked throughout central Italy scourging one another with leather whips. Their example infected populations of whole cities with a need for self-punishment. Even without punishment beauty faded before its time, as the poems of François Villon attest, and death and putrefaction haunted everyone, from Petrarch in *Meum Secretum* to peasants who yearly acted out a dance of death. Boethius, the only secular philosopher of the Middle Ages, advised the consolations of philosophy as the sole means of escaping from the dreadfulness of this world. With life thus transitory and hard the Medieval temper, inured to suffering, took refuge in a BRUTALITY that stemmed in large part from masochism.

LITERATURE.   Medieval writing abounds in reflections of the world's hardness and brutality. Medieval folk ballads are often steeped in pain: "The Wife of Usher's Well," "Lord Randall," and "The Douglas Tragedy" typify the aura of tragedy and death surrounding so many of them. And while Southern troubadours concentrated on courtly love their Northern counterparts, the Minnesingers, often commented on the cruel realities of life. "The world is very lovely, white, green, and red,/But within is colored black, as dark as death," wrote the greatest of them, Walther von der Vogelweide. The violence and bloodshed of "lying" Northern sagas in the style of *Beowulf* inject Teutonic primitivism into the mainstream of a European culture already prepared for them by plague, famine, and a Christian contempt for the things of this world. Dante's Inferno, the most human section of his epic, presents cruel and violent men like Vanni Fucci the blasphemer, and Ezzolino da Romano, who lopped off the arms and legs of the entire population of a captured city. Chaucer's "Reeve's Tale" and "Miller's Tale," despite their surface laughter, show that life is at bottom painful and cruel; his "Pardoner's Tale" is searing comment on the brutal treachery of Medieval mankind.

ARCHITECTURE.   The somber façade of the Speyer Cathedral conveys the bleak hostility of the outside world, at least in northern Europe. And the carved beasts, monsters, chimeras, goblins, and demons on Southern cathedral capitals and gargoyles[2]—Notre Dame, for example, and the Duomo of Milan—reflect how the Medieval sense of the world's brutality could penetrate even its world of the spirit.

SCULPTURE.   The ivory book cover at St. Gall (c. 900), showing wild animals tearing at cattle, and the capital of the Church of Ste. Madeleine at Vézelay depicting a woman about to be beheaded, mirror the brutal view of life. Such a view also adds darker hues to Christian concepts, as in the bronze doors made for Archbishop Bernward of Hildesheim in 1015. The "Hildesheim" doors, which portray scenes from Genesis and from the life of Christ, verge on the grotesque, and panels like *The Fall* and *The Meeting of Christ and Mary Magdalene* with their twisting bodies and menacing faces convey more fear of life than glory everlasting. In similar vein is the magnificent wood-carved *Gero Crucifixion* (Figure 4.24), where slack face and slumped body underscore the Medieval view of the agony of death here, in this world. The same view appears in part at least in Last Judgment scenes like those above the central portal of the Amiens Cathedral.

PAINTING.   The ink drawings of the Utrecht Psalter use violent scenes and gestures to illustrate the Psalms with effects much the same as in the Hildesheim doors. No painter, however, captured Medieval brutality as

---

[2] The word literally means waterspouts and is here so used.

Figure 4.24 *The Gero Crucifixion.* (c. 975). Cologne Cathedral, Cologne. [Marburg: Art Reference Bureau].

surely as Hieronymus Bosch—this although he worked at the end of the period, and almost in retrospect. In works like *Christ before Pilate* (Figure 4.25) and *The Garden of Delights,* his clusters of leering, bestial faces and imaginary monsters hatching everywhere like fears sum up with nightmare clarity the terror and brutality of the Medieval world.

Music. Music contributed two savage parodies to the gloomy world view of the Middle Ages. One was the *Carmina Burana*—collected tenth- and

eleventh-century songs of wandering students called Goliards—which cari-
catured, often obscenely, biblical and liturgical musical settings. The other
was the Donkey Mass, a public celebration with music that travestied the
most sacred of church ceremonies (see also the Latin "Song of the Ass,"
clearly an offshoot of the Donkey Mass). The sharp edges of these parodies
make it clear that despite the gleam of faith on far off mountain tops, life
here was grim and ugly and that such a state was resented. A more
outspoken version of this view was the fourteenth-century *danse macabre,*
a dance of death wherein the dead dance with the living. This dance was
performed at peasant festivals where it reminded its viewers that instead of
life moving toward death, death had come forward and moved into life.
The Medieval world demanded such a view.

The political idea unique to the Middle Ages is FEUDALISM, a concept
which reflects almost all aspects of Medieval temper. Its lord-vassal-serf
linking is a form of hierarchical order; its lord-vassal relationship is steeped
in courtly formality; its cleavage between noble and peasant is dualistic;

Figure 4.25   HIERONYMUS BOSCH.   *Christ before Pilate.*   (c. 1500).   [Courtesy of
the Art Museum, Princeton University].

and the lot of the serf was brutal and hard. Moreover the intricate cross-relationships between great and subordinate vassals and their serfs, subinfeudation, recall those in the Gothic cathedral and the motet: one scholarly commentator even sees lines of influence tying subinfeudation to the Medieval doctrine of the Trinity.

The feudal contract which yoked together serf and noble for mutual protection, to the clear advantage of the latter, was too real for the idealizing nature of most Medieval literature. Vassal heroes like Roland, Tristram, and Lancelot belong rather to the idea of chivalry (see below). Troubadour poets did perform in feudal courts, but their works were stylized or personal rather than social or political. Even protest poets like Rutebeuf and Villon dealt only with private or universal woes, and William Langland whose *Piers Plowman* opens with a Field Full of Folk mirroring feudal society soon passes on to the main concern of his poem: salvation and the true meaning of Christ's sacrifice.

In architecture feudalism gave rise to characteristic castles, especially those along the Rhine and scattered throughout England. Their towers, turrets, crenellated walls, moats, and portcullises suggest enchantment, but in reality they were defense stockades, more examples of engineering than architecture, betokening how closely the idea of feudalism clings to the ground. Sculpture had little means of expressing feudalism, but it at least suggested the idea in one predominant motif: that of Christ as feudal lord. His placement on the central portal of the Amiens Cathedral clearly suggests this motif. It receives more literal treatment in the gold carving of *Christ Adored by Henry II and His Empress Kunigunde* (c. 1020), now in the Museum of Cluny, and in the *Christ in Majesty* in the tympanum of the Cathedral at St. Julien de Jonzy. Feudalism appeared in its most direct form in the genre paintings of illuminated manuscripts like the *Gospel Book* of Otto III, which depicts life in the feudal court, and in the *Book of Hours* of the Duc de Berry, which illustrates the everyday rigors and solaces of feudal manor life.

As feudalism displayed the worldly Medieval temper, CHIVALRY allegorized the spiritual one. Like Medieval faith chivalry fused earth and heaven into Christian unity—the daily beauty of chivalric heroes' lives showed grace in action. Chivalric standards of conduct wore such Christian trappings as universal brotherhood, asceticism, reverence for vows, and induction ceremonies involving vigil and purifying baths. But the idea of chivalry had far deeper implications than a mere standard of conduct: it acted out on earth the Medieval view of what heaven would be like. The chivalric lord (such as Arthur or Charlemagne) was an all-wise Father. At his court or round table his knights were at rest, to be set in motion by him when the need arose. The spectators at chivalric tournaments resembled a heavenly host—the seating arrangement of the blessed in Dante's Empyrean is strikingly similar to theirs. And tournamental panoply and glowing costumes were physical anticipations of the joys of heaven. For this world the idea of chivalry gave birth to orders like the Knights Templars and Knights Hospitalers, but these soon turned into commercial enterprises. The reality of chivalry lay in the world of the spirit and in the world of art.

The chivalric hero was never more immediate and real than in the world of Medieval romance. Roland, Tristram, Gawaine, and Galahad are Christian ethics personified and popularized. Dante evokes universal sympathy for Paolo who, with Francisca, is condemned to the Inferno, because Paolo is chivalric and Gianciotto, Francisca's husband, is not. Chaucer's knight, the noblest of the Canterbury pilgrims, steps straight out of the world of chivalry, and the "Knight's Tale" of Palemon and Arcite uses the chivalric concept of Christian brotherhood with profound purpose: through love and death the two competing knights become a single, richer entity now worthy of the lady.

In architecture the real idea of chivalry, as an anticipation of heaven, is found not in stockade castles but in Gothic cathedrals. Then at the end of the Middle Ages when the chivalric ideal had faded, a number of fourteenth- and fifteenth-century castles *reminiscent* of chivalry were built, containing great halls, chapter houses, and knightly chapels. These appeared mainly in Germany in such places as Heilsberg, Karlstein, and Meissen. Painting illustrates the idea of chivalry at least glancingly in the lustrous Byzantine icon of the archangel Michael, now in Pisa, in which Michael wears the regalia of a chivalric knight. Since Michael was the conqueror of Satan he was often considered the first chivalric hero.

Music imitated chivalry in its northern "tournaments of song," wherein Minnesingers jousted by singing their own compositions: notable competitors include Walther von der Vogelweide (*Nu al' erst*), Wolfram von Eschenbach, author of the epic poem *Parzival*, and Tannhäuser. If knightly tournaments were shadow versions of the heavenly host, then tournaments of song echoed the heavenly choir.

Where the classical world found reason for being in wisdom, the Medieval world found it in love. For Christianity God is Love, His creation of the universe a free will act of love. Love infinite and overflowing bathed early Medieval piety in an abstract glow. God is "the first object of love" (St. Bonaventure), and mankind "in the act of loving [has] experience of an infinite good" (Duns Scotus). As this world grew more significant to Christians the focus of love narrowed, became more concrete so as to become more graspable. An idea of LOVE AS RITUAL evolved, and its implications grew richer as the Middle Ages wore on. The starting point was Mariolatry, elaborate rites in worship of the Virgin. Special offices were formulated for her worship and special Masses were said in her honor. The highest ideal of womanhood was thus made the object of a ritual of love.

In literature Mariolatry carried over into the poetry of the troubadours whose idealizing praises of the ladies they professed to love were mainly abstract formula. Their nameless ladies were *senhals,* abstract symbols of the *idea* of woman. The *Divine Comedy* of Dante carried the ritual a step forward. His Beatrice is real enough: she has golden hair and dark eyes, and she actively rewards his worship of her by interceding for him in heaven, making possible his journey to Paradise. With Dante the ritual of love celebrates a woman at once actively human and divinely blessed (the name Beatrice means blessed) who, like the Virgin, can intercede for him in heaven. Dante's successor, Petrarch, idealizes his Laura in much the same way as Dante did Beatrice and for the same hope of heavenly reward. But Laura is a cut more human than Beatrice, and Petrarch's love is more sensual; the Renaissance was approaching.

In sculpture as in literature all three stages in the idea of love as ritual appear. The free-standing ivory *Virgin and Child* with its impersonal expressions and dematerialized figures equates with Mariolatry and with troubadour love poetry. The thirteenth-century statues of the *Vierge Dorée* and of *Uta* mingle transcendent beauty with a stirring of life and denote the same humanizing of the ritual of love in stone as Beatrice did in literature. The fourteenth-century statue of the Virgin known as *La Blanche* (Figure 4.26) displays such human concern and such *chic* as to approach the final limits of the ritual of love—a reprise of Petrarch's Laura.

Painting and mosaic depict the same three stages of development of this idea. The *Virgin Enthroned* mosaic in the Hagia Sophia is as abstract and disembodied as the troubadour *senhal* and the sculpted ivory *Virgin and Child.* The *Madonna Enthroned* of Giotto parallels the sublimity-humanity of Dante's Beatrice and of *Uta* and the *Vierge Dorée.* The Virgin in Lochner's *Madonna in the Rose Garden* (Figure 4.27), primly coy in her fashionable coiffure, advances the ritual of love to the same outer limits as do Laura and *La Blanche.*

The Medieval dualism between the things of this world and those of the next at times took on a more aggressive form. Duality became conflict and, the Middle Ages being essentially spiritual, the physical world was rejected with contempt. The trait of brutality reinforced this concept of CONTEMPTU MUNDI, famine and plagues prodded it along, and the Franciscan order with its dedication to poverty, chastity, and obedience bore gentle witness to its merit. *Contemptu mundi* led men into monasteries and explained in large part the lackluster science of the Middle Ages. It infiltrated Medieval life in the form of world-rejecting pilgrimages, like the one Chaucer's travelers were making to the shrine of St. Thomas à Becket at Canterbury. And it offered an intellectual refuge akin to Stoicism in another brutal age.

Figure 4.26   *La Blanche.*   (c. 1330).   Notre Dame, Paris.   [Alinari: Art Reference Bureau].

Figure 4.27   STEPHAN LOCHNER.   *Madonna in the Rose Garden.*   (c. 1430).   Wallraf-Richarts, Cologne.   [Rheinisches Bildarchiv].

St. Augustine was the first of a long line of Christian philosophers to advocate *contemptu mundi*. His *City of God* urged men to turn away from earthly cities which could, like Rome, corrupt and decay. At the end of the line Duns Scotus denied the value of all worldly experience and turned like Augustine to the City of God. François Villon, that most worldly of poets, was obsessed with mortality; in his world as in St. Augustine's everything rotted in a day and *la belle Heaulmière* too soon became a hag with "wrinkled brow and grizzled hair." The morality play *Everyman* is an extended allegory on *contemptu mundi;* its hero, Everyman, learns the idea in graphic and painful detail.

Contemptu mundi is suggested at least obliquely in sculptures and paintings of the Last Judgment. The two-dimensional bodies in sculpture and mosaics also convey overtones of this idea. In music it appears in such later songs of Walther von der Vogelweide as *Owe war sint verswunden alliu miniu jar?* (where have my years gone to?) and in that most overwhelming of Medieval hymns, the *Dies Irae,* which sees the world dissolved in ashes. While in these latter examples *contemptu mundi* is stated in words, their musical setting intends to convey the same idea.

Mention should also be made of the concept of the WHEEL OF FORTUNE, which compared the lives of illustrious men to a course on a vertical wheel: a steady upward climb, and then a swift fall to the bottom. The idea was a carry-over from the proverbial Greek one that no man could be called fortunate until he was dead (it appears most effectively at the conclusion of Sophocles' *Oedipus Rex*). In the Middle Ages it served more as undercurrent than direct statement, mostly reinforcing the Medieval view of contempt for this world, but it did make a few notable real life appearances: in the deposition of Richard II of England and in the career of Jacques Coeur, the merchant whose loans to the crown saved France during the Hundred Years' War and whose reward was banishment and the confiscation of his property. The *De Casibus Virorum Illustrorum* (fall of illustrious men) of Boccaccio and the *Fall of Princes* of John Lydgate, modeled on Boccaccio's work, trace the idea throughout history, but filtered through the sensibilities of literary moralists. Popular homilies made much of the idea of the Wheel of Fortune. So did the Renaissance—see Shakespeare, *Richard III, Richard II, Julius Caesar, Macbeth*—which credited the earlier period with its discovery.

FORMS AND TECHNIQUES

BALLADES, RONDEAUX, VIRELAIS: In twelfth-century France ballades, rondeaux, and virelais emerged as new poetic forms, appearing in the work of Eustache Deschamps, Charles D'Orléans, and later handled supremely by François Villon (see his *Ballade des dames du temps jadis*). Composers then adopted them as musical forms. Readily available examples include the work of Guillaume d'Amiens and Guillaume Machaut: for example, Amiens, *Vos n'aler* (rondeau), *C'est la fin* (virelai); Machaut, *Je puis trop bien* (ballade), *Plus dure* (virelai).

ACCENTUAL POETRY: Rhythmic accent replaced syllabic measurement in Latin poetry by the fifth century and became the basis for all Medieval vernacular verse. Similarly, syllabic measurement in Gregorian chant gave way to rhythmic accent starting with the organa of Pérotin: for example, the two-voice organum in 6/8 time of the School of Notre Dame (c. 1175). The metric subtleties of Chaucer and Machaut represent parallel advances in rhythmic development (see Chaucer, *Troilus and Criseyde*, and Machaut, *S'il estoit nulz*).

ENCYCLOPEDIC FORM: Isidore of Seville, *Etymologiae*, and Bede, *De Natura Rerum*, used the encyclopedic form in the Early Middle Ages in an effort to preserve all knowledge for succeeding generations. Aquinas used it in his *Summa Theologica* (unfinished) for the same purpose. Dante's "teacher," Brunetto Latini, made it the method of his *Trésor*, and Dante extended the boundaries of literature to their outermost by making it the principle of his *Divine Comedy*. The *Mass* of Machaut performed a similar encyclopedic function for music.

DRAMATIZED VERSIONS OF THE BIBLE: Several art media used dramatized versions of the Bible: literature in mystery plays like the York, Towne, Wakefield, and Coventry cycles; architecture-sculpture in the biblical tableaux on cathedral façades; music in song-dramas like the French play of *Daniel*.

PARALLEL HORIZONTAL LINES: In literature, there are four levels of meaning in the *Divine Comedy*—literal, moral, political, religious—which flow alongside one another throughout the course of the epic (although in the Paradise the literal and religious levels converge); in architecture there are parallel lines of nave, triforium, clerestory, and (frequently) flat roof in the Romanesque Cathedral; in music there are the parallel lines of strict organum, for example, those of the *Scholia enchiriadis*.

LITURGICAL SYMBOLISM: The prime technique of Medieval art was liturgical symbolism, which reached into every corner of every medium. The manuscript illuminator, Jean Pucelle, in the following statement about the making of the Belleville Breviary (c. 1326), illustrates how painstakingly conscious was Medieval symbolism:

> the New Testament is all present in symbols within the Old Testament . . . . so that for each of the twelve months there is one of the twelve apostles and one of the twelve Prophets, in such a way that the prophet gives a veiled prophecy to the Apostle and the Apostle uncovers it and makes it an article of faith. . . . And since the articles of faith are the way and the gates to enter into Paradise, I am putting the twelve gates of the heavenly Jerusalem above the twelve apostles and the Virgin Mary, through whom the door was opened to us, holding a panel over each of the gates on which is painted in a picture the article of faith which the apostle has made below in words.

Examples of liturgical symbolism in Medieval art works could be cited indefinitely, and the technique offers a happy hunting ground for the student wishing to test his own perception of technical similarities among the arts. The following are a few starter examples:

The Rose.   This was the symbol of the Empyrean, as in the Mystic Rose beheld by Dante in Paradise, and in the rose windows on the façades of cathedrals.

Liturgical colors.   White, green, and red symbolize faith, hope, and charity, and gold symbolizes the light or presence of God. The gold background of most Medieval paintings symbolizes their creators' intention of producing sacred works inspired by God; white, green, and red are also used predominantly. When Dante first sees Beatrice she is dressed in red; when next he sees her she is in white.

The Circle.   A circle being without beginning or end was used to symbolize eternity, as in the halos in painting and mosaics, and the circular dome and drum of churches like the Hagia Sophia. The eternal worlds of heaven and hell imagined by Dante are constructed of circles and spheres. (Other symbolic shapes common to Medieval art include the cross [Christ, Christianity], the triangle [the trinity], and the square [this world]).

Numbers.   Liturgical number symbolism is almost inexhaustible. Each of the numbers through ten had special significances, and the digits of higher numbers were often added together to produce a single, symbolic digit: for example, Dante's *Vita Nuova* consisted of 43 parts: $4 + 3 = 7$, symbolic of the Old Testament. Its sequel, the *Divine Comedy,* had 33 cantos in each of its parts: $3 \times 3 = 9$, the miracle number, symbolizing the New Testament. Here are some Medieval uses of the Arabic numerals 3 and 8.

The number 3, symbolic of the Trinity, occurs in the *terza rima* rhyme scheme of the *Divine Comedy;* in the triple-arched portals of Gothic cathedrals; in the three-tiered Tree of Life (Eastern in origin) in Byzantine mosaics and arras; and in the three melodic lines and ternary rhythm of the medieval motet (Machaut, *S'il estoit nulz*).

The number 8 is symbolic of Resurrection and also of Christ—the shape of the number somewhat suggested Christ crucified. The Cathedral of San Vitale at Ravenna was octagonal in shape as was the Palace Chapel at Aachen. The Ambrosian hymn consists of eight strophes, and church music recognizes eight ecclesiastical modes.

SELECTED BIBLIOGRAPHY

History

Bury, John B. *A History of the Eastern Roman Empire.* 2 vols. New York: Macmillan, 1912.

Byron, Robert. *The Byzantine Achievement.* New York: Knopf, 1929.

Cantor, Norman F. *Medieval History.* New York: Macmillan, 1963.

Collins, R. W. *A History of Medieval Civilization.* Boston: Ginn, 1936.

Durant, Will. *The Age of Faith.* New York: Simon and Schuster, 1950.

Hulme, E. M. *The Middle Ages.* New York: Holt, Rinehart and Winston, 1938.

Lot, Ferdinand. *The End of the Ancient World and the Beginnings of the Middle Ages.* New York: Knopf, 1931.

Stephenson, Carl. *A Brief Survey of Medieval Europe.* New York: Harper & Row, 1941.

Strayer, Joseph R. *Western Europe in the Middle Ages: A Short History.* New York: Appleton, 1955.

Thompson, James W., and E. N. Johnson. *An Introduction to Medieval Europe, 300–1500.* New York: Norton, 1937.

Weiss, Johannes. *Earliest Christianity: a History of the Period.* New York: Harper Torchbooks, 1965.

Social and Intellectual Background

Adams, G. B. *Civilization During the Middle Ages.* New York: Scribner, 1914.

Baldwin, Summerfield. *The Organization of Medieval Christianity.* New York: Holt, Rinehart and Winston, 1929.

Bloch, Marc. *Feudal Society.* Chicago: University of Chicago Press, 1960.

Copleston, Frederick. *Medieval Philosophy.* 2 vols. Garden City, N.Y.: Image Books, 1950.

Coulton, G. G. *Medieval Panorama.* New York: Meridian, 1957.

Crump, C. G., and E. F. Jacobs. (Eds.) *The Legacy of the Middle Ages.* New York: Oxford University Press, 1926.

Freemantle, Anne. (Ed.) *The Age of Belief.* New York: Mentor, 1954.

Gilson, Etienne. *The Philosophy of St. Thomas Aquinas.* London: Herder, 1937.

———. *Reason and Revelation in the Middle Ages.* New York: Scribner, 1938.

———. *The Spirit of Medieval Philosophy.* New York: Scribner, 1936.

Hawkins, B. J. *A Sketch of Medieval Philosophy.* London: Sheed and Ward, 1946.

Huizinga, J. *The Waning of the Middle Ages.* Garden City, N.Y.: Anchor, 1954.

Leff, Gordon. *Medieval Thought: St. Augustine to Ockham.* Baltimore: Penguin, 1958.

McKeon, R. P. (Ed.) *Selections from Medieval Philosophers.* 2 vols. New York: Scribner, 1929.

Painter, Sidney. *Medieval Society.* Ithaca, N.Y.: Cornell University Press, 1951.

Pickman, Edward M. *The Mind of Latin Christendom.* New York: Oxford University Press, 1937.

Pirenne, Henri. *Economic and Social History of Medieval Europe.* Cambridge, Mass.: Harvard University Press, 1937.

Taylor, Henry Osborn. *The Classical Heritage of the Middle Ages.* New York: Macmillan, 1929.

———. *The Medieval Mind.* Cambridge, Mass.: Harvard University Press, 1959.

Thompson, James W. *Economic and Social History of the Middle Ages, 300–1300.* New York: Appleton, 1928.

Vossler, Karl. *Medieval Culture: An Introduction to Dante and His Times.* 2 vols. New York: Harcourt, 1929.

Waddell, Helen. *The Wandering Scholars.* New York: Barnes & Noble, 1949.

Wulf, Maurice de. *History of Medieval Philosophy.* New York: Dover, 1952.

Literature

Anderson, George K. *The Literature of the Anglo-Saxons*. New York: Russell and Russell, 1949.

Bergin, Thomas G. *Dante*. New York: Orion, 1965.

Chambers, E. K. *The Medieval Stage*. 2 vols. Oxford: Clarendon, 1903.

Chaytor, Henry J. *From Script to Print: an Introduction to Medieval Literature*. New York: Macmillan, 1945.

———. *The Troubadours*. Cambridge: Cambridge University Press, 1912.

Chute, Marchette. *Geoffrey Chaucer of England*. New York: Dutton, 1946.

Holmes, Urban T. *A History of Old French Literature*. New York: Russell and Russell, 1962.

Jackson, W. T. H. *Medieval Literature: A History and a Guide*. New York: Crowell-Collier-Macmillan, n.d.

Lewis, C. S. *The Allegory of Love*. New York: Oxford University Press, 1938.

Loomis, Roger S. *Development of Arthurian Romance*. New York: Harper Torchbooks, 1964.

Singleton, Charles. *An Essay on the* Vita Nuova. Cambridge, Mass.: Harvard University Press, 1949.

Tatlock, J. S. P. *The Mind and Art of Chaucer*. Syracuse: Syracuse University Press, 1950.

Toynbee, Paget. *Dante Alighieri: His Life and Works*. New York: Harper Torchbooks, 1965.

Valency, Maurice. *In Praise of Love*. New York: Macmillan, 1958.

Architecture, Sculpture, Painting

Beckwith, John. *Early Medieval Art*. London: Thames and Hudson, 1964.

Conant, Kenneth J. *Carolingian and Romanesque Architecture, 800–1200*. Baltimore: Penguin, 1957.

Dalton, O. M. *Byzantine Art and Archeology*. Oxford: Clarendon, 1911.

Dupont, J., and G. Gnudi. *Gothic Painting*. New York: Skira, 1954.

Evans, Joan. *Art in Medieval France—987 to 1498*. New York: Oxford University Press, 1948.

Focillon, Henri. *The Art of the West in the Middle Ages*. 2 vols. New York: Phaidon, 1963.

Frankl, Paul. *Gothic Art*. Baltimore: Penguin, 1962.

Gardner, Arthur. *Medieval Sculpture in France*. New York: Macmillan, 1931.

Grabar, André. *Byzantine Painting*. New York: Skira, 1953.

Holt, Elizabeth G. (Ed.) *A Documentary History of Art*. Vol. I: *The Middle Ages and the Renaissance*. Garden City, N.Y.: Anchor, 1957.

Lowrie, Walter. *Art in the Early Church*. New York: Pantheon, 1947.

Mâle, Emile. *The Gothic Image: Religious Art in France in the Thirteenth Century*. New York: Harper & Row, 1958.

Morey, Charles Rufus. *Medieval Art*. New York: Norton, 1942.

Nordenfalk, Carl, and André Grabar. *Early Medieval Painting*. New York: Skira, 1957.

Panofsky, Erwin. *Gothic Architecture and Scholasticism*. New York: Meridian, 1958.

Pirenne, Henri. *Medieval Cities*. Princeton, N.J.: Princeton University Press, 1925.

Pope-Hennessy, John. *Italian Gothic Sculpture.* New York: Phaidon, 1955.

Rice, David Talbot. *Art of the Byzantine Era.* London: Thames and Hudson, 1963.

Simson, Otto von. *The Gothic Cathedral.* New York: Pantheon, 1956.

Smith, Earl B. *Architectural Symbolism of Imperial Rome and the Middle Ages.* Princeton, N.J.: Princeton University Press, 1956.

Swarzenski, Hanns. *Monuments of Romanesque Art.* Chicago: University of Chicago Press, 1954.

Volbach, Wolfgang F., and Max Hirmer. *Early Christian Art.* New York: Abrams, 1961.

Music

Bukofzer, Manfred F. *Studies in Medieval and Renaissance Music.* New York: Norton, 1950.

Dickinson, Edward. *Music in the History of the Western Church.* New York: Scribner, 1931.

Harman, Alec, *Medieval and Early Renaissance Music,* Fair Lawn, N.J.: Essential Books, 1958.

Reese, Gustave. *Music in the Middle Ages.* New York: Norton, 1940.

Wellesz, Egon. *A History of Byzantine Music and Hymnography.* Oxford: Clarendon, 1949.

CHAPTER 5

THE RENAISSANCE

EVENTS

THE ITALIAN CITY-STATES

The first thrust from Middle Ages to Renaissance came from Italy whose diverse city-states introduced a range of changes. Venice was the earliest European state to assume the Medieval clerical functions of public welfare and charity, and by the end of the fourteenth century it added to these a pension system, public institutions, and maritime insurance. Florence introduced banking on a large scale, and the banking house of the Medici, whose emblem of gold balls persists on present-day pawn shops, used money power to dominate the state. The Italian banking inventions of accounting and double-entry bookkeeping forged an economic way of life which ultimately led European economy from the cooperative production methods of the Middle Ages to the individualistic capitalism of the Renaissance and the following periods. Florence especially, but other key Italian city-states as well, fostered the intellectual revolt known as humanism.

Humanism started as a revival of interest in Latin, and then by 1400 in Greek. Greek-speaking professors from nearby Byzantium found Italy ready and receptive to classical learning. In 1423 one such professor brought with him to Venice 238 Greek volumes. The advent of printing in 1450 ushered in a second phase of humanism: the editing of classical texts. Scholars like Marcus Musurus turned out definitive editions of Greek classics for the great Venetian press of Aldo Manuzio (1449–1516), and the Roman Lorenzo Valla (c. 1405–1457) used textual scholarship with shaking effect when he showed that St. Jerome's Latin translation of the Bible was inaccurate and that the Donation of Constantine (p. 115) was a forgery. The third and greatest phase of humanism combined classical past and Medieval echo with Renaissance present to form truly original syntheses.

Conspicuous among this third group of humanists were the Florentines Pico della Mirandola (1463–1494), who planned to show how classical, Hebrew, and Christian traditions fused into a harmonic whole, and Marsilio Ficino (1433–1499), whose *Platonic Theology* fused Platonism, Neoplatonism, and Christianity in a way consistent with the emerging secularization of the Renaissance. This surge of change in the last half of the fifteenth century raised Italian art as well as scholarship and economics to a fresh peak. Italian Renaissance achievements in architecture, sculpture, and painting rivaled those of the Golden Age Greeks, and every Italian city-state of consequence boasted its collection of geniuses.

Despite their uniformity of cultural achievement, the governments of these city-states ranged the entire spectrum of possibility, as a survey of the five key ones—Florence, Milan, Rome, Venice, Naples—will show. In the thirteenth century Florence veered toward democracy, but its wealthy families diverted it toward an oligarchy which one family, the Medici, came to control by the early fifteenth century. Cosimo de' Medici (1389–1464) gained and held power by having his puppet government throw sops to the masses and at the same time by taxing his wealthy rivals beyond endurance. Although holding no office himself, he became the acknowledged political boss of all of Florence by 1435. His grandson Lorenzo de' Medici (1449–1492) dispensed with even the appearance of a republic and replaced it with a Board of Seventy, which he appointed and directed. Under Lorenzo the Magnificent, as he was called, Florence reached an apex of culture and corruption. The legend that on his death bed he turned his face to the wall rather than kiss the crucifix held by the stern monk Savonarola tells much about his character.

In contrast to the manipulative politics of the Medici, the Visconti and Sforzas of Milan exemplify the bluntness of military dictatorship. The Visconti family established themselves as tyrants of Milan in the later thirteenth century and ruled the principality with an iron fist until 1447, when the last of the increasingly degenerate line of Visconti died out. The Milanese, free of their chains, brought in a mercenary general, Francesco Sforza, to help them in their war against Venice. After defeating Venice, Sforza forced Milan to appoint him Duke in 1450, and the Sforza dynasty continued where the Visconti had left off, remaining in absolute power until 1494.

Rome stayed the same theocracy it had been from the Early Middle Ages, but at the outset of the Renaissance its papal rulers showed a heightened interest in culture and corruption. Nicholas V (1447–1455) assembled an unrivaled library—of 5000 books!—in the Vatican and by his patronage gathered together an academy of humanists. Sixtus IV (1471–1484) went to lengths to supply his family with benefices and sold offices of the Roman Court to build his personal fortune; under his rule the Spanish Inquisition was launched in 1478. Innocent VIII (1484–1492) accepted a bribe by a Sultan not to proclaim a crusade and established an exchange at Rome for the sale of pardons—events whose consequences would reverberate throughout the Renaissance.

Venice called itself a republic all during the Renaissance. It was in fact an oligarchy run by an exclusive roster of some 1500 patrician families, nominally ruled by a duke but in truth governed by patrician committees ranging in number from 10 to 3000. These patricians worked publicly for the good of the state and in secret for individual gain. Venetian diplomatic reports were the most astute and probing political analyses of the Renaissance and greatly aided Venetian policy; Venetian elections used the most elaborate systems to guard against tampering, but were rigged by individual interests in almost every case. The combination of altruistic public service and private opportunism, along with its monopoly of trade with the East, built Venice into one of the great luxury centers of Renaissance Europe. By the later half of the fifteenth century it had reached its peak. Under its Doge Cristoforo Moro (1436–1471) it confirmed perpetual patrician rule, and when it encountered a troublesome duchess like Caterina Cornaro (in 1488) it gently deposed her and sent her to the tiny township of Asolo to form a literary circle there. Its exotic spices and palace-dwelling courtesans, its rich jewels, costumes, banquets, and public festivals dazzled the visiting foreigner and inspired him with thoughts of imitation, or conquest.

Naples seemed fated to remain a hegemony, a kingdom governed by an outside ruler, forever. Previously governed by the French House of Anjou it had weathered two notorious queens, Joanna I (d. 1382) and Joanna II (d. 1435), before passing into the hands of the Spanish Alfonso of Aragon, already ruler of Sicily. Lured by its colorful beauty Alfonso established his throne there and made Naples a mecca for scholars and free spirits. He was succeeded at his death by Ferdinand I (1458–1494), his illegitimate son, of whom a contemporary wrote: "Grace or mercy was never found in him." A caricature of the wicked tyrant, he specialized in torture and treachery and, by utter contrast with his father, completed for Naples the full gamut of the benefits and woes of monarchy.

FRANCE AND SPAIN INVADE ITALY

By 1494 the richness and variety of Italian culture and society were a model and a challenge to the rest of Europe. France first, and then Spain, Austria, and England ventured in as conquerors and left imbued with the spirit of the Renaissance. In Milan, Ludovico Sforza, uncle of the titular duke Gian Galeazzo Sforza, reigned absolutely until Gian's wife, the granddaughter of Ferdinand I of Naples, objected. To hold on to his power, Ludovico invited Charles VIII, king of France, to claim Naples as the legitimate possession of the House of Anjou and promised him free passage through Italy if he did so. With an army of 28,000 men Charles crossed the Alps in September 1494 and entered Milan where he was feted with greater luxury than he had ever known in France. He marched upon Florence where Lorenzo's son, Piero de' Medici, delivered that luxurious city to him without a struggle. He entered Rome unmolested and demanded and received bribes and royal entertainment from Alexander VI, the Borgia pope, whose conduct then and before left much to be desired. On February 22, 1495, Charles entered Naples without opposition; its newly crowned king, Alfonso II, had fled at news of Charles' arrival. Here, while enjoying the most sophisticated of vices, Charles learned that the Italian city-states were mustering armies against him. Leisurely this weak, willful, ignorant king made ready to leave, and while the Italian armies squabbled about how to organize Charles returned to France unscathed. His expedition accomplished nothing immediate, but it brought to the attention of Europe the fact that Italy was lovely and helpless. In 1498 Louis XII of France and Ferdinand and Isabella of Spain conquered Naples, and when Spain claimed sole possession Louis took over Milan. This was to be the pattern in Italy for the next three centuries; she had become a battleground for foreign kings.

At the close of the fifteenth century Italian Renaissance culture was spread out across the rest of Europe, and that culture shaped in large part the three main channels of sixteenth-century events. These were: (1) Renaissance humanism, which bore at all times the imprint of Italy; (2) the Reformation, whose hub and proving grounds were the city-states of Germany; and (3) the voyages of exploration, whose prime mover was Spain.

RENAISSANCE HUMANISM

Italian humanism affected events only obliquely, but by shaping Renaissance temper it did much to make certain situations inevitable, as will be seen. In France François I underwrote humanism by founding the *College de France* in 1530 for the teaching of Greek, Hebrew, and Latin. Under the great humanist scholar Guillaume Budé it became a focal point for French intellectual activity. A generation later a group of writers known as the Pléiade corrected texts and learned Greek from their scholar-mentor Jean Dorat, and wrote a pamphlet exhorting Frenchmen to make their own language illustrious, the way the Greeks had done. Humanists like François Rabelais and Michel de Montaigne wrote sixteenth-century classical-Medieval-modern syntheses as Pico and Ficino had done. In Germany Johann Reuchlin (1455–1522) studied Hebrew so as to make textual studies of the Old Testament and the *Cabbala*, and Martin Luther wrote his famous ninety-five theses in Latin. The Dutch humanist Desiderius Erasmus (c. 1469–1536) represented the best that humanism thought and said, and in consequence was long the spokesman of his nation. His *Praise of Folly* extols the value of humanism in an age of mass superstition. In England, John Colet (1467–1519), a disciple of Pico, studied Greek and Hebrew sources with objective clarity, and with colleagues like William Grocyn and Thomas More introduced the urbanity and inquiring spirit of Italian humanism into England. In Spain, Juan Luis Vives (1492–1540) advocated universal education and the Venetian methods of caring for the poor. At the same time Cardinal Francisco Ximenes (1436–1517) reformed the education and morals of the representatives of the church.

THE REFORMATION

In the wake of humanistic urbanity, individualism, and new concern for the things of this world, came the Protestant Reformation. Its focal point was the German city-states of the early sixteenth century, but its origins reached back into the Medieval past. John Wycliffe had fought for church reform in fourteenth-century England and German mystics like Master Eckhart (1260–1327) and Thomas à Kempis (1379–1471) had taught that man could attain union with God without the church as intermediary. The trigger cause of the Reformation was the sale of indulgences, a procedure whereby churchmen set up stalls in various cities and sold forgiveness for sins at specified rates. The traffic in indulgences by the German monk Johann Tetzel in order to augment the building fund for St. Peter's Cathedral in Rome touched off an explosion by Martin Luther (1483–1546), an ordained priest and lecturer in philosophy at the University of Wittenberg. On October 31, 1517, Luther nailed ninety-five theses attacking indulgences on the church door at Wittenberg. Typical of them was number forty-three which reads: "Christians should be taught that he who gives alms to the poor or lends to one in need does a better thing than he who buys indulgences." This incident touched off a storm of controversy in which influential humanists like Erasmus and Philip Melanchthon supported Luther.

In 1520 Luther published his famous "Address to the Christian Nobility of the German Nation on the Improvement of the Christian Estate" where in smashing language he insisted that state governments have the right to reform the church, declared every baptized Christian his own priest, and affirmed the right of every priest to marry. He followed this diatribe with *The Babylonian Captivity of the Church* wherein he attacked the sacraments of matrimony, orders, extreme unction, and confirmation. For Luther it was not ceremony or dogma but faith and faith alone that spelled salvation. Verse 1:17 of Paul's Epistle to the Romans, "The just shall live by faith," became a creed that shook the German city-states to their foundations.

Germany at this time contained some hundred city-states nominally ruled by the Holy Roman Emperor. Since 1438 the Hapsburgs, Archdukes of Austria, had served as emperors, but a powerful coalition of nobles and middle-class merchants blocked their attempts at unity. Regions such as Bavaria, Saxony, and Brandenburg were actually independent states. Emperor Frederick III (1440–1493) enjoyed the longest, least eventful reign in imperial history. His son Maximilian (1493–1519) on the other hand accomplished much. He arranged for Hapsburg succession to the thrones of Hungary and Bohemia, and while he failed to unite or even to control the

German city-states he did manage to marry his son Philip to Mad Joanna, daughter and heiress of Ferdinand and Isabella of Spain. Charles, the son of Philip and Joanna, became king of Spain in 1516 at the death of Ferdinand, and Emperor Charles V in 1519 at the death of Maximilian. Like his great grandfather Frederick III, Charles was plodding and unimaginative, yet during his dual reign Spain rose like a comet and the Reformation exploded with fullest force.

The first diet (meeting of the states of the Holy Roman Empire) convened by Charles was held at Worms in 1521. It summoned Luther for a hearing, but his entry was triumphal rather than penitent and his refusal to recant won him a surge of popular support. Excommunicated and branded an outlaw he was whisked off to the castle of Wartburg by Frederick the Wise, elector of Saxony, and there he translated the Bible into German and wrote several ringing tracts. This was the apex of his career. By 1524–1525 the Peasants' War, a revolt by peasants and city workers for better conditions, broke out. Luther, concerned with religious but not social reform, urged the soldiers to kill the peasants like mad dogs, and after their total defeat—over 100,000 peasants and workers were slain—he gained middle-class support, but lost the backing of the lower classes and of humanists like Erasmus.

In 1530 at the Diet of Augsburg, Melanchthon read a statement affirming that Lutheran doctrine proposed "nothing repugnant to Scripture or to the Catholic Church," but the attempt at reconciliation in this so-called Augsburg Confession had come too late. After the Peasants' Revolt the lower classes began to turn to a sect called Anabaptists (because they rejected the validity of infant baptism) which would evolve in time into Baptists and Quakers. Further divisions within Protestantism were led by Ulrich Zwingli (1484–1531), an extreme liberal who relied solely upon scriptural authority and who considered the Eucharist a symbolic ceremony; and by the rigidly puritanical John Calvin (1509–1564).

In 1546, the year of Luther's death, the Schmalkaldic War broke out in Germany. It pitted the Catholic emperor against a coalition of Protestant nobles—essentially it was really a struggle for power—and although a Spanish army marched in and decided the war in Charles' favor, the Lutheran nobles and their provinces remained independent of the Catholic Church. The Peace of Augsburg in 1555 allowed the prince of each state to determine the religion of his subjects, but limited his choices to Lutheranism or Catholicism. Thus state religion got under way and German rulers achieved a power almost absolute.

Where Lutheranism, aiming to restore the purity of the Medieval church, shared tracts of common ground with it, Calvinism selected certain prescriptive segments from earlier theologies and reset them in a narrow, exclusive path. Its handbook, Calvin's *Institutes of the Christian Religion*

(1536), relied like Lutheranism upon faith and the Scriptures, but the God of Calvin predestined the fate of every man and saved or damned regardless of faith or merit. The only external evidence of grace was proper moral behavior, which Calvin defined in strictest terms. From 1542–1564 he maintained a theocracy at Geneva that made adultery, blasphemy, and witchcraft capital crimes; that prohibited dancing, card playing, and ornate clothing; and that relied upon a group of twelve elders chosen by a closed council to run this peoples' government. Forbidding though life in Geneva might be—the elders might enter citizens' homes at any time and examine them on the most intimate details—the city became the showplace of Protestantism and attracted admiring visitors from all over Europe.

THE COUNTER REFORMATION

The Reformation, challenged first by forces within its own movement met a still more decisive challenge from the Catholic Counter Reformation. The popes of the sixteenth century in general transcended the self-interest of their immediate predecessors. Like the age in which they lived, they reflected a more expansive and generous concern for the things of this world. Julius II (1503–1513) translated that concern into military forays, but well-born popes like the Medici family's Leo X (1513–1521) and Clement VII (1523–1534) and the Farnese family's Paul III (1534–1549) patronized art and culture and made Rome a center of civilization. By mid-century Spain dominated Italy, and Italian culture became a strange bedfellow of the Spanish sword. The Counter Reformation combined Spanish militancy with Roman urbanity and tact. Its forum was an ecumenical council which met at Trent, then a German city just above the northern tip of Italy.

The Council of Trent which met three times from 1545–1563 unified Catholic dogma, issued a new, authoritative edition of the Vulgate, provided for a catechism, and tightened church discipline. It saw the formation of a new order, the Jesuits, whose creed as stated by its founder Ignatius Loyola in his *Spiritual Exercises* was that "Man was created to praise, reverence and serve God our Lord and thereby to save his soul." Jesuits soon served God all over the world, founding foreign missions, educating primitive peoples, helping the sick, disputing all heresies. Under Spanish influence the council also gave new sanction and fresh impetus to the Inquisition and established an Index of Forbidden Books, the first list appearing in 1559 and including works by Erasmus and Machiavelli. After 1563 the only European country in which Protestantism increased was the Netherlands, but that would not happen for another generation. The mid-sixteenth century belonged to Spain.

THE VOYAGES OF EXPLORATION: SPAIN AT ITS ZENITH

Spain was chief beneficiary of the third major factor of the sixteenth century—the voyages of exploration and conquest. Linked with the other two factors, these voyages combined the humanist spirit of inquiry—in 1484 the Florentine humanist Toscanelli sent the king of Portugal a map proving that the earth was round and that one could reach China by sailing westward—with Lutheran and Calvinist sternness of purpose. The first voyages were made not by Spain but by neighboring Portugal. Under one of the king's younger sons, Prince Henry the Navigator (1394–1460), who never made a voyage himself, Portuguese seamen explored the west coast of Africa seeking the rumored land of Ghana ruled by the legendary Christian priest-king, Prester John. They discovered Ghana, renamed it Guinea, and gutted it of gold, ivory, and Negro slaves. In 1484 Bartholomew Diaz rounded the Cape of Good Hope, and in 1497 Vasco da Gama went from Lisbon across the Indian Ocean to Calicut and returned in 1499 with a priceless cargo of jewels and spices.

In the meantime Spain, following the advice of Toscanelli, underwrote a westward search for a route to the East, for the Mediterranean route was now controlled and taxed by Ottoman Turks. On August 3, 1492, a Genoese sailor, Christopher Columbus, left Spain and sailed westward until he sighted land on October 11 of that same year. He had found the West Indies, although he thought it was Japan. He made three subsequent voyages, reaching Cuba, Puerto Rico, and the South American mainland and died convinced that he had reached Asiatic waters. One of his seamen, Amerigo Vespucci, proclaimed South America a "New World," and so it took its name from him. Columbus' legacy was a date: 1492.

For Spain 1492 was a turning point. Throughout the Middle Ages Spanish nobles had fought among themselves while the Mohammedans continued to hold Granada behind its almost impregnable fortress, the Alhambra. In 1469 Ferdinand, king of Aragon, married Isabella, queen of Castile and Leon, and the two of them forcibly unified their country. They transferred administration from nobles and clergy to lawyers and bureaucrats and thus centralized its control. They placed the church under royal control and revived the Inquisition to eliminate all heresy. In 1492 they captured Granada after a long siege, raised the cross on the Alhambra tower, expelled all unconverted Jews, and merged their territories into a single state called Spain; in that same year that marked the tight closing of Spanish society, Columbus launched the first of a series of explorations that would expand the Spanish empire.

In 1513 Vasco Nuñez de Balboa crossed the Isthmus of Darien and first set eyes upon the Pacific Ocean which he claimed, with all its coastlines, for Spain. In 1519 Ferdinand Magellan crossed the Atlantic in the dead of winter with a fleet of five ships, through the straits now named for him, across the Pacific amid hardships which saw him eating powdered biscuits swarming with worms and drinking stale yellow water. Upon landing at the Philippines he was killed by natives, but what was left of his crew sailed on. Only one ship, the *Victoria*, survived across the Indian Ocean, and on September 7, 1522, it sailed into Spain with eighteen survivors: Magellan's fleet had circumnavigated the globe. The world was indeed round, and girdled by Spain. In 1519 Hernando Cortes landed in Mexico with a force of 600 men and pillaged its enormously wealthy Aztec empire. In 1532 Francisco Pizarro invaded Peru with 183 men and looted the ancient, peaceful Incan empire whose household utensils were made of silver and gold. The wealth sent back from the New World made Spain the greatest nation in Europe.

Charles V, son of Joanna and Philip, inherited Spain, Naples, and America from his mother's line; Burgundy, the Netherlands, and the Holy Roman Empire from his father's. He ascended the throne of Spain in 1516 at the age of sixteen, the imperial throne at nineteen, and continued to hold both until he retired to a monastery in 1555. A stolid, methodical, almost dull man, he weathered the spread of challenging humanism and the shaking winds of the Reformation without being lured into excessive measures. In fact, when energetic French king François I challenged his supremacy with wars in 1522, 1525, and 1529, Charles defeated him almost casually—he even took François prisoner in 1525—and emerged in control of Italy. When he abdicated in 1555 Spain was at its crest of wealth and power. His son Philip II (1556–1598) combined a lust for power with a militant Catholicism that lured him into the excesses his father had avoided. His assertion, "I would rather lose all of my kingdoms than permit freedom of religion," led him to overuse the Inquisition to establish absolute control at home and abroad. It succeeded in Spain for the moment but caused a revolt in the Netherlands which culminated in Dutch independence. In 1571 Philip helped Venice and Rome to defeat the Turks decisively, and in 1580 he annexed Portugal, which became a Spanish territory for the next sixty years. But in 1588 his armada was destroyed in an attempt to conquer England, and in 1595 he was outfought by Henry of Navarre. The raids of English pirates on his Spanish Main cut deep inroads into Spanish wealth, and these reverses, plus his ruthless persecutions, left Spain weakened and exhausted by the time of his death.

Humanism had exposed the Italian emphasis on learning and art at the expense of military might; the Reformation, Protestant schisms, and the Counter Reformation had left Germany split; exploration and conquest had made Spain top-heavy with a wealth and power she was too insular to control. Thus the three main factors of sixteenth-century history brought their parent nations to a state of decline. Meantime, from the sidelines, three other countries—England, France, and Holland—reaped benefits from all three sixteenth-century factors and rose to greatness because of them.

THE RISE OF RENAISSANCE ENGLAND

England at the start of the Renaissance emerged from the Hundred Years' War (see Chapter 4) only to be caught up in The Wars of the Roses, 1455–1485. King Henry VI (1422–1461; 1470–1471) belonged to the family of Lancaster, which claimed its title from John of Gaunt, the fourth son of Edward III. The family of York claimed the throne on the basis of its descent from Lionel, third son of Edward III, and in the civil war that ensued Edward, Duke of York, drove Henry VI out of England and was crowned Edward IV (1461–1483). Fighting between the two houses continued intermittently—Henry VI reacquired the throne from 1470–1471—until 1485 when Yorkist King Richard III (1483–1485), brother of Edward IV, was slain at Bosworth field by Henry Tudor, obliquely a member of the House of Lancaster. The Wars of the Roses, so named because the badge of Lancaster was a red rose, the badge of York a white rose, ended with both families depleted and with the ranks of Medieval English nobility thinned.

Henry Tudor was descended from a Welsh family of middle-class origins. As Henry VII (1485–1509) he solidified his title by marrying a daughter of Edward IV, by helping the new middle class rise to power at the expense of what remained of the old nobility, by encouraging a shift in economy from agriculture to manufacture, and by using middle-class support in order to undermine Parliament and to establish himself and his descendants as absolute rulers. His son Henry VIII succeeded to a throne whose subjects were loyal and whose treasury was full.

Henry VIII (1509–1547) used caprice and temper in place of forethought and tact, and during his reign had more queens and nobles executed than any subsequent European king. His private loves profoundly affected the course of his nation. In his efforts to divorce his first wife, Catherine of Aragon, to marry one of her maids of honor, Anne Boleyn, he came into conflict with Roman church policy on divorce—this occurred at a time which coincided with the impact of the Reformation upon England. In 1534 he passed the Act of Supremacy which stated that the king "rightfully is and ought to be supreme head of the church of England." In 1535 England broke with the church of Rome, and Henry was excommunicated. Henry appointed the Lutheran Thomas Cranmer Archbishop of Canterbury, and Cranmer sanctioned his marriage with Anne Boleyn. In 1539 his prime minister Thomas Cromwell, acting under orders, seized all of the money and properties of the monasteries in England, and was beheaded for his pains. Monastic wealth created a new Protestant gentry loyal to Henry. The king meanwhile continued his matrimonial career; by 1547 he had had six wives. His descendants included a son, Edward, by his third wife, who reigned as Edward VI (1547–1553) from the ages of nine to sixteen; a daughter, Mary, by Catherine of Aragon; and a daughter, Elizabeth, by Anne Boleyn.

Mary Tudor (1553–1558) was a Catholic whose chief concern was the restoration of the Catholic faith throughout all of England. In 1554 at the age of thirty-eight she married Philip II of Spain, who was eleven years younger than she and who virtually ignored her. During her reign she had some 300 Protestants burned at the stake, including Thomas Cranmer, who in 1549 had completed the lofty, sonorous *Book of Common Prayer* for the Anglican churches, and Bishop Hugh Latimer, whose final words to his fellow martyr, Nicholas Ridley, have the surging intensity of immortality: "This day we shall light such a candle, by God's grace, in England, as I trust shall never be put out." Mary died childless in 1558 and was succeeded by her half-sister Elizabeth.

In Elizabeth I (1558–1603) the promise of the House of Tudor fulfilled itself. Like her grandfather, Henry VII, her chief concern was to strengthen England and the crown, and all of her policies reflected that concern. A Protestant, Elizabeth worked toward a compromise among the Catholic, Anglican, and emergent Puritan (Calvinist) forces in her kingdom. It is worth noting that at the beginning of her reign almost all of the common people in England were Catholic; at the end of it the majority were Protestant.

In foreign policy Henry VIII had been too sly to deceive anyone, and Mary Tudor too preoccupied with domestic affairs; Elizabeth, however, moved and manipulated brilliantly. She herself described her policy toward France and Spain as "underhand war," openly deploring while secretly encouraging attacks on Spanish shipping, for example, and at the proper moment substantially aiding the Dutch rebellion against Spain. In domestic policy she added sixty-two new parliamentary boroughs and used Parliament as a source of royal strength and support; she helped to make London a center of world trade; and she made possible a fresh infusion of Renaissance humanism by encouraging learning and the arts. The interests of England even dictated her personal policy.

She encouraged suits by Philip II, by French nobles, by ambitious English nobles like Leicester and Essex, but only when it suited England to keep those countries, or potential dissenters, at bay. When Spain seemed likely to support a claim of her cousin Mary, Queen of Scots, to the English throne, Elizabeth, however reluctantly, had this beautiful granddaughter of a sister of Henry VIII killed. Her one important military exploit was to repel the invasion of the mighty fleet of Philip II, the armada, in 1588. British seamanship, Spanish squabbling, and fortuitous storms combined to rout the armada, and the hostile coasts of Scotland, Ireland, and Holland finished most of the rest of the fleeing ships. Of some 130 ships and 30,000 men, only a small number returned home. England, victorious, faced the coming of the seventeenth century at the height of its power.

THE RISE OF RENAISSANCE FRANCE

France emerged from the Hundred Years' War with the powerful Burgundian kingdom wedged between it and Germany. Burgundian Charles the Bold (1467–1477) acquired the Netherlands and made his court one of the most luxurious and cultivated in Europe. After his death his daughter married the Emperor Maximilian, who thus acquired the Low Countries. Burgundy proper and most Burgundian holdings in France went to Louis XI (1461–1483), the French king. Cruel, secretive, oddly superstitious, shabby of dress, Louis XI wrested power away from his nobles, killing those he could not dominate, increased French territory to almost its present extent, and laid the foundations for absolute monarchy.

His son Charles VIII (1483–1498) was mainly distinguished by his expedition into Italy, but Louis XII (1498–1515) brought France into the arena of international politics. An honorable man—his sobriquet was Father of the People—he joined with Pope Julius II, Ferdinand of Spain, and the Emperor Maximilian in 1508 to form the League of Cambrai, ostensibly to wage a crusade against the Turks. The league was diverted by Julius to attack Venice, and then, with Venice rendered helpless, Julius formed a Holy League that included Venice, Spain, England, Switzerland, and the Holy Roman Empire. The Holy League drove all of the troops of Louis XII out of Italy in 1511.

François I (1515–1547) fared little better in international affairs, being beaten decisively several times by Charles V in disputes over Milan. At home he was more successful, founding the *College de France* and making his court a haven for humanists and artists; humanists like Guillaume Budé and Etienne Dolet played major roles in introducing the Reformation into France. François' son, Henry II (1547–1559), formed an alliance with the powerful Guise family which rose to a position coequal with the king. The aggressively Catholic Guises could not, however, dislodge Henry from the tolerant position François had taken, nor could his wife, Catherine de' Medici. In 1559 the Protestants held a Council in Paris during which they inveighed against religious restrictions and acquired the derisive name of Huguenots, probably derived from "le roi Huguet," a goblin of the night. Just at this time Henry was killed in an accident during a joust. His death ushered in the wars of religion, which continued unabated until 1595.

The next three kings in succession were sons of Henry II and Catherine de' Medici. Dominated by their mother, who was in turn dominated by the Guises, François II (1559–1560), Charles IX (1560–1574), and Henri III (1574–1589) championed universal Catholicism against the wishes of some 400,000 Huguenots. A series of eight civil wars were fought over the next three decades. The underlying cause of the wars, succession to the throne by the Catholic Guises or the Protestant Bourbons, became clearer as time went on. The worst massacre belonged not to a battle but to the ambush slaying of some 20,000 Huguenots on St. Bartholomew's Day, 1572. In 1589 Henry III was assassinated by a Dominican fanatic, and the Bourbon king, Henry of Navarre, besieged Paris (1590–1593) with the help of some 5000 troops sent by Elizabeth. After entering Paris and overcoming the Guises Henry became a Roman convert, explaining his action, at least according to legend, with the famous saying: "Paris is well worth a Mass." A pliant, vigorous, intelligent ruler much like Elizabeth, he reigned as Henry IV until 1610. Philip of Spain declared war on him in 1595 but was decisively defeated. In 1598 he passed the Edict of Nantes, granting liberty of worship to all, and continued to solidify and augment the French nation so that it, like England, faced the seventeenth century at the height of its power.

STIRRING IN THE NETHERLANDS

At the start of the Renaissance the Netherlands belonged to the kingdom of Burgundy. After the death of Charles the Bold the Netherlands passed to his daughter Mary, who married Emperor Maximilian and thus made them a part of the Holy Roman Empire. In 1540 the Netherlands made a brief attempt to revolt against Charles V, who defeated them without much effort. Upon his abdication Charles V gave that nation to Philip II as a territory of Spain, and when this absentee king introduced the Inquisition there in 1559 to cut off the growth of Protestantism, the Netherlands revolted in earnest. In 1567 the ablest Spanish general, the Duke of Alva, entered Brussels with a promise to make short shrift of "these men of butter." Led by William the Silent, Prince of Orange, the Netherlands resisted fiercely despite a constant stream of executions. In 1574 during the Battle of Leyden the Dutch cut open the dykes to let in the sea, thus allowing their navy, the prime source of their military power, to gain the first important Dutch victory. In 1576 the southern provinces sued for reunion with Philip, and as Belgium they remained under Philip and then under the Hapsburgs for the next two centuries. In 1579 five of the seven northern provinces, led by Holland—the other two provinces later joined them—concluded the Union of Utrecht, their declaration of independence.

The assassination of William of Orange in 1584 was a serious setback, but the intervention of an English army under Leicester in 1586 proved a turning point. Dutch naval victories, the defeat of the armada, and a decisive Dutch victory on land in 1597 brought the Spanish army in Holland to the brink of defeat. In 1609 the Peace of Antwerp ended the sporadic fighting between Spain and the new Dutch Republic. Its independence, now recognized by all powers except Spain, would have to be formalized by the Thirty Years' War (1618–1648), but by 1609 the republic was already in a position to become the leading commercial state and maritime power of the early seventeenth century.

At the same time the New World and Russia had begun to awaken. Explorations revealed with increasing impressiveness the fabulous resources of the Americas, while in Russia Basil III (1505–1533) took away the rights of his nobles and established an absolute monarchy; Ivan IV, surnamed the Terrible (1533–1584), extended Russia's empire by conquering the Tartars to the south and east and by moving westward to Poland. Hindsight shows us how significant these stirrings were, but for the present the eyes of Europe turned toward England, France, and Holland.

THE HUMANITIES APPROACH

TRAITS AND IDEAS

Where the Middle Ages had stressed the things of the next world and the seventeenth century would focus upon the world around it, the Renaissance, which came between, achieved a special kind of balance between the things of this world and those of the next. The Golden Age of Greece, like the Renaissance an age of transition, had achieved a balance too: it viewed this world as a shadow image of the universe. The Renaissance, a rebirth of Greece but of a special kind, went even farther. It fused microcosm and macrocosm together so that they became one, the way poetry imbeds an abstract idea in a concrete image. For the Greeks the trial and triumph of Aeschylus' Orestes mirrored the heavenly struggle and victory of Zeus; for the Renaissance Shakespeare's Lear was at once a suffering mortal man and God's desire for man's redemption. For the Greeks the *Athena Lemnia* (Figure 2.14) was a composite of all mortal beauty to lead the viewer upward to contemplate universal beauty; for the Renaissance the *David* of Michelangelo (Figure 5.8) *was* man and God. This FUSION OF EARTH AND HEAVEN, in a sense a secularization of the Medieval trait of faith (pp. 149–156), pervades the Renaissance more characteristically and profoundly than any other trait.

"As God is situated wholly everywhere, so is He as near to us as we can be to ourselves." Thus the philosopher Giordano Bruno restates this

trait in Pantheistic terms. Pietro Pomponazzi, the chief Renaissance Aristotelian, expresses a similar view: man "is placed in the middle between
mortal and immortal things . . . since he is neither wholly eternal nor wholly
temporal, but participates in both natures." The Renaissance Platonists, or
rather Neoplatonists, make this trait the pulse beat of their thinking. For
them God is a sublime world unity who reveals Himself through the harmonious beauty of the universe. The universe is "the essential nature of
God Himself made natural" declares Jacob Boehme, and the greatest Renaissance Neoplatonist, Marsilio Ficino, discerns a fusion of earth and heaven
in every human soul: "The soul is all things together . . . the center of
nature, the middle term of all things, the series of the world, the face of
all, the bond and juncture of the universe." Bruno reinterprets this perception with his own heroic enthusiasm: "From this infinite All, full of beauty
and splendor, from the vast worlds which circle above us to the sparkling
dust of stars beyond, the conclusion must be drawn that there are an
infinity of creatures, a vast multitude which, each in its degree, mirrors
forth the splendor, wisdom, and excellence of the divine beauty."

LITERATURE.   In *The Courtier* of Castiglione, the most popular of all Renaissance writings, Books I–III discuss the training of gentlemen and ladies in
the social arts of this world; Book IV explains how these same gentlemen
and ladies, *in this same world,* may commingle their souls and together with
God achieve a divine-and-worldly trinity of love. Rabelais in Book I
of *Gargantua and Pantagruel* has Gargantua build the Abbey of Thélème,
wherein wealth and marriage replace poverty and chastity. The Abbey is
in effect a worldly monastery (the phrase does not seem out of place in the
Renaissance) where sacred and secular are fused into one. The famous definition of God in Book III as "an infinite intellectual sphere of which the
center is everywhere and the circumference nowhere" points toward
Giordano Bruno. And Rabelais' solution to all life's problems at the close
of Book V, to drink of a wine which is at once experience and Eucharist,
reminds us again that man's soul "participates in both natures." In *The
Faerie Queene* of Spenser worldly Gloriana and spiritual Belphoebe are
both Queen Elizabeth; both also represent the ideal of woman. The earth-
to-heaven journey of the Redcross Knight in Canto 10 of Book I makes
clear that the New Jerusalem (London) is as much the heavenly city as the
vision viewed earlier. Shakespeare in plays like *Romeo and Juliet, Julius
Caesar,* and *Antony and Cleopatra,* shows us how heaven-sent dreams and
omens are acted out on earth. His Hamlet, like Sophocles' Oedipus, is at
once a noble prince and royal scapegoat who must die that the many may
be freed. But *Hamlet* differs from *Oedipus Rex* in that Sophocles' play
merely alludes to the cosmic problem: Hamlet *is* prince and Christ-figure
in the single world of Shakespeare's Denmark. Cervantes' Don Quixote is
inspired by divine madness to see divine things all about him here on

earth, and his vision catches up his squire, his district, all of Spain, and finally all of the Renaissance world before a new age encroaches and tumbles it, and him, into the dust.

ARCHITECTURE.   Greece, which saw this world as a microcosm of the next, lavished most of its architectural care on the exteriors of its buildings: in contrast to the external sweep of the Parthenon (Figure 2.5) the interior was cut up into cramped subsections. Rome, which savored most the joys of this world, built journeyman exteriors and dazzling interiors, as in the Pantheon (Figure 3.4). Renaissance architecture devised a rare balance between exterior and interior beauty, akin in achievement to the great Gothic cathedrals of the Middle Ages. But where the latter summarized Medieval faith by pointing upward and culminating in the incorporeal wholeness that is God, the buildings of the Renaissance blended the beauty of sublimity with that of the present world. This fusion was achieved in such church buildings as the Pazzi Chapel of Brunelleschi (Figures 5.1 and 5.2) whose graceful exterior and interior form a near perfect equilibrium: pilasters, Corinthian capitals, and rounded arches repeat themselves outside and in; the window shapes of the façade are traced on the interior walls; and even the medallion design of the exterior frieze is echoed within the chapel. An even clearer fusion of this world and the next were the secular buildings of the Renaissance, whose exteriors showed more concern for visual beauty than for function, and whose courtyards looked hauntingly like the interiors of churches. A prime example of this fusion is the Farnese Palace built by Antonio da San Gallo the younger (Figures 5.3 and 5.4), whose crisp outlines, perfect symmetry, and playful alternation of semicircles and triangles above the second story windows intrigue the sensual eye while its courtyard with its cadenced arches suggests a lyric version of interiors like the Cathedral of Pisa (Figure 4.18).

Another way in which Renaissance architecture mirrored this fusion of worlds was to combine the worldly Hellenistic-Roman style with the aspiring, other-worldly style of the Middle Ages. This fusion was especially favored outside of Italy. In France it set its seal on the great chateaux of the Loire Valley: Amboise, Azay-le-Rideau, Blois, Chenonceaux, Chambord. The Chateau of Chambord (Figure 5.5) consists in its lower half of a symmetrically balanced façade and wings, functional rooms, and long horizontal lines of force that hold to the ground. Its upper half is a vertical fantasy of towers, chimneys, and dormers whose Medieval effect is enhanced by the moat, bastions, and dungeon the castle also contains. In Renaissance England a Gothic-classical symmetrical style known as Tudor gave rise to structures like Hampton Court, built by Cardinal Wolsey and taken away from him by Henry VIII. The façades of Heidelberg Castle in Germany and the Escorial in Spain achieve a similar classical-Medieval fusion; the latter building was also capped with a suggestion of Moorishness.

Figure 5.1 FILIPPO BRUNELLESCHI. Pazzi Chapel. (c. 1430). Florence. [Anderson: Art Reference Bureau].

Figure 5.2   (above)   FILIPPO BRUNELLESCHI.   Pazzi Chapel, interior.   (c. 1430).
Florence.   [Dr. Franz Stoedtner].

Figure 5.3   (below)   ANTONIO DA SAN GALLO.   Farnese Palace.   (c. 1534).   Rome.
The cornice was designed later by Michelangelo and the entire palace was completed
by Giacomo della Porta, c. 1580.   [Dr. Franz Stoedtner].

Figure 5.4   ANTONIO DA SAN GALLO.   Farnese Palace, courtyard.   (c. 1534).   Rome.
[Dr. Franz Stoedtner].

Figure 5.5   Chateau of Chambord.   (1519–c. 1545).   Loire Valley.   [Trans World
Airlines, Inc.].

SCULPTURE.   Art historians like to distinguish an Early Renaissance from a High Renaissance, with the break-off point around 1492. The Early Renaissance was still in the process of achieving the High Renaissance fusion of this world and the next, and that process is especially easy to trace in sculpture and painting. The *David* of Donatello (Figure 5.6), the first free-standing nude statue since classical times, reflects the Renaissance fusion of two worlds, but with a groping, too-careful intellectuality. The theme is biblical, the slant of the hip Praxitelian; the body is slender and mortal, like those on Gothic cathedrals (Figures 4.21 and 4.22), while the face is classically impersonal; the cap is a shepherd's cap, befitting the psalmist David, but it is crowned with a laurel wreath, classical symbol for poet. The worlds are indeed fused in Donatello's *David*, but through conscious symbolism, with classical symbols representing this world and biblical ones the next. The *David* of Verrocchio (Figure 5.7) contains a more complete, more natural fusion. The face is at once human and, by its expression, remote and mysterious; the body is anatomically more realistic than Donatello's, yet at the same time radiates a subtle power due largely to the giant head of Goliath at the boy's feet. In the High Renaissance *David* of Michelangelo (Figure 5.8) earth and heaven are fused with a conviction that needs little explanation. Face and form radiate at once a personal magnetism and transcendent loftiness that simultaneously attracts and overawes. Parenthetically, while the statues of Donatello and Verrocchio stand some five feet high, that of Michelangelo stands well over thirteen feet. Michelangelo achieved a similar fusion in his *Bound Slave* (c. 1516) and in the statues on the Medici Tomb (1524–1534): in other words, where he had earlier fused the human into the divine, he came to reverse the process as well, as did High Renaissance architecture with its secular buildings and, as we shall see, painting with its secular subjects.

PAINTING.   In his *Treatise on Painting* written in 1435 Leo Battista Alberti defined the painter's purpose as the simultaneous portrayal of living people and the creation of timeless significance. Masaccio in *The Tribute Money* (Figure 5.9) had already achieved this purpose a few years earlier by taking a story of Christ and presenting it in massively human terms. The faces and even gestures bespeak mortality, and by placing Christ directly in front of the vanishing point, Masaccio also brings the world of nature into his human-divine synthesis. Other notable early examples of Christian topics that fuse the worldly and divine are the *Resurrection* of Piero della Francesca and *The Adoration of the Christ Child* by Fra Filippo Lippi. *The Birth of Venus* by Sandro Botticelli (Figure 5.10) explores this fusion by means of a classical topic. Its intellectualism recalls the *David* of Donatello, but its linear grace endows it with a special magic. To the right of Venus, a lady is about to clothe her in a red robe decorated with strawberry blossoms: red was the liturgi-

cal color for charity, strawberry blossoms liturgically symbolized righteousness and good works. To the left of Venus, two pagan gods of the winds
are breathing life into her, so that Venus (love) is born of spirit and elements,
heaven and earth.

The *Mona Lisa* of Leonardo da Vinci (Figure 5.11), uses a mortal
woman to accomplish this same fusion. Her expression and the background
against which she is set make her at once human and unearthly, recalling
Leonardo's own words about painting: "A good painter has two principal
objects to paint: man and the meaning of his soul." The *Creation of Adam*
of Michelangelo (Figure 5.12) uses God and man as protagonists and infuses each with qualities of the other to achieve a physical impact with sublime overtones rarely if ever matched. The *Four Apostles* of Dürer treats
each personage as a psychological study and as a study of the four humors—

Figure 5.6 (far left) DONATELLO. *David.* (c. 1430–1432). Bargello, Florence. [Dr. Franz Stoedtner].

Figure 5.7 (left) ANDREA DEL VERROCCHIO. *David.* (c. 1435). Bargello, Florence. [Dr. Franz Stoedtner].

Figure 5.8 (right) MICHELANGELO. *David.* (1504) Accademia, Florence. [Brogi: Art Reference Bureau].

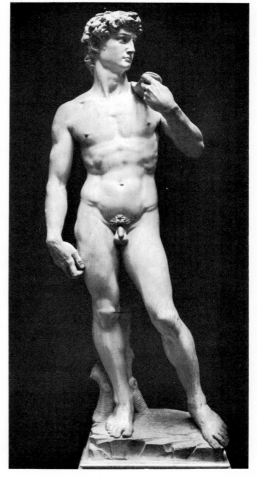

Figure 5.9 (below) MASACCIO. *The Tribute Money.* (c. 1427). Brancacci Chapel, Santa Maria del Carmine, Florence. [Alinari: Art Reference Bureau].

Figure 5.10 (above) SANDRO BOTTI-CELLI. *The Birth of Venus.* (c. 1485). Uffizi Gallery, Florence. [Italian Tourist Information Office].

Figure 5.11 (left) LEONARDO DA VINCI. *Mona Lisa.* (c. 1503–1505). Louvre, Paris. [Alinari: Art Reference Bureau].

Figure 5.12 (top right) MICHELANGELO. *Creation of Adam.* (1508–1512). Sistine Chapel, The Vatican, Rome. [Alinari: Art Reference Bureau].

194

choleric, melancholy, sanguine, and phlegmatic—thus fusing Christianity, mortality, and mental health into a single whole. Dürer's engraving of the *Fall of Man* (Figure 5.13) weaves man, nature, myth, and animals into its detailed tapestry. Adam and Eve are human, as their expressive faces show; classical, as shown by the Praxitelian curves of their bodies and by Adam's hair curled in the manner of Greek sculpture; and biblical, by virtue of their identity. The animals behind them symbolize the four Gospels; the cat at Eve's feet and the mouse at Adam's symbolize a human playfulness. The trees that bracket Adam symbolize before and after—with reference both to the Bible story and to marriage—while the goat on the precipice in the right-hand corner is about to enact, for this world, the same role that Adam will play in the spiritual drama.

MUSIC. Disembodied as music is, Renaissance music nevertheless reflects the fusion of worlds and does so in a variety of ways. During the Renaissance the Medieval elements of complexity, isorhythm, and near invisible insertions of chords based on number symbolism come to blend with the transparent simplicity of secular compositions like lute songs and dance suites. The first master of such a fusion was the Burgundian composer

Figure 5.13 ALBRECHT DÜRER. *Fall of Man.* Engraving. (1504). [Courtesy of the Museum of Fine Arts, Boston].

Guillaume Dufay (c. 1400–1474), whose works mingle complex Gothic construction with sensual Italianate melody, as in his *Mon chier amy* ballade and *Adieu m'amour* rondeau.[1] Like Donatello, Dufay found Renaissance art in a state of becoming, and his music sounds less assured and seamless than that of his great successors. A smoother fusion of Gothic complexity and secular simplicity appears in the work of Jacob Obrecht (1452–1505),

[1] See footnote 1, Chapter 4.

which like the sculpture of Verrocchio conveys a more integrated impression of fusion: for example, his *O vos omnes* motet and especially the *Kyrie* and *Agnus Dei* of his *Missa Sine nomine* (untitled Mass). The fusion begun by Dufay culminates in the work of Josquin Des Prés (c. 1440–1521), whose motets especially and chansons blend the warm clarity of secular song with the intricate detachment of Gothic polyphony in a way similar to the *David* of Michelangelo: for example, his *Tu pauperum refugium* motet and *Faulte d'argent* chanson. With Orlando di Lasso (c. 1532–1594), the last great Netherlands master, the balance begins to shift. Stylistic surprises, larger intervals, and the use of syncopation heralds the coming of a later style: for example, his *Requiem aeternam* from his *Missa Pro defunctis* (Mass for the dead) and his *Bon jour, mon coeur* chanson.

More subtly technical, but very much in keeping with the trait under discussion, is what Gustave Reese (*Music in the Renaissance*) defines as Josquin's "concern for balancing structure [the order of the universe] and sonority [the sensual sounds of this world]" which Reese calls "the outstanding trait of his classicism." With this in mind a hearing of any of Josquin's masterpieces makes Renaissance fusion inexpressibly clear.

The Renaissance is first and foremost an age of INDIVIDUALISM. Renaissance man as he beheld his universe change from earth centered to sun centered, his world change from flat to round, and his society change from regional to national, came to view himself as unique and to set a special value on himself. He was individual and, more, uniquely individual. His individualism differed both from the self-centered, almost selfish brand of the Hellenist and from our present notion of individualism as the free play of subjectivity. Renaissance man bestrode his new world like a colossus and glowed with pride in himself and in his own achievements. That *pride* and its stimulus to *self-assertion* were what characterized the individualism of the Renaissance. It affected governments, which shifted from the peer aristocracies of feudalism to individual rule; it affected commerce, which exchanged communal guilds for independent capitalism; it affected religion, which saw Luther declare every man his own priest. It helped to shape art. Where the *Athena Lemnia* was a compendium of beauty and therefore a generalized means to truth, the *David* of Michelangelo was not an objective summarizing of the beauties of all Renaissance men but a unique conception: it was Michelangelo Buonarroti's means to truth. Renaissance individualism even helped to determine how men died, for the architect Brunelleschi deliberately prolonged his death agonies until the elegant crucifix by Donatello could be brought to replace the simple one the priest had placed upon his breast. The church, plus his own esthetic sense, would win him paradise.

In his "Oration on the Dignity of Man" Pico della Mirandola declared man's achievements potentially limitless and ascribed them all to man's unbounded free will. Man could, as he willed, be lower than the beasts or higher than the angels and "is rightly called a great miracle and judged a wonderful being." Ficino's central doctrine was man's individual immortality which, in common with Pico, he ascribed to man's limitless capacity for achievement. Pomponazzi too saw man existing in a middle ground with the self-willed "power to assume either nature." Bruno held that every atom in the universe was an individual "monad" or unity, and that each individual in this new heliocentric universe was capable of unlimited achievement: ". . . for in extending and enlarging the universe, he [man] is himself elevated beyond measure and his intelligence is no longer deprived of breathing space beneath a sky that is meager, narrow, and cramped."

LITERATURE.   Niccolò Machiavelli in *The Prince* favors a ruler who is impetuous rather than cautious and whose rule is a many-sided process of self-assertion. Benvenuto Cellini sparks Renaissance individualism from every page of his *Autobiography*. Armed with visions and with his favorite saying that "God helps them who help themselves" he hailed each of his second-rate creations as "a miracle of God" and wandered through Renaissance courts, boudoirs, and prisons "not bound by any law." Michel de Montaigne prefaces his *Essays* by explaining that "I describe myself without ceasing," and illuminates the Renaissance trait of self-assertion with a special radiance of mind and understanding. The opening paragraphs of his essay "Of Repenting" display the quintessence of this trait, as do "Of Presumption" and the passage in "Of Experience" beginning "My profession and my art is living." Shakespeare's familiar characters, Falstaff and Shylock, are insistently self-assertive. And Hamlet, despite being the prototype of Renaissance prince, achieves individuality through the power of his genius and through freedom of will. His speech beginning "What a piece of work is a man!" is a straight-line summary of Pico's "Oration on the Dignity of Man." Cervantes' Don Quixote also asserts himself by means of free will. "I know who I am and who I may be if I choose," is his famous pronouncement, and he chooses to be a Renaissance individual who thinks thoughts that become increasingly profound. In time Quixote's choice becomes Sancho Panza's too, and when it does it infects him not with Quixote's own personality but with a need to be still more himself.

ARCHITECTURE.   Renaissance architects asserted themselves through their work in two ways. First, they affixed their names to what they had built: in place of Medieval anonymity there were Brunelleschi, Alberti, Bramante, San Gallo, Michelangelo, Sansovino, Lescot, to cite only a prominent few. Second, instead of adhering to a communal style such as Romanesque or Gothic, Renaissance architects broke or modified rules in order to achieve individual styles: the academic elegance of Alberti (Figure 5.19); the rich monumentality of Bramante (Figure 5.20); the ornate profusion of Sansovino—the work of these men is unmistakably theirs. Even single features of style were used to assert individuality. The massive red and green dome of the Cathedral of Florence is Brunelleschi's dome, associated automatically with the architect who single-handedly ushered in architectural individualism. The dome of St. Peter's in Rome (Figure 5.14) belongs to Michelangelo, its majestic harmony a crowning triumph to God and to its creator, its scalloped windows defiantly personal and yet inevitably in keeping with the sumptuous grandeur of the work as a whole.

In the German states where the doctrines of Luther further encouraged individualism, architecture became picturesque and various. Towering roofs, curious spires and gables, and eccentric courtyards made German palaces and villas fantastic and special, like the *Knochenhaueramthaus* in Hildesheim and the *Pellerhaus* in Nuremberg.

Figure 5.14   The Dome of St. Peter's Cathedral, and the Vatican.   (1547–1564). Rome.   [Alinari: Art Reference Bureau].

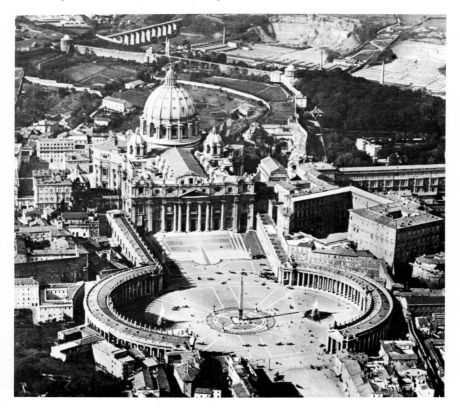

SCULPTURE.   Renaissance sculptors too asserted themselves by name. Michelangelo chiseled "I, Michelangelo Buonarroti, made this" on his most celebrated *Pietà*, and Cellini inscribed his name on the strap across his *Perseus'* chest. Individualism led sculptors to emphasize the inner nature of their subjects, and a statue of a prophet (probably Jeremiah) by Donatello was so starkly individual that he was nicknamed, for all time, *Zuccone*, pumpkin-head: most art books so identify him today. Verrocchio's equestrian statue of General Colleoni (Figure 5.15) shows both man and horse on the brink of movement. Tense, brutal, powerful, Colleoni is outstandingly a personality, and his horse, aflame with his master's strength, takes on an identity of his own.

Renaissance sculptors broke rules even as architects did to achieve individuality of style, and the styles of Donatello and Michelangelo remained dynamic and changing throughout their lives. Donatello's late masterpiece, a wooden statue of *Mary Magdalen,* conveys an intensity of anguish that brings the artist's self sharply into focus. Michelangelo's final sculpture, the *Pietà Rondanini* (Figure 5.16), breaks the mold a final time and moves his work beyond the domain of any period or tradition. Christ and the Virgin merge in mysterious unity, their features and limbs more allusive suggestion than specific form. Nothing in this work is explicitly stated. It simply is, and as the letters on its pedestal proclaim, it is by Michelangelo Buonarroti.

PAINTING.   Renaissance painters like sculptors asserted themselves by signing their works, and none did so more flamboyantly than Dürer. In his *Fall of Man* (Figure 5.13) Adam holds a bough from which hangs a sign bearing not only the artist's name but also the date of composition. In other paintings and engravings Dürer used his initials, A. D., as a signature so as to associate God with his creations. Renaissance artists also painted strikingly individualized portraits like the *Mona Lisa* of da Vinci. The most subtly probing Renaissance portrait painter, Hans Holbein, did the bulk of his work in England. His portrait of Henry VIII (Figure 5.17) depicting the monarch's surface magnificence contradicted by the beady eyes, petulant mouth, and willful thrust of the right arm with its fat, sensual fingers captures the subject's special qualities for all time.

Even more than architects and sculptors, Renaissance painters developed individual styles. The massive aliveness of Masaccio, the lyric beauty of Botticelli with its undercurrent of sadness, the dreamy mystery of da Vinci, and the sculpted power and nobility of Michelangelo, allows each of them to speak with his special voice. Titian, who *was* Venice with all of its sensuous color and atmosphere, often made the content of his paintings restate his special style, as in the *Venus of Urbino* (Figure 5.18). Venus lies sensual and alluring in the foreground, while in the background a young

Figure 5.15   ANDREA DEL VERROCCHIO.   *Colleoni.*   (c. 1482–1488).   Campo SS. Giovanni e Paolo, Venice.   [Italian Tourist Information Office].

girl, on the eve of her marriage, kneels in prayer. At the feet of Venus rests a little dog, the Renaissance symbol of fidelity in marriage. In sum, this is a wedding portrait, its angle of vision the sensual delights that marriage can give.

MUSIC.   In music too composers modified rules to assert their individual styles. Jan van Ockeghem dispensed with set cadences and composed continuously flowing, ethereal melodic lines at once rhapsodically mystic and uniquely his product, as in the *Kyrie* and *Agnus Dei* from his *L'homme armé* Mass. Obrecht in Masses like his *Missa Sine nomine* broke up the *cantus firmus* (basic melody) into short repetitive segments, an approach

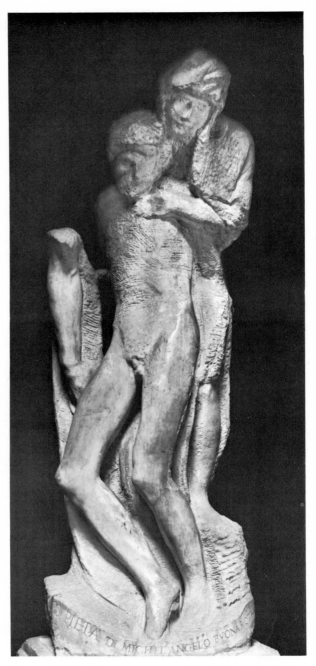

Figure 5.16 MICHELANGELO. *Pietà Rondanini*. (c.
1555–1564). Castello Sforzesco, Milan. [Alinari: Art
Reference Bureau].

Figure 5.17 HANS HOLBEIN. *Henry VIII.* (c. 1539). National Gallery, Rome. [Dr. Franz Stoedtner].

Figure 5.18 TITIAN. *Venus of Urbino.* (c. 1535). Uffizi Gallery, Florence. [Alinari: Art Reference Bureau].

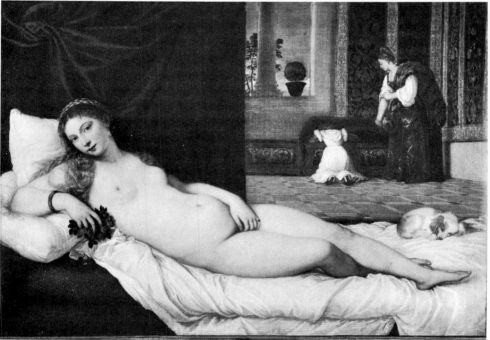

that became especially associated with him. Josquin achieved balance between structure and sonority so perfect that none could imitate him. Palestrina in works like the *Agnus Dei* from his *Missa Papae Marcelli* (Pope Marcellus Mass) combined quiet harmonies and symmetrical construction with emphasis upon a chaste, serene sonority that set the style of church music for generations to come. Di Lasso used wide intervals, syncopation, and musical surprises of every sort to stamp his compositions as his own. The ayres of John Dowland like "What if I never speed" have an intensity of emotion that single them out from among those of a host of English composers.

A type of music known as *musica reservata* came into vogue in the middle of the sixteenth century as a new expression of individualism and attracted even Josquin Des Prés. It stressed rhythmic contrasts and harmonic freedoms hitherto untried. The theorist Nicolo Vicentino described it as music "for the benefit of trained ears," as opposed to music for "ordinary ears," composed for "praising great personages and heroes." Not only its style but also its performance was individualized so that composer and interpreter alike had fresh opportunity to assert themselves. The sixteenth-century Italian madrigal became another vehicle both for individual style and individualized performance. The madrigals of Luca Marenzio represent music-painting as distinctive as the works of Titian—for example, his *Madonna mia gentil*—and were, like all Renaissance madrigals, written more for interpretive re-creation by performers than for listening audiences.

The swing toward secularization at the start of the Renaissance led men to examine the world around them with a first-hand freshness, and what they saw filled them with WORLD-JOY. In its early stages Renaissance world-joy gave rise to a zest for life that publicized with gusto the growing humanist regard for the value of man. Nothing displayed this zest for life so dramatically as the rash of practical jokes that spread over Europe. Like adolescents first let loose on the world, the men of the Early Renaissance reveled in the tricks they could play, and short story writers everywhere recorded them. A prime example is the true story of *Il grasso legnaiuolo* (Fatty the Cabinet-Maker) whom the architect Brunelleschi, with the cooperation of the entire city of Florence, gleefully drove mad. As the Renaissance wore on this zest for life subsided to an undercurrent, and world-joy became a serenity difficult to isolate, but easily sensed. It led Pico to say in his "Oration": "O highest and most marvellous felicity of man! to whom it is granted to have that which he chooses, to be that which he wills." It buoyed up Bruno, who discovered that man had encountered not only a brave new world but also a limitless universe. "Let not this contemplation discourage man," Bruno advises, "for in [God's] extending and enlarging the universe, man is himself elevated beyond measure, and his intelligence is no longer deprived of breathing space beneath a sky meager, narrow, and ill-proportioned."

LITERATURE.   Rabelais conveys the zesty aspect of world-joy by means of *le grand rire* (the giant laughter) that permeates his *Gargantua and Pantagruel*. Gargantua's famous letter to Pantagruel in Paris (Book II) on the unparalleled joys and benefits of today's world combines Early Renaissance exuberance with the serenity of the later phase. Cervantes' Don Quixote achieves a serenity that borders on the sublime when his dream world and the reality of his present become one. All of his later speeches and conduct, especially at the Duke's court, are lambent with world-joy. (It should be noted that Shakespeare and Cervantes, both of whom died in 1616, contemplated the Renaissance at a time when it had already begun to wane, and their knowledge of its deeply joyful special universe was tempered with sorrow over its present departure. Don Quixote infects the world with his serene contentment, but too late, and his final, "I was mad, but now I am sane," is a bitter and tragic Renaissance epitaph.)

ARCHITECTURE.   Impossible to illustrate, but motivating every Renaissance building was a particular kind of optimism. Unlike architects of any age before or since, those of the Renaissance felt they were building not for one generation or for several but for eternity: this feeling could produce the dome of Michelangelo. Early Renaissance architects were playful in their optimism: Michelozzo in the Medici Palace gave lessons on the texture of stone, the lower story rusticated, the next one semipolished, the top one slick. Alberti in the Rucellai Palace (Figure 5.19) flamboyantly used the Doric, Ionic, and Corinthian orders successively above the pilasters of the three stories as a tour de force of competence. In addition its façade furnished a virtuoso display of different-sized rectangles whose geometric cleverness even infiltrated the arches surmounting the windows.

The High Renaissance architect who probably best achieved an undercurrent of serenity was Donato Bramante. His *Tempietto* (Figure 5.20) adapts from the Romans (whom the Renaissance considered the most worldly of people) the recessed niches and dome of the Pantheon (Figure 3.12). He fused these elements into a harmonic, Christian whole, as the cross at the top proclaims. By its fusion of symbolic grace and well-proportioned balance of dome, drum, and peristyle the *Tempietto* achieves a serene and self-contained loveliness.

SCULPTURE.   Early Renaissance sculpture expresses zest for life through violent physical contact, as in the bronze *Hercules and Antaeus* of Pollaiuolo (Figure 5.21). In it a straining Hercules lifts a screaming Antaeus above the ground, and the deep-set satisfaction of Hercules' expression,

Figure 5.19   (left)   Leone Battista Alberti.   Rucellai Palace.   (1446–1451).
Florence.   [Dr. Franz Stoedtner].

Figure 5.20   (right)   Donato Bramante.   Tempietto.   (1502).   Rome.   [Dr. Franz
Stoedtner].

reinforced by the comfortable, almost relaxed curve of his back show him
reveling in a display of power. Based on classic models like *Laocoön* (Figure 2.24), it avoids their seriousness by being only eighteen inches high;
the total effect therefore is somehow playful, like the violence done to
Fatty the Cabinet-Maker and like Alberti's exercises in the Greek orders.
Closer to the serenity of Bramante are the *St. George* of Donatello and the
terra-cotta reliefs of Luca della Robbia, whose pretty models sometimes
evoke a happy sentimentality instead of the serenity intended.

Painting.   Early Renaissance zest for life appears here too in Pollaiuolo,
whose engraving of *The Battle of Ten Naked Men* shows his subjects
in various throes of violence. All of their writhings, however, are really
anatomy lessons, and what we are really seeing is not mayhem but sportive
bodily exercise. High Renaissance serenity is found in the *Mona Lisa*,

Figure 5.21   ANTONIO DEL POLLAIUOLO.   *Hercules and Antaeus.*   (c. 1470).   Bargello, Florence.   [Alinari: Art Reference Bureau].

Figure 5.22   SANZIO RAPHAEL.   *Goldfinch Madonna.*   (1506).   Uffizi
Gallery, Florence.   [Alinari: Art Reference Bureau].

about whose smile enough has been written, in the hopeful confidence of
Michelangelo's Adam, and above all in the Madonnas of Raphael. Raphael's
style was an amalgam of High Renaissance achievements, combining the
harmonies of Bramante, the delicacy of da Vinci, the power of Michelangelo, and Venetian love of color into a synthesis uniquely his own. His
Goldfinch Madonna (Figure 5.22), named for the finch St. John brought

to Christ, displays High Renaissance serenity to best advantage. The face of the Madonna with its oval shape and wide-set eyes is endearingly human. It is turned slightly, a gentle version of the *contrapposto* of Michelangelo, and its expression reflects the calm certainty of Renaissance humanism. The surrounding landscape makes the world of nature a vital part of the reality of this scene: the trees flanking the Virgin, like the children at her feet, are *young* trees. Through harmonious unity the artist thus achieves a world-joy whose effects are literally universal.

Music.   Contemporary with Fatty the Cabinet-Maker, with Alberti, and with Pollaiuolo were the *frottole,* accompanied songs that combined popular or original tunes with sprightly lyrics. The words themselves were trivial and frivolous, and the melodies matched their gaiety and bite. Witty, satiric, sensual, the *frottole* of the late fifteenth century reflected its zest for living: for example, the *Non val aqua* of Bartolomeo Tromboncino. Out of them developed the High Renaissance madrigal which fused poetic texts and flexible melodies into a unity akin to the *Tempietto* of Bramante and the *Goldfinch Madonna* of Raphael, as in the *Madonna mia gentil* of Marenzio. An interesting example of joyous English madrigals of the High Renaissance is the *Triumphs of Oriana* (1601), a series of tributes to Queen Elizabeth published by Thomas Morley. The motets of Josquin (*Tu pauperum refugium*) and the Masses of Palestrina (*Missa Papae Marcelli*) also communicate the High Renaissance serenity adapted from the zest for life of a generation before.

As the "Events" section points out, the Renaissance closes with the emergence of nation-states, but these are the end product of three basal sixteenth-century factors—humanism, the Reformation, and global explorations—all international in scope. Humanism spread out from Italy to all of Europe; the Reformation did the same from Germany; and exploration, though dominated by Spain, caught up all of Europe. In mind, spirit, and physical make-up, therefore, the Renaissance fostered INTERNATIONALISM. Humanism used Latin as a common language; the Reformation proclaimed the individual value of all men regardless of national origin; explorers sailed into a common unknown. Philosophers tend to be international in any age, and the monad of Bruno and the doctrine of immortality of Ficino knew no boundary lines. A more deliberate tie-in with Renaissance internationalism is the following race theory of Pomponazzi: "The whole human race is like a single body made up of various parts having different functions but all serving the common good of mankind."

Literature.   Internationalism in Renaissance literature, and in the other arts as well, shows itself most clearly in the diffusion of styles and in the free use of sources. The sonnet style popularized by Petrarch reappeared, forms, themes and all, in the writings of Ronsard, du Bellay, and other members of the Pléiade; in Sidney, Spenser, and Shakespeare; in Santillana and Boscán. The *novelle* converted into art by Boccaccio attracted Marguerite de Navarre, Rabelais, Thomas Nash, and Cervantes.

The Renaissance made use of sources in a way we find almost suspect today, borrowing plots, passages, and even word-for-word translations of entire works. Boccaccio's story of Girolamo and Salvestra was a prototype of the Romeo and Juliet story; his successor, Masuccio, adapted it, and then Luigi da Porto adapted it from him into nearly its Shakespearean form; Matteo Bandello rewrote da Porto's story, changing little more than the phrasing; Arthur Brooke then rewrote it as an English poem; Shakespeare made it a play. The plays of Shakespeare lean heavily upon the biographies of Plutarch, the *Chronicles* of Holinshed, *novelle,* and earlier anonymous English plays. *The Faerie Queene* of Spenser borrows characters, plots, and passages from the epics of Ariosto and Tasso. Cervantes' *Don Quixote* owes much to the romances of chivalry he satirizes.

ARCHITECTURE. The international spread of styles was even swifter in Renaissance architecture than in literature. Italian decorative elements soon became common European property. The Court of the Louvre by Pierre Lescot (Figure 5.23) is *in toto* a version of the geometric façade of Alberti. The use of orders also harks back to Alberti. The arcading on the ground

Figure 5.23 PIERRE LESCOT. Court of the Louvre. Paris. [Marburg: Art Reference Bureau].

floor recalls Italian courtyards, and the alternating curved and triangular pediments were a fixture of Roman Renaissance buildings. Only the roof and the relief work on the third story break away from Italian models—and turn to the style of chateaux like Chambord. In England under Elizabeth the pointed arch gave way to Italian rounded arches, and buildings like Wollaton Hall suggested Lescot superimposed upon Alberti. In Spain the University *Portal* at Salamanca is Lescot-Alberti brushed with ornate Moorish detail; the façade of the Escorial echoes that of the Farnese Palace.

SCULPTURE.   In the main Renaissance sculptors borrowed styles and techniques from classical statues being recovered at that time in abundance, and these became international property. A few examples of more contemporary borrowings can be cited, however: the *Mary Magdalen* of Donatello owes much to German sources like the *Gero Crucifixion* (Figure 4.24); the reliefs of Hans Daucher recall Ghiberti's handling of space and composition in his panels on the doors of the Baptistery of Florence; the tomb of Henry II by Germain Pilon owes much to the Medici Tomb by Michelangelo.

PAINTING.   With regard to style, the use of perspective developed in Italy spread quickly over Europe. Dürer was intrigued by it and in engravings like *St. Antony Before the Walls of Nuremberg* and *St. Jerome in His Study* he experimented with unusual angles of perspective in much the same way as the painter Andrea Mantegna (*St. James Led to Martyrdom*) had done. The detail work in Holbein's portraiture is German, but the essential style, of lucid revelation of character, derives in large part from the work of Filippo Lippi, da Vinci, and Raphael. The portraiture of Jean Clouet is similarly derived.

International borrowings of details (sources) abound in Renaissance paintings, although sometimes they are incongruous. In the somber *Judgment of Cambises* by the Netherlands painter Gerard David, Italian cherubs suddenly pop up. The *Venus Reproving Love* of Il Rosso Fiorentino, court painter to François I, adapts Michelangelo and da Vinci to the elegant, superficial world of Fontainebleau. On the other hand, the dandified *Youth Leaning Against a Tree* by the English Nicholas Hillyarde is redolent of Fontainebleau.

MUSIC.   Music made about the fullest use of international styles and sources. The Burgundian school, dominant at the start of the Renaissance, continued the style of the French Medieval school, and combined with it the English style of descant (a variation in a higher register of the main melody); French music of the fifteenth century incorporated English descant and Italian lyricism; Spanish music of the fifteenth century largely imitated French models; Italian music of the fifteenth century, especially the later half, imported Flemish somberness and ornate counterpoint. The quintessence of High Renaissance music, that of Josquin, blended northern European somberness, polyphony, muted rhythms, and mystic dreamy phrases with southern European lyricism, homophony, short phrases and accented rhythms.

Music made the same free use of sources as did literature. Parody Masses (Masses which used melodies already at hand) were about the most common type. The popular song *L'homme armé* (the armed man), for example, was treated by many composers. *L'homme armé* Masses were written by Dufay, Ockeghem, Josquin, Pierre de la Rue, and Palestrina, among others. The Geneva Psalter melodies rely heavily upon popular tunes and chansons. The lute songs of Italy were copied and adapted by France, England, Germany, and Spain. Those of Don Luis de Milan (for example, his "Fantasia for lute") are especially effective adaptations. The English madrigals of the later sixteenth century borrow Italian melodies and even translate Italian texts—Thomas Morley, the most Italianate of English madrigal composers, was also the most popular. Even so native-sounding an English form as "ayre" was in effect a close copy of the French chanson.

Jules Michelet in his monumental twenty-four volume *Histoire de France* (1833–1867) first gave the name of "Renaissance" to the period under consideration, maintaining it was a "renascence" (rebirth) of Greek and Roman culture. Subsequent historians quickly pointed out that the Renaissance was an amalgam of many elements, and so strong was the reaction to Michelet's view that the classical roots of the Renaissance are often excessively discounted. Though the Renaissance was not Greece and Rome reborn, as a comparison of the traits of those three periods can clearly show, its CLASSICISM did much to shape and color it. Fresh contact with Byzantium at the start of the fifteenth century introduced the Greek language to Renaissance Europe and made available all of the Greek literature we possess today. The humanists wrote in Latin and Greek; they turned to classical models for their style; their modes of inquiry and of synthesis were Greek; and they judged the value of contemporary literature by comparing it with classical models. Greek and Latin classics were admired second only to the Bible.

The *De architectura* of Vitruvius, rediscovered around the time of Brunelleschi, contained rules for the construction and design of every type of building which did much to determine the architecture of the Renaissance. Greek and Roman statues were rediscovered everywhere. Some were hauled up out of the sea encrusted with coral, and contemporary letters reflect the excitement of these finds and how Renaissance sculptors and artists could be inspired to feats of imitation. The birth of opera at the end of the Renaissance came from efforts to restore the chanted dramas of the ancient Greeks.

The principal Renaissance philosopher, Ficino, was at core a Platonist. (His chief opponent, Pomponazzi, was an Aristotelian.) Ficino organized a Platonic Academy and entitled his major work *Platonic Theology*. Its central purpose was to restate the Platonic theories of the immortality of the soul in a form suitable to the Christian Renaissance. Pico constructed his "Oration on the Dignity of Man" out of the Aristotelian Chain of Being. The main contribution of the most original of Renaissance philosophers, the monad of Giordano Bruno, goes back in principle to the atomic theories of Leucippus and Democritus.

LITERATURE.   *The Prince* of Machiavelli, so seminal a Renaissance work, is actually based on themes from his *Discourses*, a commentary on the Roman historian Livy. Machiavelli's famous letter to Francesco Vettori captures on a single page all of the reverence which the Renaissance felt for the ancients. No comments on the Renaissance should fail to quote at least a passage from it. "In the evening," writes Machiavelli, "I return to my house and go into my study. At the door I take off the clothes I have worn all day, mud spotted and dirty, and put on regal and courtly garments. Thus appropriately clothed I enter into the ancient courts of ancient men where, being lovingly received, I feed on that food which alone is mine and which I was born for." Montaigne's favorite author was Plutarch, his favorite person Sophocles. His *Essays* shimmer with the relativity, disillusion, and sense of change of Hellenistic skepticism. The manifesto of the Pléiade, the *Défense et illustration*[2] *de la langue française*, had a dual purpose: (1) to show how French could be a language worthy of Greek so that (2) it could be better used to imitate the ancients. *The Faerie Queene* of Spenser abounds in Platonic myth, and Plutarch, Montaigne's favorite, also supplied Shakespeare with sources for *Julius Caesar, Timon of Athens, Coriolanus* and *Antony and Cleopatra*.

ARCHITECTURE.   The rediscovery of Vitruvius led to a number of Renaissance treatises based on his work. The extensive *On Architecture* by Alberti was the most important. It followed Vitruvius' dictums in many places and also advocated Pythagorean number relationships and a Hellenistic-inspired concern for exterior beauty. Treatises by Giacomo Barozzi da Vignola (1562) and Andrea Palladio (1570) also imitated Vitruvius. In his Rucellai Palace Alberti used a different Greek order for each story, a classical history lesson frequently copied by other Renaissance architects. In remodeling the Church of San Francisco at Rimini, Alberti intended to surmount it with a Roman triumphal arch. He never completed the remodeling but did crown his Vitruvian San Andrea at Mantua with a modified version of one. Other façades with strikingly classical elements include the *Tempietto*, the Farnese Palace, St. Peter's, the Court of the Louvre, and the Palace of Charles V by Machuca and Berruguete.

---

[2] To make illustrious.

SCULPTURE.   A number of close and conscious resemblances can be found between Renaissance and classical works of sculpture. The ten reliefs of Ghiberti's so-called *Gates of Paradise* that form the eastern doorway of the Florentine Baptistery echo the spaciousness, the dignity, and the lovely modeling of the *Altar of Peace*. The *Gattamelata* of Donatello is similar in stance and appearance to the equestrian statue of Marcus Aurelius. In 1506 the *Laocoön* (Figure 2.24) was discovered in the Baths of Titus, and its twisting tension led Michelangelo to the use of *contrapposto* in statues like *Bound Slave, Moses,* and the *Pietà Rondanini*. The *Nymphs* of Jean Goujon for all their mincing poses wear the rippling draperies of the Parthenon goddesses and trace at least a hybrid descent from them.

So much of classical sculpture is available for comparison that we may profitably compare the Renaissance borrowing of elements as well as whole subjects. To cite a few, the stance of Donatello's *David* forms a Praxitelian "S" curve; so do the *Davids* of Verrocchio and Michelangelo. The *Zuccone* of Donatello shifts his weight onto one foot in the approved classical manner, as does the *David* of Michelangelo; and the latter's hair was curled by boring holes in it, the way the ancients used to do.

PAINTING.   Renaissance painting had few classical models to refer to, giving us no opportunity to make direct source parallels. However, the works of Andrea Mantegna reproduce classical structures as background at every opportunity, suggesting the impact of classicism on him. Renaissance painters frequently turned to classical subjects: Botticelli's *The Birth of Venus;* Raphael's *The School of Athens;* Titian's *Bacchus and Ariadne;* and Giorgione's *Sleeping Venus* are only a few examples out of many. One can also find such classical elements as the "S" curve of Botticelli's Venus and the Greek style curled hair of Dürer's Adam throughout the painting and engraving of the Renaissance.

MUSIC.   Like the Greeks the Renaissance humanists saw music as ennobling the *ethos,* the spirit. Ficino advocated medicine, music, and theology for the whole man, saying that the first ministered to the body, the second to the spirit, and the third to the soul. Renaissance musical theorists began going back to original classical sources instead of to their early Medieval mediator, Boethius. The Swiss theorist Franchino Gafori (1451–1522) had all extant Greek musical treatises translated into Latin and used them much as architects were using Vitruvius. The title of Vicentino's basic work, *L'Antica musica ridotta alla moderna prattica,* ancient music converted to modern use (1555), describes its purpose and bears witness to the impact of classicism.

Not only theorists but also practicing composers turned back to the ancients. The vocal music of Josquin placed new emphasis upon length of syllables (actually, upon more important words in context, as in the chanson

Faulte d'argent) the way Greek music was supposed to have done. This emphasis was hardened into formula by the sometime Pléiadist-poet, Jean-Antoine de Baïf, who founded in Paris an *Académie de poésie et musique* in 1570. The academy purposed to write and perform *musique mesurée*, in which the long and short syllables of the text were set to correspondingly long and short notes. Medieval music, such as Gregorian chant, had distinguished between long and short syllables only by pitch (the long syllable was set higher than the preceding short one). During the Renaissance de Baïf aimed at making length as well as pitch conform to ancient practice. The imitation succeeded academically, but even good examples of *musique mesurée,* those of Claude le Jeune (*D'une coline*), justify most historians' contention that the Renaissance is not solely a rebirth of Greece and Rome.

The Renaissance fusion of this world and the next came to be reflected in a Renaissance state of mind. Two worlds meant two views of things; their fusion meant that both views could seem equally valid: hence the Renaissance idea of CONSIDERING BOTH SIDES OF A QUESTION. Thus Pomponazzi could declare that while he could not believe in angels and demons as a philosopher, he could do so as a Christian. Pico, despite his excitement over the possibilities of unlimited free will, points out that while its exercise can raise man higher than the angels it can also sink him to the level of the lowest beasts. Religious change could evoke Erasmian tolerance and the intolerance of Mary Tudor, and the Renaissance could accept both viewpoints as valid. Political forces in the sixteenth century gave rise to absolutism and to democracy at the same time, and out of the same causes. Earth and sun were both the center of the universe in the minds of many, and Jesuit dialectic could find advantages on either side of any argument.

In literature Rabelais dramatizes the validity of both sides of a question by giving double-edged answers as to whether Panurge should marry. Montaigne consistently blends skepticism with tolerance; in his essay "Of Cannibals" he writes: "While judging the misdeeds of savages we are blind to our own. I think there is more barbarism in eating a living man than a dead one." It is Hamlet's capacity to think out both sides of a question—not indecision—that delays him from taking his revenge, and his "To be or not to be" soliloquy is a classic articulation of this capacity. It is less easy to detect the consideration of both sides of a question in the other arts, overshadowed as it is by the fusion of this world and the next. But hints of it can be found in those very examples of fusion: in the façade and courtyard of the Farnese Palace, in the *David* of Donatello, in the *Birth of Venus* of Botticelli, and in the attention paid to homophony *and* polyphony in music, as in the chanson *Bon jour, mon coeur* by di Lasso.

The Renaissance gave special meaning to the form of the PASTORAL, a meaning that appears full blown in the *Arcadia* of Jacopo Sannazaro (1504), with its dancing youths and preoccupation with games. The pastoral was to the High Renaissance what chivalry was to the later Middle Ages. Both conveyed the idea of an ideal world, like the Greek pastoral from which both derived. But where chivalry connoted heaven, as did the Greek pastoral world to a large extent, the Renaissance pastoral conjured up the innocent world of childhood. It was a world of self-indulgence and freedom from responsibility where shepherds sang and loved in an eternal summer, untroubled by cares or obligations. For the Renaissance, with its maturity of vision, sought escape not from the grim present, as had the Middle Ages, but from that very maturity. Thus, even when responsibility and death entered the pastoral world, which they did as early as the *Arcadia,* they came from the world outside.

In literature the drama *Aminta* by Torquato Tasso is Renaissance pastoral in its purest form: Aminta who languishes in his garden for love of Silvia wins her at last and all live happily thereafter. Montaigne inserts the idea of the pastoral in his essay "Of Cannibals" by describing how his noble savages turn their world of nature into a bountiful, ideal commonwealth. Shakespeare in *As You Like It* presents a prismatic view of the pastoral idea: for his hero and heroine the forest of Arden is freedom from care; for others who see it through this world's eyes it is a place of toil, of ignorance, of absurdity. In such later plays as *Cymbeline, Winter's Tale,* and *The Tempest* Shakespeare gives himself over more fully to the Renaissance idea of the pastoral. Cervantes, by having Quixote plan to be a shepherd after having been a knight-errant, comments on how the pastoral idea has superseded that of chivalry.

In architecture the chateaux of France were often modeled to suit the pastoral idea, especially the palace of Fontainbleau which François I made into an escapist world of gardens, forests, fountains, and waterfalls. In painting, the trees of Raphael's *Goldfinch Madonna* represent the youthful innocence of nature. Other examples (out of many) of the pastoral idea as landscape include Lippi's *Adoration of the Christ Child,* Giorgione's *La fête champêtre,* Schongauer's *The Birth of Christ,* and Cranach's *Apollo and Diana.*

In music the leading Italian madrigal composer, Luca Marenzio, used pastoral lyrics for most of his texts, matching the first-time freshness of the form with pastoral sentiments. The leading English madrigalists—Thomas Weelkes, Thomas Morley, John Wilbye—often did the same (for example, Wilbye's "Adieu sweet Amarillis"). English ayres, whose very name connotes pastoral liberty, also made frequent use of pastoral texts (for example, Morley's "It was a lover and his lass"). Mention should be made of *The Fable of Orpheus* (1494) by Angelo Poliziano, a superb lyric narrative that combined the Renaissance idea of the pastoral with lyrics so fresh and delicate that they were set to music and presented dramatically. The *Orpheus* was the earliest direct ancestor of the opera.

The Renaissance took one of its ideas from the ancients from whom it was "reborn," the idea of *arete*, highest worthiness and competence (pp. 49–50). On occasion it used *arete* unaltered, calling it *virtù:* for Machiavelli the *virtù* of the Prince was his ability to control his state by any means. In the main, however, the Renaissance adapted *arete* to suit its own temper. With its fusion of worlds, it sought to fuse all aspects of *virtù* together somehow; with its special individualism, it sought to attribute those aspects to a special kind of person, dubbed a UNIVERSAL MAN. (In Italian, *uomo universale;* the concept was invented in Italy.) Pico, in his *De ente et uno* proposed to show how classical, Hebrew, and Christian cultures formed a universal whole, the idea of universal man in philosophical abstraction; Bruno extended that abstraction to include the boundless universe. Leonardo da Vinci brought it to life. Leonardo's competences were many and he could practice them several at a time. While writing and directing Milanese court pageants he devised a system of hydraulic irrigation for the plains surrounding the city. While serving as papal architect he was also chief engineer for the Roman army. One of the greatest painters of all time, he also made important contributions in the areas of sculpture, architecture, civil engineering, mathematics, physics, botany, anatomy, physiology, hydrodynamics, aeronautics, literature, and philosophy. A "lesser" universal man was his contemporary Michelangelo, merely one of the greatest painters, sculptors, architects, and poets of his or any other century. In literature Castiglione's courtier is formed in the image of a universal man. Shakespeare's Hamlet, philosopher, sage, and man of action, is the universal man held up as a mirror to nature.

In his influential *Treatise on Architecture* (1567), Philibert Delorme claimed that to be a significant architect one had to be first and foremost a universal man. Presumably he had in mind the architect Leo Battista Alberti (1404–1472), who, though less well known than da Vinci or Michelangelo, probably had greater abilities in a wider range of areas than either of them. Like da Vinci he was extremely powerful and could bend a horseshoe with ease. His *On Architecture* was the first printed work of its kind and a cornerstone of architectural theory. He was also a major practicing architect. His *Treatise on Painting,* though less important than *On Architecture,* makes valuable early contributions to the science of perspective. His *Treatise on the Family* is a seminal sociological study for anyone concerned with the rise of the middle class. He was probably the most important prose writer of the fifteenth century; his *Momus* is a masterpiece of literary satire. A mathematician and physicist, he devised rules to measure the arc of projectiles and invented a device for raising sunken ships. He was one of the most gifted organists of the fifteenth century, and its leading Platonic philosopher until Ficino. He was an early teacher of Lorenzo de' Medici, who turned out to be an excellent banker, financier, soldier, politician, poet, philosopher, composer, and dramatist.

The Middle Ages had made a ritual of love, through Mariolatry and then by idealizing woman as a kind of semidivine mediator between man and God—Beatrice had served Dante in this way. The Renaissance, fusing this world and the next, made the ideal woman a means to grace here as well as hereafter—Beatrice shaded into Shakespeare's Juliet and Portia. As Renaissance woman mediated between man and God in heaven, so she also mediated between man and sublime happiness on earth, through the sacrament of marriage. Thus developed the Renaissance idea of MARRIAGE AS HEAVEN ON EARTH. The idea did not affect all women or all marriages, for Medieval antifeminism persisted too. Renaissance women had the legal status of minors, lost all property rights through marriage, and their husbands were allowed by law to beat them. "Let [them] bear children till they die of it. That is what they are for," wrote Luther, actually a feminist sympathizer. Machiavelli's witty novella, "Belfagor," shows a devil better off in hell than being married. But in the Renaissance as in the Middle Ages some women were exceptions, and these made marriage a fusion of physical and spiritual joy. The exceptional ladies of the Renaissance were more individual, more real, more interesting than their Medieval predecessors. Like Juliet and Portia they could demand love as well as bestow it, and with them marriage became a peer relationship, akin to friendship. For Ficino the two states are essentially the same, a bond between two persons and God nurtured by awareness and contemplation. For Tasso in a philosophical dialogue entitled *Manso*, love and friendship were both based upon reciprocal *virtù:* that is, the *arete* of both parties combined to form a completed whole.

In literature the idea of marriage as heaven on earth probably first appears in embryo form in the capstone (one-hundredth) story of Boccaccio's *Decameron* (c. 1354). In it Griselda is "purged" by her husband for thirteen years and thus made worthy of him: ". . . this which I have done I have wrought to an end foreseen, willing to teach thee to be a wife," her husband explains to her. Griselda, by nature subordinate because she is a woman (according to Medieval thinking), serves as transition between Beatrice and the Renaissance idea of marriage as heaven on earth. The epics of the Italian Renaissance present this idea at least in part in the Ginevra and the Isabella episodes of Ariosto's *Orlando Furioso* and in the Tancred-Erminia, Rinaldo-Armida love affairs in Tasso's *Gerusalemme Liberata.* Spenser conceives the idea full blown in his plan to make the marriage of Arthur and Gloriana the grand culmination of *The Faerie Queene.* Rabelais touches upon it in his Abbey of Thélème, which accepts only the noblest and most attractive votaries whose service to God *in excelsis* is marriage. In *Romeo and Juliet* Shakespeare presents two youthful lovers with reciprocal *virtù* who "grace for grace and love for love allow," but whose potentially perfect marriage is tragically cut short. In *Antony and Cleopatra* Shakespeare depicts a Romeo and a Juliet full grown and explores with unparalleled sublimity the Renaissance idea of marriage as heaven on earth. The love of Antony and Cleopatra "must needs find out new heaven, new earth," and at Antony's death the whole universe grows stale:

> The odds is gone,
> And there is nothing left remarkable
> Beneath the visiting moon.

Cervantes' Don Quixote was the last survivor of the Renaissance full formed. Quixote too viewed marriage as heaven on earth and created a worthy lady, Dulcinea, to be his companion. But throughout the novel she never appears, because by that time (1615) the Renaissance and its ideas had begun to fade.

In painting as in literature we can trace the step-by-step development of the idea of marriage as heaven on earth. By comparing the *Madonna Enthroned* of Giotto (Figure 4.23) with the *Venus* of Botticelli and then with the *Venus* of Titian, we can view the extent and final limits of the development. The Titian painting, moreover, comments directly upon the Renaissance idea of marriage.

A special appeal of Botticelli's Venus is her subtly sorrowful expression, attributed by critics to the Neoplatonic tradition to which Botticelli adhered. For Neoplatonists, spirit was divorced from matter, and thus the sensual delights of Venus, so lyric in the Botticelli painting, lead only to dust. Hence her fugitive sadness, which offers a near perfect transition to the *Mona Lisa* of da Vinci: Mona Lisa (in English, *Mrs.* Eliza!) has a voluptuousness far more in keeping with this world than does Botticelli's Venus, and her serenely contented expression bespeaks her conscious awareness of marriage as heaven on earth. Michelangelo's *Creation of Adam* also alludes to this idea, for Eve, cradled in God's arm, is depicted, as is Adam, with a sensual fullness matching the spiritual beauty of their expressions. How thoroughly aware the Renaissance was of this idea of love can be seen in Titian's *Sacred and Profane Love* (Figure 5.24). The clothed figure seated stiffly, her face almost devoid of expression, represents profane love. Sacred love, whose expression is ardent and joyful, whose body is supremely sensual, and who is seated on the red robe symbolic of charity, is contrastingly alive. Behind her is a nature scene of tranquil innocence, and behind that the spire of a church, making flesh, nature, and God aspects of a single actuality.

Figure 5.24   TITIAN.   *Sacred and Profane Love.*   (c. 1520).   Borghese Gallery, Rome.   [Alinari: Art Reference Bureau].

This Renaissance adaptation of a Medieval idea had so great an impact on Western culture that by the nineteenth century instead of being the property of a fortunate few it was claimed as a right of the many. Marriage as heaven on earth became a feature of Romantic love, and its frequent failure to bring about that fusion became a basis for Realistic and Naturalistic reactions. In the twentieth century the idea persists in our mass media and in the stereotype Sunday newspaper photographs of earthily angelic brides. For today's serious artists the idea has become an ideal which they are seeking to recreate in a different way (see Part II, Chapter 9).

FORMS AND TECHNIQUES

As a rebirth of Greece and Rome alongside a continuation of the Middle Ages, the Renaissance made widespread use of earlier forms and techniques. It borrowed so often from the classical period that the practice became almost automatic. It also made frequent use of Medieval liturgical symbolism but for a broader purpose, as the Venus paintings of Botticelli and Titian (Figures 5.10 and 5.18) demonstrate. Although its most prominent forms and techniques were classical and Medieval, the Renaissance did develop its own examples as well.

DISCRETE PLANES: A series of tiered surfaces, moving from front to back. Examples of discrete planes are the inner and outer shells of

Brunelleschi's dome on the Cathedral of Florence and of Michelangelo's dome on St. Peter's, the ten panels of Ghiberti's *Gates of Paradise,* each of which is composed of a series of recessive planes with a separate action or scene depicted on each plane; the *Colleoni* of Verrocchio, a statue in the round which uses recessive planes much as the *Gates of Paradise* panels do; a majority of Renaissance paintings, including Botticelli's *Birth of Venus,* Raphael's *Goldfinch Madonna;* Dürer's engraving *Fall of Man;* Titian's *Sacred and Profane Love.*

ENCLOSING BORDER: The boundaries of an enclosing border arrest a work and turn it back toward its center, as in the three sallies of Don Quixote, during each of which he reaches a circumscribed point and then returns to the center, in this case the village; in Ghiberti's panels, whose lines of force thrust back from the edges toward the center; in a majority of Renaissance paintings, some examples being Botticelli's *Birth of Venus,* da Vinci's *Mona Lisa;* and Michelangelo's *Creation of Adam.*

TRIAD: Relationships by threes were called triads. Examples are found in three-story secular buildings, each story linked in an optical relationship with the others, by texture of stone, as in the Medici Palace of Michelozzo, or by use of orders, as in the Rucellai Palace of Alberti; in the related triads of figures on the Medici Tomb whose triadic relationship Michelangelo intended, although even he was unsure of the precise meaning of that relationship; in the major and minor thirds that became the basic harmonic units for Renaissance and for all subsequent music.

MADRIGAL: An especially effective and popular form in Renaissance literature and music was the madrigal. In literature the madrigal was a brief lyric poem that could deal with virtually any topic: see the madrigals of Poliziano, Ronsard, Christopher Marlowe. The madrigal in music mirrored the text with special vividness; for example, Marenzio's *Madonna mia gentil.*

VERSE DRAMA: This form reached its highest development in the Renaissance in the dramas of Shakespeare; Italian theorists of the High Renaissance, in trying to bring the form even closer to its Greek origins, evolved the opera, verse drama set to music.

MONUMENTALITY: Actually, not one technique but a sum total of several combined to achieve the technical effect of massive high seriousness. In literature *King Lear* achieves monumentality by means of grand characterizations, cosmic forces, and powerful language; the *Tempietto* of Bramante achieves it through sweep and harmony, the dome of Michelangelo through harmonic grandeur; the *David* of Michelangelo achieves it through size, power, and fine integrity; *The Tribute Money* of Masaccio achieves it through theme, gesture, and physical bulk; the Masses of Ockeghem and the motets of Josquin achieve it through solemnity of melody and through "imitation," polyphonic overlapping to achieve a monolithic effect; for example, Ockeghem, *Kyrie* and *Agnus Dei* from *L'homme armé* Mass; Josquin, *Tu pauperum refugium*.

THE HUMAN FORM AS EXPRESSION: The Renaissance learned to use the shape or posture of the body as a means of statement. Shakespeare's Falstaff conveys his worldliness through his bulk. The contours of Don Quixote and Sancho Panza, and the contrasts between them, indicate to a large extent what they represent. The physique of Michelangelo's *David* spells out his heroism; the pose of Michelangelo's Adam bespeaks his yearning and his faith; the bodily thrusts in da Vinci's *Last Supper* reveal loyalty or betrayal.

In the course of this period, which forms a transition to a new age as well as away from an earlier one, there are stirrings in science and in politics (absolutism, democracy, nationalism) which may be detected during the Renaissance but which do not influence its essential nature. They do actively affect the century to come, however, and will be dealt with—including their Renaissance origins—in Chapter 6 in Part II.

SELECTED BIBLIOGRAPHY

History

Cheyney, E. P. *The Dawn of a New Era: 1250–1453*. New York: Harper & Row, 1936.

Durant, Will. *The Renaissance*. New York: Simon and Schuster, 1953.

Ferguson, Wallace K. *Europe in Transition, 1300–1520*. Boston: Houghton Mifflin, 1962.

Green, V. H. *Renaissance and Reformation, 1450–1660*. London: Arnold, 1952.

Lindsay, T. M. *History of the Reformation*. 2 vols. New York: Scribner, 1928.

Lucas, H. S. *The Renaissance and the Reformation*. New York: Harper & Row, 1960.

Smith, Preserved. *The Age of the Reformation*. New York: Holt, Rinehart and Winston, 1920.

Social and Intellectual Background

Burckhardt, Jakob. *The Civilization of the Renaissance in Italy*. New York: Phaidon, 1950.

Cassirer, Ernst, *et al*. (Eds.) *The Renaissance Philosophy of Man*. Chicago: University of Chicago Press, 1956.

Chastel, André. *The Age of Humanism: Europe 1480–1530*. New York: McGraw-Hill, 1963.

Craig, Hardin. *The Enchanted Glass*. New York: Oxford University Press, 1936.

Dulles, Avery R. *Princeps Concordiae: Pico della Mirandola and the Scholastic Tradition*. Cambridge, Mass. Harvard University Press, 1941.

Ferguson, Wallace K. *The Renaissance in Historical Thought*. Boston: Houghton Mifflin, 1948.

Gilmore, Myron P. *The World of Humanism: 1453–1517.* New York: Harper Torchbooks, 1952.

Kristeller, Paul Oscar. *Renaissance Thought.* 2 vols. New York: Harper Torchbooks, 1961, 1965.

Pater, Walter. *The Renaissance.* New York: Random House, 1951.

Roeder, Ralph. *The Man of the Renaissance.* New York: Meridian, 1960.

Santillana, Giorgio de. (Ed.) *The Age of Adventure.* New York: Mentor, 1956.

Schevill, Ferdinand. *The First Century of Italian Humanism.* New York: Appleton, 1928.

Singer, Dorothea W. *Giordano Bruno, His Life and Thought.* New York: Schuman, 1950.

Symonds, John Addington. *The Renaissance in Italy.* 2 vols. New York: Random House, 1935.

Taylor, Henry Osborn. *Thought and Expression in the Sixteenth Century.* New York: Macmillan, 1920.

Thorndike, Lynn. *Science and Thought in the Fifteenth Century.* New York: Columbia University Press, 1929.

Tillyard, E. M. W. *The Elizabethan World Picture.* London: Chatto and Windus, 1948.

Young, George F. *The Medici.* New York: Random House, 1930.

Literature

Bush, Douglas. *The Renaissance and English Humanism.* Toronto: University of Toronto Press, 1939.

Dunn, Esther C. *The Literature of Shakespeare's England.* New York: Scribner, 1936.

Einstein, Lewis. *The Italian Renaissance in England.* New York: Columbia University Press, 1903.

Lee, Sidney. *The French Renaissance in England.* New York: Scribner, 1936.

Lewis, C. S. *English Literature in the Sixteenth Century.* New York: Oxford University Press, 1954.

Pinto, V. de Sola. *The English Renaissance, 1510–1688.* New York: Dover, 1950.

Symonds, John Addington. *The Renaissance in Italy.* 2 vols. New York: Random House, 1935.

Sypher, Wylie. *Four Stages of Renaissance Style.* Garden City, N.Y.: Anchor, 1955.

Tilley, Arthur. *Literature of the French Renaissance.* 2 vols. Cambridge: Cambridge University Press, 1904.

Architecture, Sculpture, Painting

Benesch, Otto. *The Art of the Renaissance in Northern Europe.* Cambridge, Mass.: Harvard University Press, 1945.

Berenson, Bernard. *The Italian Painters of the Renaissance.* New York: Meridian, 1957.

Blunt, Anthony. *Art and Architecture in France, 1500–1700.* Baltimore: Penguin, 1953.

Dewald, Ernest T. *Italian Painting 1266–1600.* New York: Holt, Rinehart and Winston, 1961.

Holt, Elizabeth G. (Ed.) *A Documentary History of Art.* Vol. I: *The Middle Ages and the Renaissance.* Garden City, N.Y.: Anchor, 1953.

MacLagen, Eric. *Italian Sculpture of the Renaissance.* Cambridge, Mass.: Harvard University Press, 1935.

Mather, Frank J., Jr. *Western European Painting of the Renaissance.* New York: Holt, Rinehart and Winston, 1939.

Panofsky, Erwin. *Meaning in the Visual Arts.* Garden City, N.Y.: Anchor, 1955.

————. *Studies in Iconology.* New York: Harper Torchbooks, 1962.

Pope-Hennessy, John. *Italian Renaissance Sculpture.* New York: Phaidon, 1958.

Scott, Geoffrey. *The Architecture of Humanism.* Garden City, N.Y.: Anchor, 1956.

Symonds, John Addington. *The Renaissance in Italy.* 2 vols. New York: Random House, 1935.

Vasari, Giorgio. *The Lives of the Most Eminent Painters, Sculptors, and Architects.* Edited by Betty Burroughs. New York: Simon and Schuster, 1946.

Wittkower, Rudolf. *Architectural Principles in the Age of Humanism.* London: Warburg Institute, 1952.

Wölfflin, Heinrich. *Art of the Italian Renaissance.* New York: Schocken, 1963.

Music

Bukofzer, Manfred F. *Studies in Medieval and Renaissance Music.* New York: Norton, 1950.

Dickinson, Edward. *Music in the History of the Western Church.* New York: Scribner, 1931.

Fellowes, Edmund H. *The English Madrigal.* New York: Oxford University Press, 1947.

Harman, Alec. *Medieval and Early Renaissance Music.* Fair Lawn, N.J.: Essential Books, 1958.

————, and Anthony Milner. *Late Renaissance and Baroque Music.* Fair Lawn, N.J.: Essential Books, 1959.

Morris, Reginald O. *Contrapuntal Technique in the Sixteenth Century.* Oxford: Clarendon, 1922.

Pattison, Bruce. *Music and Poetry of the English Renaissance.* London: Methuen, 1948.

Reese, Gustave. *Music in the Renaissance.* New York: Norton, 1959.

Stevens, Denis, and Alec Robertson. (Eds.) *Pelican History of Music.* Vol. II. *Renaissance to Baroque.* Baltimore: Penguin, 1964.

INDEX

°Page numbers in italics denote illustrations.